THE NAVIGATION ACTS

AND THE

AMERICAN REVOLUTION

CONTENTS

TABLES

INTRODUCTION

THE TIME has come to reëvaluate the trade and navigation acts and their relation to the American Revolution. Lawrence A. Harper has blazed a new trail of scholarship in his *English Navigation Laws*. At last we know what they were and how they worked in the seventeenth century. There are other excellent studies of parts of the field. This volume deals with the operation of the mercantile system as a factor in disrupting the first British colonial Empire.

For a century the Navigation Acts have been prominently mentioned as one of the important causes of the Revolution. This explanation was strongly influenced by the nineteenth-century economic concepts of free trade. English statesmen had embraced Adam Smith's theories and made them a part of the national policy, much as Russia has done with the theories of Karl Marx. The apparent success of England profoundly influenced the thinking of the Western World. This thinking was reflected in the historical explanations for the separation of America from the rest of the Empire.

It has long been obvious to students who have examined contemporary opinion on the eve of the Revolution that there was a wide discrepancy between ascertainable facts and the current descriptions of the workings of the British colonial system.

Today British statesmen have completely abandoned their century-old theories of the infallible righteousness of the doctrines of free trade. Tariffs and other trade regulations are again a reality in England, and protection of home markets against foreign competition and encouragement of exports is a fixed practice. Planned economies are the order of the day. In addition there are being created most elaborate monetary and priority systems to promote trade within the Empire and to develop colonial resources. It is an almost feverish rush to devise ways and means to set up and again secure to the mother country and the colonies the advantages of the close-knit, economically efficient commercial and industrial organization that was terminated by the American Revolution.

We also see the United States embarking upon a system of extreme regulation of trade and industry and subsidization of foreign markets without parallel in Western nations since the days of Montesquieu. With such reversals of theories and practices in progress, it seems opportune to examine anew the evidence upon which it has been assumed that the old trade and navigation laws were a material cause for the separation from England.

The object of this study is to assemble the evidence. Four main lines of investigation have been undertaken: (1) the attitude of representative Americans toward the trade and navigation acts; (2) the attitude of representative British groups; (3) the specific provisions of the acts affecting the colonies and how they were working; (4) the anti-trade policy adopted after 1764 and how it operated to destroy imperial unity.

To supply a background of information on contemporary opinion between 1765 and 1775, the author has gone over *in extenso* the chief sources from which men living at that time could have known what was going on. He undertook to find and to read what adults might have read and what could well have been the current subjects of discussion in various local areas.

The chief sources of current information were the almanacs, the printed sermons, the local newspapers, the ephemeral broadsides, and the contemporary expository and controversial pamphlets. To these should be added the solid volumes of history, government, science, and economic and political theory that were widely circulated at the time. Only the well-to-do and the professional classes could secure the latter, but the public generally had pretty free access to the other kinds of material.

The first systematic search was for the colonial newspapers. Every important file was located and read in the preliminary search. They were examined, not for information upon a single item, but for what they contained. The object was to discover what the contemporary newspaper reader could have known from that source, the nature of the news service, the type of contributed article, the kinds and sources of copied items, evidences of the expression of opinion by local editors, the influence of other newspapers, and the content and character of the advertising carried by each. The files of British newspapers in our libraries are not so extensive, but they too were searched for news from America and articles dealing with American affairs.

Examination of contemporary pamphlets involved many difficulties. Evans' list of American imprints is a good beginning; but there is no convenient location list to indicate where they can best be consulted. In the case of the British pamphlets it was necessary to assemble lists as one worked, since there was nothing comparable to Evans for British imprints. Shelf lists turned out to be more practicable than the general card catalogue, because one had to work in the absence of definite information as to authors and titles. The collections that were found especially useful were those at the William L. Clements Library at Ann Arbor, which is not only the best collection west of the Alleghenies, but is especially strong in British titles; the collections of the Widener Memorial Library, the Boston Public Library, and the Massachusetts Historical Society; the John Carter Brown Library at Providence, Rhode Island; and the Rare Book Room of the Library of Congress at Washington, D. C. The last mentioned has the most complete collection of both British and American pamphlets in this country. The American Antiquarian Society's collection is also useful and contains some items not found elsewhere. The collection at the New York Public Library is excellent, but was not used so extensively as the others. The British Museum was found to contain many items not available in American libraries.

Broadsides were found chiefly in Boston, New York, and Philadelphia, which apparently were the places where they were most used. Contemporary almanacs were consulted mainly at the Library of Congress, which has a very complete collection. They contain much besides the usual astronomical data, especially those published in Boston.

Manuscripts were consulted chiefly at the Massachusetts Historical Society, the Historical Society of Pennsylvania, and the Manuscript Division of the Library of Congress. The unpublished Orme papers were examined at the Essex Institute at Salem, Massachusetts. Wherever printed sets of papers were available, they were used instead of the manuscript copies.

As the examination of contemporary materials progressed and the point of view of those living in 1765 to 1775 became clearer, the need of revision of many current historical statements became evident. This was especially true of the trade and navigation laws as an important cause for the separation from Great Britain.

As thousands of pages of colonial newspapers were turned and hundreds of American and British pamphlets examined, the absence of any adverse references to the long-established commercial relations between the colonies and the mother country became impressive. Writers were not discussing that subject; but they were discussing constitutional relationships, theories and incidence of taxation, and past practices along these lines. They were profoundly interested in the future development of America and the Empire as a whole. There was active and positive difference of opinion, and clear evidence of the gradual stratification of that opinion into definite political groups. The Americans had grievances; but, if the century-old navigation system was prominent among them, it is not adequately reflected in their contemporary literature.

With ample negative evidence accumulating that the traditional treatment of the Navigation Acts as a cause of the Revolution did not properly reflect the attitude of popular opinion in America, the published and unpublished papers of those who became most prominent on the American side of the controversy were examined. Was there evidence that they found the trade and navigation system especially burdensome and were secretly plotting to escape from it, but for various reasons wished to put forward other issues for popular discussion? Again the evidence was either negative, or expressive of a surprisingly widespread general satisfaction with the system as it existed prior to 1764.

At this stage it was determined to make a detailed examination of the entire regulation of colonial trade on its way to and from England to the colonies and also in its passage to its ultimate markets. The simple assignment of the navigation laws to three or four important statutes so commonly found in standard treatises at once was revealed as a very dangerous oversimplification. The trade of the Empire was discovered to be an economic whole with a complicated mass of legal regulation. Hundreds of laws with no reference to America profoundly affected colonial trade. The descriptions of the mercantile system as found in certain well-known philosophical treatises were also quickly revealed as the crudest caricatures of what was actually going on.

Finally the search led to the vast collection of Treasury and Customs papers in the Public Record Office in London. These were examined for details of the trade of the Empire—imports, exports, duties, bounties, rebates, discriminating and differential tariffs, seizures, important ports, destination of exports, etc. It was an almost unworked field. Among these papers were found extensive portions of the presumably lost papers of the American Customs Commissioners. Examination of records of this type is a slow and laborious task. The meaning of hundreds of pages of closely written statistical records cannot be determined by a single survey. Thousands of pages were microfilmed so they could be examined, studied, and compared as needed. The study has taken many years.

It is anticipated that this volume may provoke considerable discussion and sharp differences of opinion. It is realized that many of its conclusions are not in accord with those commonly held, and with some that have been accepted and supported by names of great respectability. However, they are based upon evidence drawn from sources that have been largely unused.

This study reveals the serious need for additional research on all phases of the enumeration policy. Every enumerated product thrived under enumeration and became a sick or dying industry after the advantages of enumeration were lost. We need to know why.

In the case of all the important enumerated products we need to know where the distribution trade centered in Great Britain; who the chief merchants were and how they were financed; where the ultimate markets were and the means of supplying them; the extent to which the colonial producers were furnished with working capital by the distribution machinery in the home country; and the services necessary to prepare the raw colonial products to satisfy the ultimate consumers. A part of this has been done in the case of tobacco, but the study is far from complete. Similar studies on a far more extensive scale need to be made of the other enumerated products. Exploitation of colonial producers of enumerated products by the home country is an economic myth. We need to know who gained or lost by the arrangement—British merchants or colonial producers. Possibly the major profits went to neither, but to society at large.

This volume is divided into two main sections. The first describes conditions of trade that were in fact the cement of empire. This condition had existed for a hundred years and had enabled the British Empire to outstrip all other colonial empires. This was the century of the trade and navigation systems where the chief motive was to encourage British trade and commerce. It worked.

The second section deals with the change of policy beginning in 1764, where the dominant motive was not regulation and development, but regulation for the sake of revenue and political exploitation. In ten short years the cement of loyalty had been eroded and dissolved. It is a story based upon evidence and attested by practically every customs officer on duty in America. The hostility was not to the old navigation and trade system, but to a new policy contrary to that system. This is not a new theory. It was the situation as understood by the men who made and won the Revolution, and admitted by those who opposed it.

The prediction is freely made here that if modern empires are to survive they must be tied together by such mutually advantageous economic arrangements as so successfully integrated the

British colonial Empire under the complicated trade and navigation laws. Mutual prosperity and protection for all sections of a
far-flung empire is a cohesive element of enormous adhesive power.
It generates loyalty to the whole empire. It has to be modified to
meet new conditions. What worked in the eighteenth century
could not be expected to work in the twentieth century.

OLIVER M. DICKERSON

Greeley, Colorado, January, 1951.

Part I

THE CEMENT OF EMPIRE

I

THE BRITISH MERCANTILE SYSTEM
IN OPERATION

A CENTURY AGO England, with the first tools of the industrial revolution in her possession, was shifting from a complicated system of protected and managed economy to a system of free trade. Manufacturing and shipping interests displaced the landed interests in Parliament. It was to their advantage to have ample labor, cheap raw materials, and low wages. Their success depended upon underselling their competitors in the markets of the world. For the time free trade seemed the road to national prosperity. British agriculture was sacrificed—it could not compete with the virgin lands of America. Her example profoundly affected economic theories in the United States, and the devotees of the new theories of economic orthodoxy rewrote our colonial history in terms of the accepted ideas of their group.

Today the hands of the clock of time have completed their circuit and we see the British rebuilding a system of tariffs, trade preferences, and controls as the only way of preserving the Empire. Free-trade ideas of a century ago are obsolete. England must export or die. Food must be produced on English soil or her people will go hungry. Regulated and controlled economics are again the order of the day. Discriminations in favor of British trade are now the cement of empire. It is possible that the commercial regulations of the eighteenth century were also an integrating force tending to bind the Empire together instead of disrupting it.

3

The time has come for a reëxamination of the commercial system of the old colonial empire in terms of how it actually worked and how it affected people and conditions at that time.

The Problem

What we have to explain is how a system of trade regulation that worked without serious friction for more than a century, built up the greatest overseas European population in the world, and made British America the mecca for peoples of other nations, could suddenly become a cause of the disruption of the greatest colonial empire of its time.

If the navigation system was a cause of American revolt, then it must have worked in such a way as to produce either real or fancied economic distress among the colonists. Historically it is about as important to know what people thought of an economic system under which they lived as to know how it worked. A system may work well; but if important groups of the population are opposed to it, they may insist it works badly and agitate for its change. In either case contemporary evidence is usually adequate to determine the actual conditions.

Were the Navigation Acts an active cause of the American opposition to the British imperial system between 1765 and 1775? To answer our question we need to know: (1) what the Navigation Acts included and how they operated. (2) What did Americans at the time think of the system? Did they make it the subject of active complaint and protest? (3) What was the attitude of the British toward the system? Did they consider it a distinct advantage and essential to their welfare? Did they think the Americans were trying to break through the system, and hence adopt measures to retain the Americans within it? (4) What were the observations and testimony of historians contemporary with the events themselves, and hence cognizant of the current popular opinion and discussion that was too intangible to be preserved in the written and printed records of the time?

It is not intended to enter into an elaborate description of the Navigation Acts and their administration. Professor Harper has done that job so thoroughly that it must be considered a definitive historical study.[1]

A concise statement of the main features of the system is essential, however, to a consideration of the major question. One must, of course, know what the Navigation Acts were and how they operated before he can pass upon them as a cause of serious discontent.

In 1765 the thirteen American colonies were a part of the second largest colonial empire in the world in point of area, and the largest in point of wealth, population, and material resources. It included the kingdom of Great Britain and Ireland with the outlying islands in Europe; colonies on the Gold Coast of Africa; India, Ceylon, and some minor islands in Asia; Newfoundland; Hudson Bay, Nova Scotia, Quebec, Massachusetts Bay, Rhode Island, Connecticut, New York, New Jersey, Pennsylvania, Delaware, Maryland, Virginia, North Carolina, South Carolina, Georgia, East Florida, West Florida, and proposed new interior colonies on the continent of North America; the Bahamas, Bermuda, Jamaica, Antigua, Barbados, and the Leeward and Windward groups of minor islands in the West Indies; and the settlements of Belize in Central America.

Literally the American portion was an Atlantic ocean empire, the parts of which were connected with each other and with the home islands by water communications as the parts of an inland empire are connected by roads. Any government has to exercise control over the vital lines of communication which tie it together. The British colonial Empire's lines of communication were all by water. Consequently, the commercial regulations which bound together this far-flung extension of the homeland were, and remained, controls over ocean-going commerce. For all practical purposes they began at one port and ended at another. The few attempts to extend them over inland production and commerce proved futile because there was no administrative machinery to deal with conditions and commerce except by sea. It is important to keep this in mind. The British colonial Empire did not, and never has, developed the direct governmental agencies for the control of interior areas that have made the United States government so effective.

This vast empire was economically self-contained. The navigation laws were only a few of the many regulations built up in the course of a century and a half. The system was inevitably highly complicated, and in many ways it was very much like the intricate protective tariffs and the commission-controlled, rate-making transportation systems of the United States. As regulations increased in complexity, the number of persons affected by even the slightest change also increased. This is true of all schemes for regulating economic affairs by law. What benefited one group might inconvenience another.

The system may have been founded originally upon the general mercantile theory that trade was valuable only when it yielded a net return in gold and silver, and that colonies were chiefly sources of supply for raw materials and outlets for manufactured goods of the home country; yet in actual practice it included all sorts of variations from this theory. Again it was not unlike the American tariff system. There are well-known theories of free trade and of protection as means of promoting commerce or of building up infant industries; but when it comes to tariff-making, the general theories have very little bearing upon specific provisions written into the laws. A single item in a tariff schedule cannot be changed without affecting other schedules and industries in the most unexpected ways. If some unprotected industry secures protection, a number of already protected industries demand additional protection to cover the increased costs of their raw materials or the changes in their markets incident to the new rates.[2] Gradually this condition came to exist in the British Empire of the eighteenth century. No greater error can be made than to assume that the system in operation at a given time corresponded even roughly to the mercantilist theories expounded by the well-known writers.

So far as the commercial system directly affected the colonies, there were five main groups of laws: (1) laws regulating the nationality of the vessels, their crews, and ownership, in which goods could be shipped; (2) laws regulating the destination to which certain goods could be shipped; (3) extensive tariff regulations so adjusted as to promote specific industries; (4) an elaborate system of rebates, drawbacks, export bounties, and export taxes; (5) direct prohibition of industries that tended to develop competition with other industries that were already established, or were being promoted by other favorable legislation. These will be taken up in the order indicated.

The Navigation Acts

Acts regulating shipping go far back into British history. As early as the reign of Richard II foreign shipping had been excluded from the business of carrying goods from one British port to another; that is, the coasting trade was limited to vessels of British nationality. As new dominions separated from the mainland developed, British coast lines increased and the principles of the coastwise trade inevitably expanded.[3]

So far as the American colonies are concerned, navigation acts had their immediate inception in the laws of 1649 and 1651 of the Commonwealth period. These were reënacted with modifications in 1660 by the Restoration Parliament and became the permanent, basic Navigation Act which is customarily referred to in discussions. This law was designed to protect the British shipping industry from Dutch competition. It provided that after December 1, 1660, no goods or commodities whatsoever should be imported into or exported out of any colonies or plantations in Asia, Africa, or America, that belonged to, or might in the future be acquired by, the King of England, except such as were shipped in English-owned vessels of which the master and three-fourths of the crew were English. The phraseology specifically defined as English, residents of the colonies as well as those of the British Isles;[4] and this inclusion of colonials in all regulations concerning shipping remained a permanent feature of the navigation system until the Revolution. Section two of the same act excluded aliens from the privilege of acting as factors or merchants in the plantations. Section four provided that foreign goods could be imported into England only in English ships or in ships belonging to the country where the goods were produced; also that imports in foreign vessels could come only from the place of production or common origin.

Section three limited the importation into England of goods produced in Asia, Africa, or America to such as were imported in English ships. This section, together with section four, effectually transferred the European and colonial distributing trade from Dutch to British ports. Heretofore Holland had been the center of such trade for more than half a century. Her ships visited all parts of the world and brought their products to Dutch ports, from which they were reshipped to other places where they were wanted. By the operation of sections three and four of this act, Dutch ports and vessels could no longer supply the British market. Instead, English vessels now brought goods to English ports, there to be reshipped to other countries and to other portions of the British colonial Empire.

This law confined the carrying trade between various parts of the British Empire to English ships, giving to them a complete legal monopoly. It applied to this vast commerce not only the common principles of a coastwise trade, but it very greatly limited the trade of foreign vessels at English ports, and excluded them completely from colonial ports. The direct traffic between the colonies and foreign countries was confined to such trade as was carried in English ships. England was the only part of the vast empire to which foreign vessels were admitted for trading purposes.

The provisions of this basic Navigation Act were reinforced from time to time and extended by clauses dealing with the import and export of specific commodities, which required in all cases that they be shipped only in English vessels. Thus there was built up, both within and without the Empire, an extensive commerce entirely confined to and monopolized by English shipping. Colonial vessels were English, and shared in the profits of this protected trade just the same as if their owners were resident in England. The term "English" meant nationality and not geographic place of residence. Virginians were just as much Englishmen as those living in London.

Supporting and protecting this vast carrying trade was the power of the British navy: sweeping the seas free of pirates; holding the Barbary states in awe and compelling them to refrain from molesting British vessels engaged in the Mediterranean trade; and, in time of war, supplying the physical protection for commerce that enabled this business to go on with a minimum of costs for insurance, and the least possible interruption from enemy operations.

Capital employed in British shipping was thus insured a better prospective return on the investment and a smaller danger of total loss than capital invested in any other shipping industry in the world. British shipping increased rapidly after 1660,[5] and no portion of it more rapidly than the part of it that was colonial. In this development New England especially shared. The navigation system was the foundation upon which her shipbuilding industry and her vast carrying trade were built.

In the practical operation of the laws regulating shipping, the coastwise trade from one American colonial port to another, including the vast trade from the New England colonies to the West Indies, fell mainly into the hands of colonial shipowners.[6] A large part of the direct trade from England to the colonial ports to bring back the bulky colonial products, the coastwise trade in Great Britain, and much of the trade from Great Britain to European ports was concentrated in the hands of shipowners resident in the British Isles. There was an extensive colonial trade, carried on by colonial ships, directly from the colonies to the Mediterranean and south European ports. There was also an extensive trade directly from the colonies to the British African ports.[7]

The gradual settling of trade into channels served by shipowners whose home ports were British or colonial did not rest so much upon provisions of the law as upon practical considerations. The ships built for trans-ocean service were large and too expensive to operate in the coastal service. Costs of entering and clearing ports varied with the size of the vessel. Thus, pilots' fees alone at the port of Charleston, South Carolina, in 1768, as stated in the annual almanac, varied from £7-10s for a vessel drawing six feet of water to £62-10s for a vessel drawing seventeen feet. Such costs practically forced the master of a large vessel to secure his entire cargo at a single port.

The small colonial vessels, on the other hand, were not suited to compete with the large cargo carriers for the direct trade between colonial ports and England. Shipowners decided for them-

selves what type of trade they wished to enter. Colonial shipowners had the same legal right at any time to engage in the direct
trade with England as did owners who lived in Britain. An Englishman was an Englishman regardless of where he resided.

How could the part of the system just described be a cause of
the Revolution? When the laws were first enacted, there were protests from both Massachusetts, the chief shipowning province; and
from Virginia, the chief tobacco colony. The laws threatened tem-
porarily-increased freight rates to the Virginia tobacco planters.
Concessions were granted Virginia, assuring her that the system
was not to operate as a tax upon her chief industry; and Massachusetts ultimately ratified the laws in 1674 when informed by
emissaries from Charles II that obedience to them was expected.[8]
From this time forward complaints about the shipping clauses of
the Navigation Acts were nonexistent.

COMMODITY CLAUSES

The second phase of the navigation system, as originally adopted,
was the policy of listing or enumerating specific colonial products
which had to be shipped to ports within the Empire and could go
to foreign countries usually only from ports in the mother country.
At first this list included only tobacco, sugar, indigo, cotton-wool,
ginger, fustic and other dyewoods.[9] This original list included no
product of New England and only one grown in Virginia. All but
the first item were the products of the tropical or semi-tropical
colonies.

As the chief world market for these articles was in England, this
regulation helped create a large direct trade between the colonies
where they were grown and the mother country. There were advantages in this plan for the colonial producers. It brought them
into direct relation with the great wholesale merchants, enabled
them to secure the services of agents to look after their orders for
supplies, insured them an adequate amount of shipping at the
time their crop had to be moved, and permitted them to arrange
for the credits necessary to carry on the plantation type of agriculture.

Frequently there were other compensations. In the case of tobacco the American planters were given a monopoly of the home market in Great Britain. This result was brought about by very high tariffs upon Spanish and other foreign tobacco,[10] and by a legal prohibition of tobacco culture in England, Ireland, and Guernsey.[11]

As time went on the list of enumerated articles was extended to include naval stores,[12] hemp,[13] rice,[14] molasses,[15] beaver skins,[16] furs,[17] and copper ore.[18] Of this new list, all but molasses were products of the continental colonies. The enumeration of rice was relaxed when it was found that the cost of unloading and reshipping in England seriously interfered with the market for rice in Portugal.[19]

The Sugar Act of 1764 added coffee, pimento, cocoa nuts, whale fins, raw silk, hides and skins, pot and pearl ashes, to the list of enumerated articles. The first three were products of the Caribbean Islands, whale fins were largely supplied by the northern fisheries, and the rest came principally from Georgia and the Carolinas. No major industry in any colony was involved. In addition the same law forbad the exportation of iron and lumber to Europe.[20] Two years later it was made illegal to export any non-enumerated goods direct to Europe north of Cape Finisterre.[21] These provisions probably affected the course of trade only slightly as the direct exports of these articles to the proscribed areas was very small.

It should not be understood that the American colonies, including those in the West Indies and Central America, were alone singled out for a policy of enumeration. The same policy applied to the East India settlements in Asia[22] and to gum senegal from Africa.[23]

As colonial products increased beyond the needs of the British home market, drawbacks were provided so that the colonial products could pass through the British market without being so heavily burdened as to hamper their sale in competition with similar products in the world markets. This policy will be treated in detail in another chapter.

ENCOURAGEMENT OF SPECIFIC INDUSTRIES

The object of all systems of protection is to increase production, expand markets, and prevent home producers from being driven out of their occupations by cheaper, foreign competition. Such a policy was not limited to industries in England, but included those in the overseas dominions.

The first colonial industry to receive this special attention was that of naval stores. An ample supply of tar, pitch, turpentine, resin, and hemp was essential to shipping, both naval and commercial. Navies could not operate without such articles in time of war, and large quantities at reasonable prices were needed for the expanding British carrying trade. These products were as essential to the shipping industry then as coal and oil are today.

Prior to 1700 the main source of supply had been the Baltic regions. Commencing in 1704 extensive efforts were made to develop this industry in the colonies. After the failure of efforts at direct production under government agents,[24] the policy of encouragement by bounties upon importation into England was adopted and continued down to the Revolution.[25]

Colonial shipowners had the opportunity of buying tar and pitch of their own production; and these products received, in addition to the preference of the colonial market, a liberal bounty on delivery at the customhouses in England, plus a practical monopoly of the British home market. As colonial production increased, import duties on the Baltic product were increased so as to shut it out as an effective competitor.[26] A similar policy was followed in the case of hemp.[27]

Under this policy of special protection the very important colonial naval-stores industry was built up, especially in the Carolinas, although tar was also produced in paying quantities in many other colonies—at least it appears as an important item in their exports. Under similar encouragement of an import bounty of six pence a pound,[28] indigo became a leading crop in South Carolina, Georgia, and Florida,[29] after its cultivation had been practically abandoned in Jamaica.

Raw silk imported from the American colonies was not only

not seem to have been burdensome to the industry where it had natural advantages.[64]

The dependence upon wood for fuel probably meant the ultimate failure of most iron works, except in sections where forests were still undisturbed and the land was not attractive for farming. Even here the furnaces quickly used up the available wood supply within profitable hauling distance. Thus the fuel supply was exhausted far more rapidly than the supply of ore, but exhaustion of either was fatal to the local enterprise. Lack of a permanent fuel supply was the chief handicap to the iron industry in England,[65] and it proved to be a similar handicap in America. Any effective permanent iron and steel industry had to await the development of the use of coal in blast furnaces as a dependable fuel supply.

REGULATION OF COLONIAL CURRENCIES

The various acts of Parliament regulating the value of foreign coins[66] and limiting the issue of paper money were more important, effected more people, and were probably productive of more friction and irritation than all of the other regulations combined. The creation of an adequate circulating medium, adjusted to the varying needs of the different colonies, was one of the most serious problems of imperial administration. The rapidly expanding trade of the colonies with each other and with other parts of the Empire, along with the extensive credit system upon which nearly all trade was conducted, made any local solution of such an issue impossible.

The long credits given to merchants, and by them to buyers, and the common practice frequently sanctioned by law, by which even customs duties were not paid until some months after goods were imported, made it impossible to estimate profits and costs of doing business, unless there was reasonable stability to the medium in which debts were discharged. Conditions of trade also made local forms of currency vary considerably in purchasing power when transferred to other places—hence, the attempts of British merchants to have all prices, charges, and legal payments regulated in terms of coin.

A common monetary system for the entire British colonial Empire was an unsolved problem at the time of the Revolution and has never been effectually resolved by the post-Revolutionary Empire. The difficulty was fundamental in the type of control developed over the colonies. There was no administrative machinery that reached beyond the control of ocean-borne commerce. The British colonial Empire was not, and has never become, a centralized government like the United States with its far-flung dependencies. Even the United States may find its imperial controls break when it faces the problem of control over colonial currencies.[67]

WERE THE NAVIGATION ACTS OPPRESSIVE?

BANCROFT says "American independence, like the great rivers of the country, had many sources, but the headspring which colored all the stream was the Navigation Act."[1] Other writers join in the general condemnation, but few are specific as to just who was hurt and by what provisions of the acts. Let us examine the operation of the system in detail.

Whatever may have been the opinion of some Americans in 1660 in regard to the basic law limiting the carrying trade of the British Empire to English vessels, by 1760 all opposition had disappeared, and a careful search of contemporary newspapers, pamphlets, and other publications discloses no record of anyone seriously proposing an abrogation of that law. Certainly New England, whose fishing, trading, and shipbuilding industry rested upon this law, would not be expected to ask for changes that would bring in the competition of foreign ships. The only sections of the colonial empire that could theoretically have found such a regulation even an imaginary grievance were those engaged in plantation types of industry, where markets were distant and freights heavy.

There may have been a time when freight rates were influenced by the presence or absence of the foreign-owned ships, but after 1700 the expansion of English shipping, especially from New England sources, had become so great that there was ample competition.[2] American ports swarmed with shipping, some owned in

England but much more of it in the colonies. In 1768 more than two thousand vessels cleared from the American continental ports for the West Indies alone. By 1771 it required more than one thousand vessels to serve Virginia and Maryland, and over eleven hundred for the two chief ports in Massachusetts, Boston and Salem. In 1770 a total of 4,171 ships, with a combined tonnage of 488,724, cleared from the various continental ports.[3]

The trade to the West Indies was indeed notable, employing more ships with a greater total tonnage than England was using in her trade with Holland, and far more than she used in her direct trade with Norway, Sweden, and the Eastland countries of the Baltic.[4]

In addition, colonial shipping enabled Britain completely to dominate the Mediterranean trade. In 1768 the clearances from American ports for south Europe totaled 436 ships, with a combined tonnage of 37,093. At that time England was only using 23,113 tons in her trade to the Straits of Gibraltar, which encountered less than one per cent of foreign competition. Clearances from America are not included in this figure, so the American tonnage is in addition to the English figure, but is included in the percentage of English ships passing the Straits.[5]

The expansion of colonial shipping continued to the Revolution. By 1775 nearly one third of all the ships in Britain registered as English were colonial built. Instead of being oppressive the shipping clauses of the Navigation Act had become an important source of colonial prosperity which was shared by every colony. As a device for launching ships these clauses were more efficient than the fabled beauty of Helen of Troy's face.

There was another important compensation in having a shipping industry under the British flag adequate for all commercial purposes. The plantation industries, such as tobacco, rice, sugar, and indigo, had to depend upon an annual market of their staple product and an assured supply of food, clothing, tools, and other necessities that were not produced locally. This supply was dependent wholly upon the annual fleets that visited their ports. So long as England effectually controlled the seas, English shipping could serve them in time of war about as freely as in time of peace. Had they been dependent upon foreign shipping, the outbreak of a war might have meant complete suspension of their industries.

Business of any kind needs stability of conditions under which large investments of capital are made. The plantation colonies were conducted under conditions of as large individual investments of capital as were the manufacturing industries of the time. It was sounder economic practice to pay somewhat higher freight rates, if necessary, than to face the economic losses incident to a dependence upon foreign shipping; besides, there is no proof that freight rates within the British Empire were not as low after 1700 as those outside. Certainly there is no evidence in contemporary publications of any agitation to repeal this provision of the Navigation Act, nor did prominent Americans express any desire for a general relaxation of its major requirements.

ENUMERATION

Enumeration of commodities of colonial production has been pictured as an outstanding sin of mercantilism. The English continental colonies had three products of major importance, tobacco, rice, and indigo, included in the enumerated list. All were agricultural and were grown commercially only in the southern colonies.

It should be clear that no one would engage in producing enumerated commodities unless he expected to make a profit. If he found his venture unprofitable he could shift his energies to other crops. No one was under any legal compulsion to grow the enumerated products. In spite of the extravagant language that has been used to condemn the system, the grower of enumerated commodities was not enslaved by the legal provisions of enumeration. Obviously growers continued to produce rice, indigo, and tobacco because they made larger cash profits from their cultivation than they could make by using their land, labor, and capital in any other way.

The most cursory examination of these industries reveals that each had its list of wealthy planters who had accumulated fortunes in a few years by growing the enumerated crops. These men and their families were the aristocrats of the South. No similar conditions existed elsewhere in the vast agricultural regions of the colonies. Let us examine the conditions of each industry.

TOBACCO

Tobacco, the most important of all colonial exports, suffered from all the disadvantages of other agricultural crops. Late frosts could destroy the tender plants in the seed beds; and early frosts could damage the mature crop before it was harvested. Favorable seasons could produce unusually heavy yields; and heat and lack of moisture could seriously lighten a crop. There were recurring surpluses and shortages. Also there were worms, plant diseases, and soil depletion. All of these and many more were hazards that the grower had to face in colonial times and still does. All are interesting details of the burdens of the tobacco planter, but they have no possible connection with the Navigation Acts. They existed without benefit of law and always will.

Tobacco growers in many cases were debtors. That condition was not peculiar to the tobacco industry and again has no possible connection with enumeration. Farmers who engage in commercial farming always have been in debt and always will be. Farming is a business. It requires land, buildings, equipment, labor, good clothing, and shelter for those engaged in it. Costs for these have to be met for months before a crop can yield any return. Unless inherited, these things had to be supplied by the farmer himself from savings or from borrowings. Most farmers chose the latter course and hoped to make the business ultimately clear itself. In this respect tobacco raising was not different from other business enterprises.

The great assembling and processing markets were in Great Britain, as were also the bankers who supplied the essential working capital. Growing tobacco was one job, marketing it was another. Both were essential parts of the industry.

Tobacco was not only the most important colonial enumerated product, it was an essential source of revenue to the British government. It was one article that could stand enormous taxation without materially reducing its consumption.

Prior to the union with Scotland tobacco could be shipped only to England or Wales; but after 1707 it could go to Scotland as freely as to England. Soon there developed most active competition between Scotch merchants, mostly in Glasgow, and the English tobacco merchants with headquarters in London or the English "outports." The customs service kept three sets of books: one for London, another for the "outports," and a third for Scotland. All of these have to be consulted to get the entire picture. Ireland remained a foreign country so far as tobacco was concerned.

The decade preceding the Revolution was one of rapid expansion for the tobacco planters. American tobacco was supplying a steadily expanding world market. The most important fact in the

TABLE 1. TOBACCO IMPORTATIONS INTO GREAT BRITAIN[7]

(in pounds)

	London	Outports	Scotland	Total
1767	25,723,434	13,417,175	28,937,891	68,078,500
1768	23,353,891	12,103,603	33,237,236	68,694,730
1769	24,276,259	9,480,127	....	....
1770	26,758,534	12,419,503	38,708,809	77,886,846
1771	42,952,725	15,006,771	48,269,865	106,229,361
1772	36,265,788	15,101,682	45,259,675	96,627,145
1773	37,918,111	18,010,718	44,544,230	100,473,059
1774	36,859,641	19,186,837	41,348,295	97,394,773
1775	45,250,505	10,210,997	45,863,154	101,324,656

complicated expanding tobacco trade was the rise of Scotland as a chief primary market. Scottish imports rose from 12,213,610 pounds in 1746 to 48,269,865 pounds in 1771, a growth of more than four hundred per cent in twenty-five years.[6] Finding, servicing, and holding an additional market for 36,000,000 pounds of tobacco was a real feat of merchandising. At the same time the London merchants were increasing their importations, but at a slower rate. The merchants in the English "outports" just about held their own. From 1767 to 1771 Scotland imported nearly as much American tobacco as did London and the "outports" combined and remained the chief market to the Revolution. Table 1 shows the course of the tobacco trade for the nine years preceding independence.

Enumeration clearly did not hamper the expansion of the tobacco raising business in America. Any industry that enjoys an expansion of its total production of more than fifty per cent in five years and holds that growth has at least the appearance of prosperity.

This expansion of tobacco raising in America could not have occurred without the aid of the great tobacco marketing centers. The merchants at these centers found and developed new markets in Europe; graded, processed, and repacked the tobacco to suit the varying tastes of tobacco users; supplied, on their own personal security, the liquid capital to buy, ship, and store the annual crops; and found additional funds for loans to planters in America with which they bought land, slaves, and equipment to start new plantations.

The marketing of the tobacco crops each year employed enormous sums. The mere payment to the planter at the lowest price of two pence a pound would have required $4,000,000. In addition there was freight, insurance, export duties, port charges, duties in England, unloading, cartage, warehousing, that had to be paid for. That was only the beginning. No merchandise sells itself. Purchasers had to be found. The tobacco had to be prepared to meet varying demands. Some could be reëxported in the original hogsheads in which it was imported. Some had to be made into snuff or various types of smoking and chewing tobacco. A very important tobacco manufacturing industry was developing at the centers. A keen set of merchants sought out the varying demands and supplied the tobacco in the form desired. The results are impressive.

At the beginning of the century Spain was an important supplier of tobacco for the English market. She had under her control the finest tobacco lands in the world. But after 1760 Spain was actually importing more than a million pounds of American tobacco annually from Glasgow and London.[8] In addition, American-grown tobacco was being exported to Great Britain, processed, and shipped back to the American colonies to be sold in the very areas where it was originally grown. In 1772 American customers bought more than 500,000 pounds of American tobacco processed in Great Britain, nearly one-fifth of which was imported at New York.[9]

On the eve of the Revolution America was raising tobacco for a world market, created by the merchandising skill of the English and Scottish merchants. Only a small part of the tobacco annually reaching Britain was ultimately consumed there. Johnson says that four-fifths of the total annual importations were reëxported.[10] He does not give the source for his statement nor the time when it was true. His estimates for conditions just before the Revolution are much too low. Total British importations in 1772 were 96,627,145 pounds and total exports that year were 92,845,714 pounds, which is more than ninety-five per cent of the imports.[11] The trade through Scotland that year shows an even higher ratio of reëxports to imports. In 1772 Scotland imported 45,259,675 pounds of tobacco and exported 44,450,543, leaving only about a million pounds for home consumption,[12] or a little more than two per cent.

The course followed by American tobacco as it traveled from its three great primary markets to its ultimate consumers is shown in the following tables, one for England and another for Scotland:

TABLE 2. TOBACCO REËXPORTS FROM ENGLAND, 1772[13]
(in pounds)

Countries to which Exported	From London	From Outports	Total from England
Flanders	3,788,691	710,937	4,499,628
France	7,019,949	2,880,006	9,899,955
Germany	7,579,297	587,156	8,166,453
Holland	16,462,701	2,093,280	18,555,981
Ireland	29,714	1,655,517	1,685,231
Norway and Denmark	616,048	952,972	1,569,020
Spain	854,275	39,281	893,556
Sweden	456,929	990	457,919
Elsewhere	1,805,526	889,588	2,695,114

TABLE 3. TOBACCO REËXPORTS FROM SCOTLAND, 1772[14]
(in pounds)

Countries to which Exported	Amounts	Countries to which Exported	Amounts
Flanders	710,937	Norway and Denmark	789,329
France	22,514,188	Spain	130,081
Germany	3,096,706	Sweden	7,914
Holland	14,075,349	Elsewhere	252,930
Ireland	2,873,109		

Western Europe was the chief market, with France, Holland, and Germany taking more than 76,000,000 pounds in 1772, which was an average year, or more than seventy-five per cent of the total crop exported from America. Scotland was the chief supplier for France and Ireland and a keen competitor for the German, Dutch, and Scandinavian trade. Flanders was almost entirely supplied by the English merchants.

If the tobacco planters were oppressed by enumeration they should have prospered when freed. But what happened? There was a temporary rise in exports to the pre-Revolutionary levels, but the growers quickly learned that the markets gained for them by the British, and especially by the Scotch, merchants could not be held. An attempt by Jefferson, while Minister to France, to sell tobacco directly to the French government did not succeed. The French complained that the tobacco was not up to grade and canceled the contract.[15] Under the old plan of buying in the great central market at Glasgow they could select just the kind of tobacco that best fitted their needs. There was no such market in America and the growers had neither the experience nor the capital to set up such an organization of their own. Grading by public inspectors proved to be wholly inadequate as compared with the grading in the great merchandising and processing centers.

Instead of thriving, the decades following the Revolution show that tobacco was a sick industry, gradually losing an important part of its former export trade. The Napoleonic wars and the War of 1812 caused wide fluctuations in exportations from year to year; but when these are averaged by five-year periods the steady decline is obvious. The full story of this decline is easily read in Table 4.

TABLE 4. TREND OF AMERICAN TOBACCO EXPORTS BEFORE AND AFTER THE REVOLUTION[16]

Years	Average Yearly Exports in Pounds	Years	Average Yearly Exports in Pounds
1767-1770	71,223,398	1805-1809	54,525,206
1771-1775	100,249,615	1810-1814	51,544,857
1790-1794	99,665,656	1815-1819	84,533,350
1795-1799	70,625,518	1820-1822	79,369,141
1800-1804	85,935,914		

The same countries of Europe that bought 96,727,147 pounds of American tobacco in 1772 bought only 68,327,550 pounds fifty years later. Holland was buying only 23,692,034 pounds as contrasted with 32,631,330 in 1772. France had taken 32,414,143 pounds in 1772 but was buying only 4,665,670 fifty years later. Flanders, that had bought 5,210,565 pounds in 1772 was not even mentioned in our exports for 1822. Exports to Germany remained essentially unchanged from what they had been in 1772.

Partially to compensate for the heavy losses in our export market for tobacco in northern Europe new outlets had been found for a little more than six million pounds in other portions of Europe, and additional exports of ten millions of pounds to other parts of the world. Thus there had been some development of direct new markets, but the total market for American tobacco was millions of pounds short of our exports in 1772.[17]

Most of the loss was in drastic reductions in our exports to Scotland. Direct exports to England had shrunk from 51,367,470 pounds in 1772 to 26,740,000 in 1822, but in the same period exports to Scotland had fallen from 45,259,675 in 1772 to only 1,142,000 fifty years later.

The Revolution not only separated the American colonies from official control by the British government, it separated the tobacco planters from the great banking and marketing organizations that had developed their former world market. A very large proportion of the debts due British merchants and creditors after the Revolution were in the southern states. From what we know of the conditions of agriculture, a large percentage of these must have been advances to the tobacco planters. A total of nearly $35,000,-000 in such claims was filed before the claims commission created by the Jay Treaty and ultimately compromised in 1802 for $2,664,-000.[18] The Scottish merchants seem to have been the chief losers, since they do not again appear prominently in the world tobacco trade. It was three-quarters of a century before the American tobacco industry could replace the great central marketing machinery that had been built up under enumeration.

RICE

Next to tobacco, rice was the most important commercially grown agricultural crop of the continental colonies. Like tobacco it was enumerated, but on the eve of the Revolution had a free market in Europe south of Cape Finesterre and in America south of Georgia. It was an important crop in the lowlands of South Carolina and Georgia.

It has been assumed by many writers that enumeration imposed a serious burden upon the rice planters. The ascertainable facts do not support this assumption. In the years preceding the Revolution the rice industry was prosperous and expanding. Rice exports from Charleston, South Carolina increased from an average of 80,631 barrels per year for the five years, 1760 to 1764, to an annual average of 120,483 barrels for the years 1770 to 1773. The exports from Georgia, the other important producer of rice, rose from an annual average of 5,152 barrels for the years 1760 to 1764 to an average of 21,910 barrels during the years 1770 to 1773.[19] Planters made fortunes during these years.

American rice growers, like American tobacco planters, were producing for a world market. Where was that market? In 1772 rice exports from America totaled 155,741 barrels; of which 97,563 went to Great Britain, 10,066 to South Europe, and 48,112 to the West Indies.[20] This shows that more than sixty per cent of all American rice exported was finding its world market by way of Great Britain and only about seven per cent was exported to that part of Europe that was free from enumeration.

Something other than mere enumeration was attracting rice to the British markets. In 1773 total British imports were 468,915 hundredweight, of which only 11,842 hundredweight were landed in Scotland.[21] The latter can therefore be eliminated as of any importance as a market for rice, after 1770, although it had been a market of major importance ten years before. The world market centered in England and continued to do so for many years.

Analysis of reëxports of rice from Great Britain in 1773 reveals the ultimate market for American rice. A total of 365,325 hundredweight were exported. Of this amount, 242,693 went to Holland; 81,764 went to other parts of Europe north of Cape Finesterre;[22] and 24,684 hundredweight to southern Europe, of which Spain imported 16,657 and Portugal 5,612.[23] Thus, even southern Europe imported more than half as much American rice by way of England as it did directly from the colonies by way of the open market.[24]

What happened to America's world market for rice when the Revolution freed it from enumeration? In 1822, after the world had adjusted itself to peace, our exports of rice totaled 87,089 tierces. Of this amount 40,735 tierces went to Europe; 24,073 of which were imported by the British Isles; 15,526 went to Europe north of Cape Finesterre; and 1,136 tierces to southern Europe. Translating tierces into hundredweight we have the following results: 216,657 hundredweight exported to the British Isles in 1822, as contrasted with 468,915 in 1773; 139,734 hundredweight to continental northern Europe in 1822, as contrasted with 324,407 in 1773; and 10,224 to southern Europe in 1822, as contrasted with combined total direct exports from America and reëxports from Great Britain of 69,981 in 1773. Our total European market for rice was only 366,615 hundredweight in 1822, as contrasted with 484,320 exported to the same area fifty years before.

Like the tobacco planters the rice planters faced changed conditions after the Revolution. While England remained their best market, total exports for the five years beginning in 1782 were less than half what they had been in the five-year period before the war. The war had brought to an end a long period of prosperity for the rice industry. Much of the advantage of the old central market in England was lost. Importations were burdened with new duties, although drawbacks on reëxportation were permitted. Shipping regulations of other countries hampered our trade. Even our ally, France, would not admit our rice-laden ships to her ports in 1788, so that cargoes bound for that country had to be unloaded at Cowes on the Isle of Wight for transshipment to French vessels.[25]

There is nothing in the evidence to support the theory that the rice planters were handicapped or oppressed by enumeration or that they benefited from the freedom to find markets where they could. The advantages of the one great central market still operated as the magnet to attract imports and exports. The planters not only lost a large part of their former markets, but what was even more serious, they lost the financial help they had received from the British merchants. Freedom involved the necessity of finding their own financing as well as their own markets.

INDIGO

Indigo was the third most important enumerated product of the continental provinces. Unlike rice and tobacco, indigo found its ultimate market in Great Britain. It was not only enumerated but was also encouraged by a direct British bounty.

On the eve of the Revolution the indigo planters were very prosperous and production was increasing rapidly, as shown by the tables of exports reported by Sellers[26] and by Gray.[27] Both reports are based upon fragmentary American sources. These show that exports nearly doubled between 1765 and 1773. These estimates are too low. Actual importation by Great Britain in 1773, all certified as produced in the British plantations, was 1,403,684 pounds,[28] or twice that reported by Gray. This is nearly three times the colonial exports reported by Macpherson for 1770,[29] and his reports seem to be based upon official records. Any industry that was so obviously prosperous cannot be called oppressed.

The Revolutionary War quickly brought to a close this period of prosperity for the indigo planters. They soon discovered that the industry could not exist without the former bounties. British aid and encouragement were transferred to Jamaica, which was still within the Empire. American production declined and just about disappeared. By 1822 the reported exports totaled only 3,283 pounds. In the meantime importations of foreign indigo had risen from zero to 1,126,928 pounds, or nearly as much as our exports were in 1773.

THE BALANCE OF TRADE

The relative values of imports from Great Britain into the colonies and exports from them to the home country are frequently cited as proof of economic exploitation. In the form they are usually given they are misleading. The American colonial empire was one economic whole. The products of the West Indies were used by all of the other colonies and their products in turn

Both of these independent studies are in substantial agreement as to the basic facts. Both agree that British legislation had very little effect in retarding colonial manufacturing. We will discuss each measure separately.

WOOL AND WOOLEN GOODS

The prohibitions against exporting wool and American-made woolens has generally been referred to as oppressive. The impression given is that Englishmen in America were being treated less well than those in England.

There is no foundation for this inference. England had developed the wool-growing and wool-manufacturing industry far beyond that of other countries in western Europe. It was an economic advantage of first importance—a sort of atom bomb of the seventeenth century. Under no circumstances was England willing to permit her special advantage to get away. To this end there was enacted a long series of laws regulating wool and possible wool exports, commencing with the Restoration under Charles II and extending through the reign of William III. The American woolens act was a minor item in those regulations.

The restraints imposed upon Englishmen in America who engaged in wool growing or processing were mild in comparison with those faced by Englishmen in England.

There, in addition to provisions against the export or shipment of wool similar to those in the American law, the owners of sheep had to give notice of their plans to shear sheep. They also had to report the exact number of fleeces at shearing time and give official notice of any removal from their farms, as no wool could be moved from one place to another without a permit. Buyers in certain areas had to be licensed under bond, and no raw wool could be loaded on a horse cart to be moved by land except in the daytime and at hours fixed by law.[36] All of the above restrictions remained in force until the Revolution and are listed in the same customs manuals with the American regulations.

As has already been pointed out the prohibitions were not upon production or manufacture but upon water export of such goods. Consequently, household and neighborhood production went on unhampered, as did distribution of such products throughout the colonies and the rapidly expanding back country. Little can be added to the extensive studies of Clark. The back country clothed itself. There was very little cloth made for the market. Colonial newspapers, published in the larger port towns, printed very few advertisements of homespun cloth for sale.

There was no effort to compete commercially with imports from the home country. Textile production was still in the handicrafts stage. Weavers were not well paid and spinners very poorly paid. Working in such industries was associated with extreme poverty.[37] It just did not pay to produce cloth under American conditions when goods of as good or better quality could be had from abroad for less money. Where family labor had no commercial value and money and money-crops were scarce there was extensive production.

American conditions remained largely unchanged long after the Revolution. In 1821 woolen goods of American production is not listed among our exports. On the other hand there appears in the list of goods imported into the United States woolen goods of various kinds to a total value of $11,971,933 out of total imports valued at $41,955,134, or nearly thirty per cent of all our imports.[38]

It is obvious that the failure of colonial America to develop a large export of woolen goods and other textiles rested upon factors entirely separate from a parliamentary act of the seventeenth century.

HATS

The hat act did prevent the shipment of hats by water and may have had a temporary effect upon a developing export trade in New England hats. But the act had no effect upon the steady development of hat manufacturing in America. It was more advantageous for hatmakers to migrate with their skills to new neighborhoods than it was to live in one place and make hats for merchants who, in turn, sold them where they could find a market. Hat manufacture, especially of wool, became widely diffused and was so far advanced that Hamilton in his "Report on Manufactures" in 1791, in discussing the wool industry, stated: "Household manufactures of this material are carried on in different parts of the United States to a very interesting extent; but there is only one branch, which as a regular business can be said to have acquired maturity. This is the making of hats."[39] That statement could hardly have been justified concerning any other manufacturing business. The industry was better developed than any other. In 1810 Tench Coxe reported 842 hatteries operating in the United States, some of which were in the western territories of Indiana, Michigan, and Mississippi. The center of the industry was not in New England, but in Pennsylvania, where 532 operating hatteries were reported.[40]

IRON AND STEEL

The law prohibiting new rolling and slitting mills, plating forges and steel furnaces, passed in 1750, is mentioned in all accounts. In some cases writers have expanded this into an instance of real oppression. Bining, who has made the most detailed study of the colonial iron industry, agrees with Clark that such legislation did not check the development of the iron industry. He even insists that on the eve of the Revolution there were more iron furnaces in operation in America than there were in England and Wales combined and that the total output was greater than that of the iron furnaces of Great Britain.[41] Most of the pots, pans, and other hollow ware used in the colonies were made at local iron works. The growing farming, milling, and extensive wagon transportation demands for iron were absorbing most of the bar iron that could be produced. As a result the British bounties, which attracted increased colonial exports of bar iron from a bare 39 tons in 1761 to a total of 2,234 tons ten years later, proved ineffective after 1771 and exports rapidly declined.[42] The reason was steadily growing demands for domestic use.

Most of the iron works were relatively small and were designed to supply a neighborhood market. In the main they represented personal investments. All of the large colonial iron works were erected by foreign capital and employed imported labor. All of the larger works proved financially unprofitable, largely because of the gradual exhaustion of the local supply of charcoal. That the law was not interfering with the growth of the iron industry is proved by its rapid expansion westward in Pennsylvania and by the fact that the great American Iron Company was set up in 1764 with London capital by Hasenclever, who quickly expended a total of more than a quarter million dollars on the project. It was the largest capital outlay in any colonial manufacturing venture.[43]

Production of steel on a commercial scale came slowly. In 1810 Tench Coxe could report only four steel furnaces in the entire United States with a combined capacity of nine hundred seventeen tons, presumably per year.[44]

Bining did not find a single case where any iron work was discontinued, a slitting mill or steel furnace destroyed, or even an attempted prosecution of an iron works operator. Clark also failed to find a single case in any of the other colonies. An extensive search of the Treasury papers in the Public Record Office in London by the author also failed to reveal a single such prosecution, although there is much material on other clauses of the trade and navigation laws. There is but one conclusion, and that is that the iron industry was not materially hampered by any British legislation and that its development was rapid and continuous.

OTHER MANUFACTURES

British legislation did not apply to other forms of colonial manufacture except to promote them. Naval stores were encouraged by direct British bounties. The Navigation Acts directly encouraged shipbuilding and all of the allied services such as rope-making, and manufacture of anchor chains, bolts, etc. American distilling of rum was on a large scale as was also sugar refining. Enormous quantities of forest products were worked up and exported to all parts of the empire and to South Europe. Millions of staves and shingles were exported annually. Much furniture shows in the list of exports coastwise and to the West Indies. Thousands of tons of bread and flour were manufactured and exported each year.

The major amount of manufactures, however, do not show in the list of exports as they were produced for domestic consumption and were sold within the colonies in the immediate vicinity where they were made.

While no case can be made for any charge that limitations on colonial manufacture were real, the measures discussed above were a part of the controversy. The iron bill carried a potential threat that real interference with domestic manufactures might be attempted. Thus it produced uneasiness in certain circles in America. The growth of colonial manufactures created a fear in England among workers, capitalists, and trading and shipping circles that unless this movement were checked in America they would lose their best markets and face a future of poverty and high taxes. This was the fear upon which the Americans played with their nonimportation agreements.

BOUNTIES

The bounty system certainly was not an item of complaint on the part of American producers. As the bounty policy was one of the most important phases of the general mercantile system, it is of course included in any general denunciation of the industrial and commercial relations of the colonies to the mother country.

The following industries were directly dependent upon such bounties: (1) naval stores, including tar, pitch, resin, turpentine, masts, spars, yards, bowsprits, and hemp; (2) lumber; (3) cooperage materials made of white oak; (4) indigo. The bounties were authorized over such periods that producers could plan production intelligently, and merchants in England could count on a continuous, artificially-attracted supply of such products over a period of years. By 1765 the policy of enacting bounty laws for periods of only a few years was abandoned, and laws were passed fixing bounties for periods as great as twenty years.[45] The total sums expended by the British government for bounties on colonial products were very large and extended over a period of nearly seventy years. They were at their highest point on the eve of the Revolution and were reported by the Comptroller General as amounting to £186,144 during the years 1761 to 1776.[46]

Of the four groups of articles that received bounties, all were produced in colonies that revolted; and the sums expended by the British government in behalf of these industries went wholly to the continental group. It was the southern colonies, rather than the northern, that benefited most from this policy. Naval stores other than masts and spars came largely from North Carolina, South Carolina, and Georgia. Indigo grew chiefly in South Carolina and Georgia, and the most desirable lumber and cooperage materials were the products of the colonies south of Pennsylvania.[47] New England supplied mainly masts and spars, and the bounty on these was relatively insignificant.

It should be noted that the policy of granting bounties continued until the close of the colonial period. Those on lumber and cooperage materials were adopted in the reign of George III; in fact, the first bounty on such products was expected to soften the reception of the Stamp Act in America. The framing of bounty laws in permanent form was also a characteristic feature of the legislation of his reign. No part of the commercial policy was more firmly established than that of bounties, and the sugar interests advocated them as more efficient in promoting their favorite industry than tariffs. Below is a very plausible contemporary argument for such a policy.

"Suppose the bounty (on sugar) should be two shillings six pence per hundredweight, and 12,000 hogsheads, at 12 hundredweight each, should be sent to foreign markets, one year with another the bounty will be no more per annum than £18,000. The value of these 12,000 hogsheads at twenty-five shillings per hundredweight will amount to £180,000 sterling, which will be returned to Great Britain; and according to the common course of the sugar trade may be computed as follows, viz.:

It will pay,

For freight to British seamen and shipping	£ 30,000
To factors, insurers, and customs house officers for charges in marketing it	£ 18,000
Merchandise from Great Britain	£ 36,000
Negroes from Guinea, bought chiefly with British and East India goods	£ 24,000
	£108,000
Remains to the sugar planters and merchants	£ 72,000
	£180,000

"This sum of £180,000 that may be thus saved to this nation by the exportation of 12,000 hogsheads of sugar only, amounts to ten times the proposed bounty."[48] In these days of accumulating farm and other surpluses, this argument has a familiar ring.

The same author, while he favored confining the continental colonies to the supply of sugar and molasses available in the British sugar islands, advocated compensatory bounties on the products of those colonies to make up for the losses incident to their exclusion from the direct trade with the foreign sugar islands.[49]

If the bounty policy was a cause of the Revolution, it operated in a decidedly different way from what has been so confidently asserted by those who condemn the Navigation Acts. The bounty payments were a considerable burden upon the exchequer; and, when the load of taxes after 1763 became a matter of public complaint, the existence of the bounties, their continuance, and the impression made upon public opinion by the figures of total payments during the eighteenth century, became an added reason why the people in America, who apparently benefited from such bounties, should assume their fair share in the costs of Empire.

To the extent that the bounties were a burden upon the British taxpayer and an excuse for taxation of the colonies by the home government, they were a cause of the Revolution. They were certainly not a cause in the sense that such payments produced discontent in America.

Several industries practically disappeared at the end of the Revolution because they could not exist without the bounties. As the beneficiaries of the bounty system were essentially all in the thirteen continental colonies that revolted, it is highly probable that the bounty phases of the navigation system produced a conservative element of loyal supporters of the imperial system—at least so far as men permitted themselves to be influenced by their direct economic interests. There may be a direct relation between the British financial encouragement of colonial industries and the loyalist movement in America. It was definitely strongest in those colonies that benefited most directly from this practice.

PREFERENTIAL TARIFFS

The policy of preferential tariffs and export bounties could not have been a cause of economic complaint on the part of Americans, who thus secured access to the best market in Europe on better conditions than other producers. There was no possible ground for complaint on the part of American consumers when the British government allowed drawbacks of its own import and inland duties upon goods exported from England to the colonies, or when it encouraged both production in England and colonial consumption by export bounties, as it did in many cases. These regulations gave the colonies especially favored treatment, and were causes of prosperity and not of complaint.

INFLUENCE ON GENERAL PROSPERITY

Were the navigation and trade laws so generally burdensome upon the colonies as to interfere with their development, and thus produce general poverty and distress? Again the answer must be negative; just the opposite condition existed. The colonies were prosperous and wages of labor were admittedly higher in the continental colonies than elsewhere in the world.

Population in continental America was doubling every twenty-five years, while in England it was scarcely doubling in a century. In fact the population of England seems to have doubled only once from 1066 to 1600, and again by about 1760, although a very marked increase in population was to characterize the reign of George III. In no other section of the world was there a white population expanding from natural increase so rapidly as in continental America. Marriages occurred early and families were large. The British colonies on the continent were attractive to emigrants, especially from the British Isles, and there are numerous references in the British periodicals, published in the decade, 1765 to 1775, to artisans of all kinds migrating to the new world.[50]

Another measure of their prosperity was the expansion of trade that had occurred during the eighteenth century. Other evidences of wealth were the multiplying educational institutions, churches, newspapers, magazines, and other publications. Many of the finest specimens of colonial church architecture date from the period just before the Revolution.

The wealth acquired by American merchants and planters was a real cause of jealousy on the part of residents in the mother country. There had grown up in America a new race of untitled nobility with estates and palaces that compared favorably with the possessions of the titled classes in England. Their houses were not only well, but even luxuriously, furnished. Their consumption of British and European goods was not limited to necessities, but included luxuries of all kinds. The best evidence of this is the elaborate offerings of goods, including finery of all kinds for both men and women, found in the extensive advertisements in the newspapers of the time. The population of the seaboard was no longer clothed in homespun. Many men wore silk and velvet regularly. Joseph Warren had on his usual silk waistcoat when he was killed at Bunker Hill.

One of the best tests of real prosperity is the rapidity with which a population can sink its public debts following a war. The French and Indian War had been a real world contest so far as the British Empire was concerned. Colonial exertion on the part of the northern colonists, especially, had been on a scale not unlike that of Canada and Australia in the last world war. Many of the colonies levied heavy taxes during the war, and came out with large debts. The total colonial debt according to Charles Lloyd, who prepared the statistical data for the Stamp Act, was £2,600,-000. Yet this was sunk so rapidly that in 1765 it was estimated that only £767,000 remained, and the greater part of that would be sunk by 1767.[51]

The estimate of the time within which the colonies could extinguish their remaining obligations was too optimistic; but past accomplishments made a profound impression upon people in England, who could not hope to reduce their own national debt to the level of 1754 in less than a generation.

The ability of the colonies to sink their heavy war debts at the rate of about twenty per cent a year was a startling performance to thoughtful Englishmen. The economic recovery of the American continental colonies was not unlike that of the United States during the first ten years after World War I. The soreness of many British taxpayers, as they looked forward to long years of heavy taxation of their own people, while their fellow citizens across the Atlantic would soon be free from all but the lightest taxes, especially in view of their belief that the war had been fought and the burdens incurred for the benefit of the Americans, was not unlike the feeling aroused over the war debts in the years immediately following World War I.

A few extracts from the extensive contemporary discussion of this subject may give a better understanding of the way many Englishmen viewed America.

The taxes paid at present by Americans bear no proportion to the burdens of the English. In less than five years, most of their burdens will cease, as their debts will be discharged; there is no hope of relief here, as the total revenue pays only interest and ordinary expenses of government. A future war would increase the taxes to pay interest; Americans have no future wars to dread, as British fleets and armies are a protection against foreign invaders: They can look forward to plenty and security in a wholesome climate and extremely prolific soil. The people of England have to look forward to increasing debts and taxes, frequent wars waged against them because of their burdens, poverty and insecurity, an exhausted people and a deserted country.[52]

England labours under a great load of debt, and heavy taxes; England has a very expensive government to maintain; the Americans have a government of very little expense; and consequently we must dwindle and decline every day in our trade, whilst they thrive and prosper exceedingly. The consequence of this will certainly be that the inhabitants will run away as fast as they can from this country to that, and Old England will become a poor, deserted, deplorable Kingdom— like a farm that has been over-cropped.[53]

It is something remarkable, that ever since the regulations were made last year, concerning the North-American trade, we hardly read a news-paper that does not mention manufacturers of one kind or another going from England, Scotland, or Ireland to settle in those colonies; which, if true, is certainly a matter that should to the last degree prove alarming to these kingdoms.[54]

Your abilities even to share our burthens are unquestionable, seeing that when eight millions of us pay ten millions of taxes, which amounts to twenty-five shillings on each person, three millions of you pay only seventy-five thousand pounds, or six pence on each person, and this in a country where a labouring man gets three times the wages that he does in England, and yet may live on half the expense.

When you tell us that you are unable to pay taxes, pardon us for once in this Address, if we tell you that we do not believe you. . . . For you we submit to monopolies; for you lay restraints on our trade; for you we are taxed; and for you impose similar hardships upon other parts of our dominions.[55]

British officers who served in America were struck by the vast real wealth here: the number of horses, cattle, hogs, farms, thriving cities, bountiful food supplies, and the lavish scale of living they found everywhere in the older parts of the country. Certainly they saw no evidences that the commercial system was reducing the Americans to poverty. On the contrary, they saw evidences of a people acquiring wealth and property more rapidly than elsewhere, with a vision of becoming the richest and most powerful nation in the world. The wealth and prosperity of the Americans was probably one of the causes of the Revolution. It excited both the envy and the fear of some British citizens, and led them to support the taxation policy. It also fired the imaginations of Americans, and led them to think and talk in terms of the vast empire that they conceived would develop here in the next century.

American and British writers prophesied that within half a century the population of the continental colonies and its resultant military and naval strength would exceed that of England. The realization of this fact was one of the reasons for the attempted imperial reorganization between 1763 and 1770, and was largely responsible for serious thinkers abandoning plans for a consolidated imperial legislature made up of representatives from the dependencies as well as the British Isles. Charles Lloyd, Grenville's chief financial lieutenant, urged in 1767 that force should be used to execute the taxation program because, if the Americans were not forced to submit to the authority of Parliament then, their growing strength would make any successful attempts in the future impossible.[56]

No case can be made out for the Navigation Acts as a cause of the Revolution on the grounds that such laws were economically oppressive and were steadily reducing the Americans to a condition of hopeless poverty. It is true that evidences of hard times in the colonies may be found; but such conditions were periodic and were preceded and followed by other periods of over-trading, extravagance, and luxury.[57] There was unquestionably high taxation in some of the colonies during and after the French and Indian War. In places there were price readjustments due to deflation and the termination of large governmental activities. Such conditions were not evenly distributed. There were times when merchants and newspaper publishers complained of slow collections; but such conditions can be found in any region where credit is easy, and they can also be found at times in even the most prosperous countries. The evidence indicates far less depression in the colonies than in the home country in the same years.

It is true that after 1770 there was a serious depression in the tobacco business in a portion of Virginia, which is reflected in the newspapers. In accounting for their economic distress and suggesting possible remedies, the planters in no case charged their distress to the Navigation Acts. Their ideas of what was wrong and of proper remedies sound strangely modern. They charged their economic condition to the too easy credit supplied by the Scottish merchants, and to the organized monopoly of the buyers. One writer seriously proposed active coöperative organizations to handle their tobacco crops, with paid factors in Britain to care for their sales and arrange for their purchases.[58]

Professor Andrews[59] and Professor Schlesinger[60] have assembled a good many items from the correspondence of merchants indicating some economic distress. Such data, however, are not convincing. The conditions complained of are local and periodic where they are not due to the chronic absence of an adequate medium of exchange. They should not be interpreted as indicating a general lack of prosperity for America as a whole, covering the period between 1763 and 1775. They more probably indicate that a tidal movement of prosperous and dull times was characteristic of American economic life long before the formation of the federal government.[61]

Conditions for the period as a whole must be considered. A country that was a Mecca for immigrants;[62] that was importing slaves in large numbers;[63] that was rapidly expanding its settled area into the back country; that could order from overseas expensive marble statues of its favorite English politicians as did South Carolina[64] and New York;[65] that could squander large sums on the public funeral of a royal governor and bury him in a sepulcher as elaborate as was accorded to royalty in England;[66] that could find the funds for better church buildings than it ever had before in its history; that could sink public debts more rapidly than other countries; and whose population could live on a far better scale than similar classes in any other part of the world; was not suffering from economic ills that lead to permanent poverty.

REFERENCES

CHAPTER 2

1. George Bancroft, *History of the United States* (6 vols., 1st ed. New York, 1834-74), V, 159. In the last revision "Colonial Mercantile System" is substituted for "Navigation Act" (III, 60).

2. See Emory R. Johnson, *History of the Domestic and Foreign Commerce of the United States* (Washington, 1915), Vol. I, Chap. iv.

3. Total number of vessels clearing from the more important centers in the various years were:

	1768	*1769*	*1770*	*1771*	*1772*
Massachusetts	927	1172	1110	1143	1181
New York	480	795	612	741	700
Philadelphia	658	699	750	729	759
Maryland and Virginia	839	965	940	1005	1088
Charleston	429	433	455	489	485
Savannah	104	143	150	124	161

Compiled from *Customs* 16:1.

4. The number of ships and their tonnage clearing for the West Indies in 1768 were:

	Ships	*Tonnage*
New England	936	49,234
Middle Colonies	419	23,208
Southern Colonies	649	30,703

Ibid. For comparable data for England's trade see Harper, *English Navigation Laws*, p. 317, fn. 81.

5. American figures are from *Customs* 16:1; English totals are from Harper, *op. cit.*, pp. 286-92.

6. *Customs* 14:1B.

7. Compiled from the records, *Customs* 17:1-4, and *Customs* 14:1B. Public Record Office, London.

8. *Customs* 17:1-2.

9. *Customs* 14:1B and *Customs* 17:I.

10. *Domestic and Foreign Commerce of the United States,* I, 24.

11. *Customs* 17:I.

12. *Customs* 14:1B.

13. Compiled from *Customs* 17:I.

14. *Customs* 14:1B.

15. Gray, *History of Agriculture in the Southern United States,* II.

16. Exports to 1775 are from *Customs* 17:1-3; those after 1790 are from Gray, *op. cit.,* II, 1035, and from *American State Papers,* X, XI.

17. All references to exports in 1822 are based upon the official figures in *American State Papers,* X.

18. J. B. Moore, *International Arbitrations,* I, 298.

19. Compiled from Gray, *History of Agriculture in the Southern United States,* II, 1022-23. See also Leila Sellers, *Charleston Business on the Eve of the American Revolution,* p. 157.

20. *Customs* 16:1.

21. *Customs* 14:1A.

22. Sellers, *op. cit.,* estimates that 60 per cent of the rice went to northern Europe. This is approximately correct if one includes Great Britain with northern Europe. In 1773 only a little over 40 per cent went to the continent of Europe north of Cape Finisterre.

23. *Customs* 17:2.

24. The 10,066 barrels exported to southern Europe in 1772 are equivalent to 45,297 hundredweight according to the formula used by the customs service for converting barrels to hundredweight.

25. The best study of conditions facing the rice growers after the Revolution is in Gray, *History of Agriculture in the Southern United States,* II, 593-610.

26. *Charleston Business on the Eve of the Revolution,* pp. 165-77.

27. *History of Agriculture in the Southern United States,* II, 1024.

28. *Customs,* 17:2.

29. *Annals of Commerce,* III, 572-73.

30. In 1770 a total of 685 ships with a combined tonnage of 83,300 cleared from the continental ports for Great Britain; 1,959 ships with a tonnage of 97,680 cleared from the same ports for the West Indies; and 3,868 vessels with a total tonnage of 117,692 cleared from the same ports to others on the continent. *Customs* 16:1.

31. Compiled from *Customs* 3:69-71.

32. Johnson, *History of the Domestic and Foreign Commerce of the United States,* I, 92.

33. *Customs* 3:69.

34. *History of Manufacturing in the United States.* (Washington, D. C., 1916.)

35. *British Regulation of the Colonial Iron Industry* (Philadelphia, 1933).

36. 12 Charles II, c. 32, secs. 1-3; 14 Charles II, c. 18, secs. 2, 3, 8, 9; 7-8 William III, c. 28, secs. 2, 3, 4; 9-10 William III, c. 40, secs. 1, 3, 22; 10-11 William III, c. 10, secs. 2, 6, 19.

37. Clark, *History of Manufactures in the United States,* Chap. vii. Good spinners in Ulster earned forty cents a week, or seven cents a day, and fine weavers two dollars a week. *Ibid.,* p. 157. Colonial manufactures could not compete with such cheap labor.

38. *American State Papers,* XI, 686, 709.

39. *American State Papers,* I, 142.

40. *Ibid.,* VI, 666 ff.

41. Bining, *British Regulation of the Colonial Iron Industry,* pp. 26-31.

42. *Ibid.,* p. 133 and *Customs* 16:1. In the table of American exports in 1770 in Macpherson, *Annals of Commerce,* III, 572-73, reproduced in Johnson, *History of the Domestic and Foreign Commerce of the United States,* pp. 118-19, the total export of bar iron, of 24,064, is erroneous. It is clearly a mistake in addition. *Customs* 16:1 gives the correct figure as 2,156 tons.

43. Bining, *op. cit.,* p. 18.

44. *American State Papers,* VI, 666 ff.

45. By 4 George III, c. 26, the import bounty on hemp and rough flax was arranged as follows: 1764-71, £8 per ton; 1771-78, £6 per ton; 1778-85, £4 per ton. By 5 George III, c. 45, the bounties on lumber were established to 1775. By 11 George III, c. 50, the bounties on white oak staves and headings were authorized to 1778. While it had been customary to reënact bounty laws when they expired and no important ones, in fact, were allowed to lapse, this plan of extending them for longer periods should have been beneficial to the favored industries, as it made investments of capital more secure and gave those who were embarking in such industries definite rewards upon which they could base calculations over a period of years.

46. *Treasury* 38: Bundle 363, Public Record Office, London.

47. See Sheffield's discussion of this industry. He says that the bounty of five shillings, sixpence per barrel on tar was frequently more than the original price. *Observations,* 2nd ed., pp. 77-88.

48. *Present State of the British and French Trade to Africa and America,* etc. (London, 1745), pp. 39-40.

49. *Ibid.,* pp. 52-56.

50. Dora Mae Clark, *British Opinion on the American Revolution,* pp. 26-28; 70-71.

51. *Conduct of the Late Administration Examined* (London, 1767), p. 63. This pamphlet was written for the British public, but has all the appearances of being based upon information secured from official sources. At the time of its publication it was popularly assumed that it was the work of Grenville. There is some discrepancy between the estimates in this pamphlet and the official compilation in the treasury papers; but the latter includes £150,000 for New York, which was supposed to have been paid off in 1763, and does not include any estimates for Pennsylvania, Delaware, North Carolina, South Carolina, or Georgia. It is possible that Lloyd's statement of the total debts and the amounts outstanding in 1765 may be more accurate than those in the earlier Treasury estimates. Below are the official data supplied for the information of Grenville on the eve of the enactment of the Stamp Act:

Colony	Debt at Close of War	Unpaid in 1765	Provisions for Sinking
New Hampshire	£ 67,000	£ 18,000	Taxes 1766-67-68.
Massachusetts	810,000	160,000	
Connecticut	280,000	All paid	
Rhode Island	Uncertain	70,000	
New York	290,000	150,000	Supposedly all in 1765.
New Jersey	210,000	150,000	In about 19 years.
Maryland	50,000	All paid	
Virginia	390,000	290,000	In 1769.
	£2,097,000	£838,000	

Treasury 1, Bundle 430.

52. An unsigned article evidently contributed by an admirer of Pitt. *London Chronicle,* February 18, 1766.

53. Another unsigned article, probably contributed by an admirer of Pitt. *London Chronicle,* February 20, 1766.

54. *Ibid.,* February 3, 1765. This was copied into the *Newport Mercury,* April 15, 1765.

55. Sir Charles Dalrymple, *The Address of the People of Great Britain to the People of America* (London, 1775), p. 17.

56. "To impose with success on the Americans that portion of the public burthen, which they ought to bear, seize the opportunity, while a general peace leaves you at liberty to employ in this service, whatever force may be necessary for it: and while the infirm and disjointed state of the provinces renders a small force equal to the work—if you suffer this important hour to pass unimproved, it is lost forever: The Americans will cease to be the Colonies of England, and we shall have more than doubled our national debt in a war—the successes of which were all to their advantage, to enable them to pour the benefits of their trade into the bosom of our commercial rivals. The declaratory law—will hold forth *only a delusive and nugatory affirmative of the right of the legislature of this Kingdom,* if not followed by some bill which shall exert it—if now, you neglect to pursue those measures—the whole new world ceases forever to be subject to your authority." *The Conduct of the Late Administration Examined* (London, 1767), pp. 157-59.

57. In the debates over the repressive legislation in 1774, Mr. Glover pointed out that the distress in England was partly due to the collapse of the paper money in 1772, and that he could point out the exact time when the collapse happened. Hansard, *Parliamentary Debates,* XVII, 1119.

58. Purdie's *Virginia Gazette,* October 21, November 25, 1773.

59. *Boston Merchants and the Non Importation Movement* (Publications, Colonial Society of Massachusetts, XIX), pp. 180-91.

60. *The Colonial Merchants and the American Revolution* (New York, 1918), p. 106.

61. This is practically conceded by Schlesinger in his account of the economic recovery after 1770. *Ibid.,* Chap. vi; Virginia D. Harrington, *New York Merchants on the Eve of the Revolution,* describes the periods of varying good and hard times in New York, but also advances a theory that merchants'

letters are a better indication of business conditions than are the statistics of trade. She states that the bottom of the business depression in New York was in 1769, pp. 289-319.

62. Between August 3 and November 29, 1773, at the ports of New York, Philadelphia, Charleston, New Jersey, Halifax, and Newport there landed 6,222 immigrants from Ireland, 1,400 from England and Scotland, and 56 from the Isle of Man. *Pennsylvania Packet,* Sept. 5, 1774. Immigrants do not flock to a region where economic conditions are bad and the future unpromising.

63. The importations of slaves at Charleston for twenty years, from 1753 to 1772, were:

1753	1,398	1758	3,177	1763	1,145	1768	178
1754	2,532	1759	1,879	1764	3,057	1769	4,612
1755	1,436	1760	3,449	1765	7,184	1770	149
1756	1,952	1761	1,395	1766	101	1771	3,079
1757	1,438	1762	602	1767	12	1772	4,865

South Carolina Gazette, June 14, 1773.

This makes an average of more than two thousand per year for twenty years. Other colonies were also importing in large numbers as is evidenced by the notices of arrivals and advertisements for sale of the slave cargoes in the current newspapers. Large numbers were also coming to the West Indies. Ragatz, *The Fall of the Planter Class in the British Caribbean,* pp. 81-90.

64. John Wilkes.

65. William Pitt.

66. Governor Boutetourt of Virginia. This may still be seen in Williamsburg.

3

EVASION OF THE NAVIGATION ACTS

ONE OF THE most difficult questions to answer is the extent to which the Navigation Acts were enforced or, what is more to the point, voluntarily observed without compulsion. Some writers assert they were dead letters; one says that they "were systematically evaded, although so far as the European traffic is concerned the amount of smuggling seems to have been less than is commonly supposed."[1] This writer gives no authority for the first part of his statement, nor does he take the trouble to indicate what parts of the laws were "systematically evaded." He leaves the impression that this applied to all portions of the acts.

It is possible that the Americans were as much interested in having some portions of these acts enforced as were their fellow citizens in England. Enforcement, observance, and evasion are relative terms. There is probably no law that is never violated, nor is there ever a general condition where each and every violator is publicly punished. The finding of a few instances of evasion or smuggling is not sufficient evidence to warrant a conclusion that the law was a dead letter or that all seamen were smugglers.

ACT OF 1660

It may be helpful to make a preliminary analysis of the navigation and trade laws to determine the points of probable interest in evading them, then consider such data as can be found on the suspected items. The first basic element in the navigation system was the limiting of the carrying trade between ports in the British

Empire to English ships. Was this fundamental regulation, that only English ships could carry goods from one English port to another or import products of Asia, Africa, or America into any English port, whether home or colonial,[2] a provision that either was or could be easily evaded?

So far as the law applied to ports in Great Britain, its enforcement was in the hands of customs officials in those ports. It was to the interest of all English shipowners, masters, and seamen to protest against any evasion of this law by a foreign vessel. Only merchant importers could possibly be interested in employing the non-English vessels. As such employment deprived English seafaring men of work and profits and their families of support, there was an ample body of public opinion available to compel customs officers to do their duty. If they failed, there was the financial temptation of one-third of the value of the offending ship and cargo, which, upon confiscation, went to the informer to insure complaint; and an informer in this case would be amply supported by public opinion. The whole weight of the English seafaring population and shipowners must have been back of enforcing this phase of the system.

Conditions in American ports were not unlike those in England. Every local shipowner, his friends, relatives, and employees must have been in favor of preserving the carrying trade as a privilege of the English population. It is possible that in a region where there were neither shipowners nor sailors, but only plantation owners, a different view might have been held; but the foreign ship would have been instantly recognized and complained against by the seamen on English ships who would be injured by the competition.

The laws specified that proofs of the character of a vessel had to be given at the port of loading as well as at the port of arrival. The certificates, bonds, and other regulations made it practically impossible for any foreign vessel to conceal her identity, evade the regulations, and compete with native carriers.

The same law required that the master and three-fourths of the crew should be English in time of peace. There was an authorized relaxation in time of war so as to release a certain proportion of the sailors for the navy. It is obvious that such provisions would enforce themselves. They were there to provide jobs for English sailors, and public opinion in the ports would not tolerate the employment of foreigners at the expense of natives, especially as the native could profit by informing against the offending ship. The records show that the most minor violation of this rule was quickly prosecuted.

In support of these general conditions that would lead to the assumption that the above features of the law must have been effectively observed are the lists of arrivals and departures at the various ports that were published in the local newspapers and obviously supplied by the customs officials. The arrival of a ship was important news to the families of the members of the crew and their friends; to its owners; to the owners of the cargo it carried; to the master, who sought a market for his cargo or new freight for his return trip; and to the public that might be interested in incoming passengers, mail, news, freight, or have merchandise for outward shipment. All of these factors tended to make news of ship arrivals and departures among the most regularly reported items in practically all colonial newspapers. The data are so full that a fairly complete marine register for all of the colonies could be compiled from such reports.[3]

The most cursory glance at these lists reveals at once that the vessels were English by their names, the ports from which they came, and the names of their masters. The presence of a foreign vessel in an American port was almost unknown in the period between 1765 and 1775.

The other evidence is the news items in the same newspaper. These reveal the arrival of no foreign ships. There is a record of one French vessel entering the port of New York under claims of distress, but she was not permitted to transact any business. The sailors were even prevented from selling articles in a "piddling way," as a local chronicler puts it.[4] There are also the official reports of entrances and clearances kept by the customs officers. These reveal no arrivals or departures of foreign vessels at colonial ports in the period under consideration. Finally there is the absence of reports of seizures or condemnations of vessels for violation of this section of the act. So far as the evidence is available, this part of the Navigation Act seems to have been enforced as nearly one hundred per cent as any law ever was. Harper, who has made the most detailed study of the Navigation Acts from their passage, arrives at a similar conclusion.[5]

The regulation that European goods must enter British ports in either English vessels or ships of the country where the goods were produced also enforced itself. Even the vessels and sailors engaged in the extensive smuggling along the coast of the British Isles appear to have been English.[6] As European goods could be imported into the colonies in the main only by way of England, the enforcement of this section was largely a problem of British customs officers in the British Isles.

Enumerated Articles

Practices in regard to enumerated goods were more complicated. The important items, so far as quantity and value were concerned, were tobacco, sugar, molasses, rice, indigo, and naval stores. There was a time prior to 1700 when there seems to have been some evasion of the tobacco enumeration through an export of tobacco from the northern colonies direct to Europe. Long before 1765 this practice seems to have disappeared. Certainly after that date, and probably for a considerable period before, there was little evasion of the tobacco enumeration, unless in a very small way connected with the Mediterranean trade. With known registered imports into Great Britain of more than 100,000,000 pounds annually there could not have been any appreciable smuggling of this article to foreign countries.

There was little chance for profit in an illicit export of tobacco from the producing areas. Tobacco was bulky. It was difficult to conceal because of its positive odor, and market conditions favored the trade through England. The system of direct shipments to the home market in complete cargoes meant low freight. Smugglers had to sell for cash because of the hazardous nature of their business. The regular trade was conducted on a well-established credit basis.

The wholesale merchants of England and Scotland, at the center of the tobacco trade of the world, always had available information of the market conditions at the various trading centers and could ship when conditions were most favorable. The colonial merchant or planter had no such information and frequently lost by sending his ships to an unfavorable market, thereby wasting both money and time. In addition, tobacco had to be sorted, graded, and prepared for the various markets. This was a highly specialized business that could best be conducted in connection with a great central market.[7] These conditions, coupled with the policy of drawbacks of the import duties upon exportation to the continent, made the enumerated market more attractive than a direct trade carried on illegally.

The amount of tobacco carried directly to continental Europe in the period after 1765 appears to have been extremely small. This conclusion is based upon the very large known receipts in England and Scotland; the large exports from Britain to the continent;[8] the aggressive control of the Virginia tobacco trade by Scotch merchants; and the very few American vessels that are known to have been at Hamburg, the reputed center of the continental trade.[9]

Rice, because of its bulk and the fact that culture developed after the commercial regulations had become thoroughly established, seems never to have been a large item of trade contrary to the navigation laws. The change in the law by which it could be shipped directly to southern Europe,[10] the West Indies, and the Spanish and Portuguese colonies seems to have given ample outlet for this crop.

Sugar and molasses were constant trouble-makers. The world supply of these commodities centered in the Caribbean. The English sugar islands, particularly Barbados and Jamaica, came first into production, followed in the early 1700's, by the French sugar islands, especially Haiti. Both of these sugar-producing areas offered profitable markets for the large quantities of nonenumerated products, cooperage materials, food, animals, and miscellaneous goods supplied by the continental colonies. These colonies in turn used vast quantities of the raw sugar and molasses obtained through this trade. Practically all of this interchange was within the law prior to the enactment of the Molasses Act of 1733.

Both sugar and molasses were enumerated products that could not be legally exported to a foreign market except by way of England.

In the seventeenth and early part of the eighteenth century, there was probably a considerable indirect trade to Europe of sugar from the British sugar islands by way of the northern colonies. After 1730, however, the supply of French sugar was so great that it tended to displace the English product in the European market. As it was cheaper than the English, such evasion as seemed to exist was probably French sugars carried by colonial vessels engaged in the European trade.[11] The permission to ship sugar from the English West Indies direct to Europe[12] effectually destroyed any incentive that may have formerly existed for the northern colonies to carry on an irregular trade by exporting British sugars to the continent in a clandestine manner. Molasses was mainly converted into rum for export to Europe and Africa, and in that form was not enumerated. Operation of the laws taxing colonial imports of sugar and molasses will be discussed later.

Ginger, fustic, dyewoods, and furs, while enumerated, were minor articles of trade and had to be shipped generally with other cargoes. These conditions would have caused practically all such commodities to have been taken to England without any enumeration, as quantities were seldom sufficient to supply cargoes of such articles alone, and partial cargoes eastward were little temptation to the irregular trader, as the main course of trade was toward Europe. If ships did not have profitable cargoes eastward, the voyages were losing ventures; for there was little opportunity for paying cargoes on the westward voyage.[13]

The two remaining important items of enumerated goods, indigo and naval stores, including masts, yards, etc., present new conditions. These articles received import bounties at the English customhouses, coupled with favorable tariff duties. The bounties on naval stores were enough to make the voyage to England a profitable one under ordinary conditions. This treatment was sufficient to attract all the available export surplus without enumeration. It was only in time of war, when enemy nations, cut off from other sources of supply, offered very high prices for these articles delivered either in their own ports or to their fleets at sea, that there was any problem of enforcing the enumeration in regard to such goods. England had the best world market for naval stores and continued to receive the bulk of our exports of these articles after independence, which is additional proof that there must have been very little financial inducement for persons to embark in irregular trading in such commodities in violation of the enumeration clauses.[14]

EUROPEAN AND ASIATIC GOODS

The provisions of the basic Navigation Acts that appear most susceptible of successful and profitable evasion were the requirements that all European and East India goods should reach the colonies by way of English ports. Thus the Americans who wished to live within the law had to (1) go without, (2) manufacture for themselves, (3) use British manufactures, or (4) supply themselves with European and Asiatic goods by way of England.

It has been assumed that such conditions offered a large and lucrative opportunity to the colonial smuggler, and that the legal restriction was of little importance.[15] It is possible that such assumptions may be warranted for some of the colonies during a part of the seventeenth century. Most of the instances of evasion cited by historians belong in that period; but it is only the known evasions that have been systematically reported, possibly because it makes interesting or easy reading. In this respect such information is like the crime news in modern newspapers, which gives no space to the citizens who observe the law. One needs tables of legitimate trade during this time even to infer the relative amount of such irregular trade. When all of the known evasions are consolidated and compared with the known legitimate trade, the proportion of irregular trade is exceedingly small. Writers seem to assume that the occasional case of smuggling was representative of general conditions. There is no adequate foundation for such assumptions.

Such evasions as were practiced diminished steadily during the eighteenth century and certainly constituted a very small part of the total importations of East India and European goods after 1765. This conclusion is based upon (1) the more than 600 per cent increase in British exports to the colonies forming the United States between 1700-70;[16] (2) the fact that the nonimportation agreements produced real scarcities of goods in common use; (3) the nature of the offerings of merchants advertised in the newspapers; (4) the absence of foreign goods generally in the advertised list of articles for sale;[17] (5) upon the relatively large known importation of certain articles from England;[18] (6) upon the very common statement in merchants' advertisements that they have just imported the various articles from some particular English port, giving the name of the vessel in which imported and the port from which she came; and (7) upon the fact that such goods were chiefly secured from England after the Revolution. This mass of data clearly indicates that nearly all of the "European goods" came from England, and that the outstanding demand on the part of the purchasing public was for goods of English manufacture.[19]

How had such a condition come about in relation to articles that frequently were of such high value and small bulk that it must have been physically possible to conduct an extensive illicit trade? The reason is to be found in the provisions and workings of the navigation and trade acts themselves.

The incentives for smuggling were far less than has been supposed. The navigation system sought to make the British market not only the center of supply for colonial products, but for all other goods in common demand as well. Had the latter object depended upon a policy of compulsion only, it would have been a prolific source of smuggling. There was a distinct effort to make the British market attractive to colonial purchasers by employing methods similar to those used to attract colonial products to England and to develop colonial industries.

Just as there were import bounties on, and preferential tariffs favoring, important colonial commodities, there were also export bounties on important British manufactures largely consumed in the colonies.

There were six separate export bounty acts. The first on the important article of sailcloth, was passed in 1713.[20] It granted a bounty of one penny per yard on sailcloth made in England. Four years later this amount was doubled, making the permanent export bounty two pence per yard.[21]

The next group of British manufactures encouraged by export bounties was that included in the silk industry. In 1721 extensive bounties were authorized as follows on each pound *avoirdupois* weight:[22]

Ribbons and goods made entirely of silk	three shillings
Ribbons and goods made entirely of silk mixed with gold or silver	four shillings
Stockings, gloves, fringes, case thread for sewing or stitching, made entirely of silk	one shilling, three pence
Material made of silk and grosgrain mixed	three pence
Materials made of silk and linen or cotton	six pence
Materials made of silk and worsted	six pence

The object of these bounties was to promote the use of English-made silks in place of the Persian, Chinese, and East India products. This policy was still further promoted by the provisions in the Sugar Act of 1764, by which all foreign silks imported into the colonies from Great Britain had to pay a duty in American ports of two shillings per pound, whether the goods were pure silk or of mixed materials.[23]

Another article of extensive use in America was gunpowder, which could be had from many sources. The English manufacturers secured legislation in 1731, by which they were given an export bounty of four shillings per barrel. The funds to pay the bounty came from the general customs duties on imports.[24] This law, like others of its kind, was continued by successive reënactments and became a part of the settled commercial policy of the Empire.

In 1742 the linen industry received similar aid through a simple bounty of one penny per yard on all British and Irish-made linens exported, provided the value of the goods was from six pence to a shilling a yard, and a half penny for goods worth less than six pence per yard.[25]

In this case the debenture plan was involved, and the term "debenture" is expressly used in the act. The funds available to pay the bounty came from additional duties levied upon imports of foreign cambrics, and these duties were set aside for the payment of the bounties authorized by this act. The encouragement was not for a general export, but was applicable only in case the goods were exported to America, Africa, or Portugal. Obviously the large market was in the American colonies, and the quality of goods was that in greatest demand by the poorer and middle classes. The cheaper grades supplied slaves' clothing in the southern colonies.[26]

The operation of the export bounty laws has escaped notice because they were not a part of any laws applicable to America, but were a part of laws purely British in content. They were, however, just as much a part of the trade act system as the Navigation Acts themselves. The information concerning their operation is scattered and difficult to consolidate. Writers generally give the English figures only and omit those from Scotland and frequently from the outports of England. Only samples can be given in this discussion. Scotland exported mainly British and Irish linens to America and almost no foreign linens. There was practically no export of British and Irish linens to foreign countries. In 1772 Scotland exported to America 2,425,285 yards of British linen, 543,758 yards of Irish linen, and only 384,300 yards of foreign linens.[27] The bounties on this linen for that year alone totaled £13,556, in addition to the drawbacks on the foreign linen.

Scotland's heavy linen trade went to the colonies from which she had a large import trade in tobacco. The total amounts of linen sold to certain colonies is almost unbelievably large.

TABLE 6. SCOTCH EXPORTS OF LINEN TO AMERICA, 1772[28]

	British Yards	Irish Yards	Foreign Yards	Total Yards
New England	103,128	27,181	......	130,309
Pennsylvania	170,267	22,799	......	193,066
Maryland	171,085	112,230	61,800	345,115
Virginia	939,004	313,949	314,300	1,567,253
North Carolina	110,129	24,823	3,600	138,552
South Carolina	119,241	625	......	119,866
Jamaica	438,080	14,798	2,000	454,878
Totals	2,050,934	516,405	381,700	2,949,039

The exportations that year were not abnormal and were obviously following the usual course of trade which persisted after the Revolution. Below is a comparison of the exports of linen to Virginia for two years before the war with two years immediately after the treaty of peace.

The export bounties on linen shipped to Virginia, alone, from Scotland averaged more than £5,000 per year for the two years preceding the Revolution and £6,000 per year for the two years following its close. That these bounties were attractive to exporters is attested by the recurrence of elaborate legislation to prevent foreign linens from securing the bounties authorized for the native product.[30]

The exports of linen from England to America exceeded those from Scotland with consequently larger bounty payments. Bounty

TABLE 7. SCOTCH EXPORTS OF LINEN TO VIRGINIA[29]

Virginia	1773 Yards	1774 Yards	1784 Yards	1785 Yards
British	594,815	717,060	1,078,662	772,134
Irish	309,909	283,986	199,659	199,477
Foreign	38,154	16,634	40,474	99,276
Total	942,878	1,017,680	1,318,795	1,070,887
Bounties	£4,771	£5,324	£6,836	£5,254

payments on British and Irish linen exported from England to America were compiled by the customhouse in London from 1757 to 1775 inclusive. These payments totaled £455,098.[31]

The Scotch bounties can be estimated in terms of the ratio the known payments held to English payments the same year. In 1772 the Scotch linen bounties amounted to £13,546 and the British bounties for the same year were £22,403. This gives a ratio of approximately sixty per cent. If the known British bounties of £455,098 for the years 1757 to 1775 are increased by sixty per cent so as to include the Scotch bounties, we have a total of £728,166 paid out over a period of nineteen years to encourage the export of British and Irish linens to America, or an average of more than £38,000 per year.

In addition there were export bounties on sailcloth,[32] gunpowder,[33] silk manufactures,[34] cordage, and refined sugar which, together with some minor bounties, averaged about the same as the bounties on linen exports from England.

The relative importance of these bounties was increased by the provisions in the Sugar Act of 1764 which levied import duties in America on foreign linens, thus giving the British product still further advantages in the American market.[35]

Finally, in 1766, the British cordage manufacturers secured a debenture plan by which they were paid a bounty of one shilling and three farthings per hundredweight upon all cordage exported, provided it was made of American or British-grown hemp. The funds to pay such bounties were taken from the duties levied upon the importation of foreign hemp.[36]

Sugar exports from England were encouraged by an extensive system of drawbacks. These were gradually combined with export bounties upon British refined sugar, which were finally consolidated and increased to a flat bounty of fourteen shillings per hundredweight on British refined sugar exported after 1765.[37] It has generally escaped notice that this policy coincides in time with the levying of import duties in America upon foreign refined sugar. As the Sugar Act levied an additional import duty in America of twenty-two shillings per hundredweight on foreign sugar, and the act just cited granted an export bounty of fourteen shillings on refined sugar reëxported from England, the combined result was to give the British sugar refiner a differential of forty-one shillings per hundredweight over his foreign competitor.[38]

The effect was to increase the demand for English refined sugar in the colonies. Exports from England increased from an average of 4,337 hundredweight for the years 1763-64 to an average of 12,391 hundredweight for the years 1766-73, or an increase of nearly three hundred per cent. What was more significant, the American market was taking only three per cent of the total British export of refined sugar in 1762-63 while in the eight years following the change in the law it took an average of thirty-five per cent and at the close of the period was absorbing one half of the total British export of refined sugar.[39] Obviously there was not much profit left in smuggling that article.

Drawbacks were refunds of all or part of the import duties

when foreign goods were reëxported. The American colonies were especially favored in the complicated mass of legislation providing for such drawbacks, but the customs officials kept no separate lists of American drawbacks. Totals were kept but these were not arranged by countries. It is possible to compute the amounts of the American drawbacks if one assumes that they held the same ratio to the total value of foreign exports as was true of the total trade. Using this technique we have the following results.

The total exports from Great Britain to the colonies for the years 1770-74, inclusive, were £24,075,831. Of this amount £4,685,891 were foreign goods reëxported and on this there was paid out £1,611,834 in drawbacks, or an average of £322,367 a year.[40]

These calculations ignore the exports from Ireland to America; but as these were largely domestic products, the total drawbacks are not very important.

We are now in a position to consolidate the total payments from the British treasury to promote the American trade with the home country.

TABLE 8. TOTAL PAYMENTS FROM THE BRITISH TREASURY TO ENCOURAGE TRADE WITH THE AMERICAN COLONIES FOR FIVE YEARS PRECEDING THE REVOLUTION

	1770	1771	1772	1773	1774
Bounties on Imports from America, England	£ 14,577	£ 13,768	£ 12,751	£ 17,827	£ 16,694
Export Bounties on British Goods, England	39,338	61,133	48,484	37,395	59,403
Export Bounties, Linen, Scotland	12,436	17,406	13,556	12,594	14,483
Drawbacks on Goods Exported, Computed	268,956	409,064	344,699	270,560	318,555
Total	£335,307	£501,371	£419,490	£338,376	£409,135

In the face of these facts, it is not surprising that Englishmen complained that Americans could buy both foreign and English-made goods cheaper than could the resident of England, and that the Englishman was taxed for the benefit of the American.[41] Disregarding this feature of the controversy, the amount of the drawbacks and bounties was sufficient very greatly to reduce the possible profits in an illegal trade to foreign countries to secure goods of their production, rather than use articles secured in the legal manner from England.

Woolen goods was the largest single item of British exports to the colonies. In 1721 this had amounted to £147,438, or more than half of the total exports of £294,586.[42] In 1773 exports of woolen goods had increased more than three times to £472,763 but constituted only about one-fifth of the total export of British goods to the colonies. The colonies north of Virgina were the largest importers, with the chief markets in the very areas where reports indicated there was the greatest prospect of American manufacture. The colonies from New Hampshire to South Carolina imported £427,054 of such goods, or ninety per cent of the total colonial consumption.

That profit in smuggling woolen goods from European markets was highly improbable is indicted by the fact that Europe itself was an importer of British woolens to even a larger extent than were the colonies. The exports in 1773 to that area totaled £520,491.[43] British woolens were the best and the cheapest to be had in any market. There was every inducement for the Americans to use them.

Manufactures of all kinds coming from England must have enjoyed an advantage in freight rates that commodities secured in other markets did not have. The shipment of bulky enumerated products to the English market created a system of one-way freights, and many vessels sailing westward had to come out in ballast. Such a condition must have created intense competition for such shipments as existed, with resultant low freight charges for the westward voyage.

There is other evidence of an even more convincing character that there was relatively little irregular trade in the general mass of manufactured goods. The period of rigorous enforcement of the trade and revenue laws that was set up after 1767 reveals almost no convictions for violation of the clauses dealing with textiles and manufactured goods.

We have also the evidence revealed by the committees to enforce the nonimportation agreements. It is possible that public opinion would have protected those who sought to import by way of foreign countries; but the leaders of the nonimportation movements had to avoid the charge that their agreements were designed to favor smugglers and to promote the trade of England's commercial rivals. Practically all of the persons who had their operations denounced, however, were engaged in bringing in goods from England in defiance of the nonimportation agreements. The exposures made by John Mein in his efforts to discredit the association of Boston merchants,[44] which were given wide publicity throughout the colonies, include no cases of importation from foreign countries; but they do include much evidence that John Hancock and others were violating the agreements by importing goods directly from England in violation of their solemn pledges not to do so.

Furthermore, one of the chief reasons for having the Boston tea ships come into port and tie up at the British wharf in 1773, instead of returning to England without entering the port, was because they had on board the major supply of goods for the winter trade.[45] All of this evidence fails to make out a case for Boston being a city that set the Navigation Acts completely at naught, but does show that most of the trade was unquestionably in legitimate channels.

Finally, there is evidence of what happened after independence. Importation of manufactured goods in contravention of the navigation laws would not have been carried on with its attendant expense and risks unless it were profitable to do so. If goods could be had in England more cheaply than elsewhere, there was no object in going to foreign countries for them; nor was there any real hardship in being confined by law to the British market.

A comparison of the trade under the navigation and trade laws with that of the years immediately following independence supplies relevant data on this point. Chalmers contributes the following figures: during the years 1771-73, the average exports to the colonies that revolted were £3,064,843 and imports from the same source were £1,742,311; in 1784, the first full year of peace, there were exports from England to the same destination of £3,397,500 and imports of £749,329.[46]

The years 1771-73 were a good average, during which there was no serious boycott of British imports, but some acceleration due to the past period of nonimportation and, to some extent, by the fear of another approaching period of the same. The year 1784 was somewhat abnormal, due to the large importations at the close of the war to replace exhausted stocks; but this was offset by the dislike of things British created by the war, and by the inevitable destruction of purchasing power in America. The fact that Americans turned at once to the old market for their supplies, and in larger measure than before, would seem to indicate that the former trade was not unnaturally forced by the navigation and trade laws and that the profit from breaking through them was far less than has been assumed.

The assertion of Jefferson that the cost of goods secured under the old conditions had been artificially enhanced two and three times over the cost of similar goods from other sources seems to have been inspired by his enthusiasm for the doctrine of free trade, rather than his positive knowledge of commercial conditions,[47] or else he had in mind small articles of relatively unusual demand.

Even during the war, the funds supplied by the French government for clothing for the American troops were used by the Americans to buy British cloth through Dutch merchants, rather than French or other foreign goods. The French protested against this practice, and pointed out that, since France supplied the money, it should be laid out for French merchandise. The American agents defended their action on the ground that more and better cloth could be had for the money in the purchase of British cloth than in any other way.[48]

Chalmers also asserts that, during the war, importations of British cloth into America went on by indirect means to such an extent that France protested strongly against the trade; and that the popularity of the English product was such that merchants advertised their Dutch and French cloth as English as an inducement to purchasers to buy.[49] If these statements are even approximately true, the clauses of the Navigation Acts that sought to make England the chief source of supply for manufactured goods were not burdensome, and there was neither inducement for, nor profit in, the systematic evasion of them between 1760 and 1775.

COLONIAL EXPORT DUTIES

The provisions of the act of 1672, levying small duties upon enumerated products exported from the place of their production to places other than England, set up a series of export duties in America about equivalent to the import duties in England.[50] The object of this act was not to burden the intercolonial trade, but to prevent the high import duties imposed in England from driving the great colonial staples away from the home country and creating new distributing centers in America, especially New England. It is obvious that if the New England shipowners could carry colonial staples to Europe free of duty by stopping in a New England port on the way, similar products going through England and paying the regular tariffs would meet with unfair competition.

Probably the duties imposed by this law were the first effective means of compelling ships to enter and clear regularly, which was essential to the enforcement of the other provisions of the navigation laws. The law imposed export duties on enumerated products exported elsewhere than to England as follows:[51]

Sugar, white	5s. per hundredweight
Sugar, brown	1s. 6d. per hundredweight
Tobacco	1d. per pound
Cotton wool	½d. per pound
Indigo	2d. per pound
Ginger	1s. per hundredweight
Logwood	£5. per hundredweight
Fustic	6d. per hundredwieght
Coconuts	1d. per pound

As enumerated products could be carried legally nowhere but to England or to another British plantation, this law imposed a tax upon certain phases of the intercolonial trade. British custom-house reports usually refer to the sums arising from such taxes as the "plantation" duties.[52] As these were export and not import taxes, they had to be collected in the ports of the colonies where they originated. As tobacco and indigo, and later rice, were the only enumerated products produced on the continent, the bulk of these duties was collected in the colonies that did not revolt. There may have been some evasion of these export taxes, but how much it is difficult to determine. The situation can be checked only roughly. We have the total reported collections for considerable periods;[53] but we do not have the corresponding record of exports from the southern ports, where the products originated, with which to compare them. Even data of that kind would be only approximately correct, because, by the simple device of underestimating exports to ports other than those of Great Britain, the tax could be partially evaded.

There are available reports of the imports and exports from some of the large continental ports, such as New York and Philadelphia. Lord Sheffield, who gives the exports from the latter port for 1771-73, does not include tobacco in his long list of articles. In the case of New York he lists imports of 285 hogsheads in 1774 and 340 hogsheads in 1775, with exports of 95 and 35 hogsheads in the corresponding years.[54] The *Pennsylvania Magazine* table of exports for the port of Philadelphia for the three years, 1771-73,[55] gives the same data as Sheffield. If there had been any extensive evasion of the regulations concerning tobacco in the form of illegal imports, they would have been revealed by exports in excess of imports. No such condition is disclosed. Exports are either nonexistent or considerably smaller than recorded imports.

Sugar was one of the chief items involved in the third Navigation Act (1672), which levied a duty of five shillings a hundredweight upon raw sugar exported from one colony to another. This tended to discourage the use of British colonial sugar in the continental colonies, because it made it that much higher in price. At the same time there were neither British restrictions nor British colonial duties upon the importation of foreign sugars. Until 1733 it was legal for colonial vessels, unless forbidden by temporary trading-with-the-enemy acts, to secure sugar from any of the foreign islands. If they broke any law, it would not be British.

From the standpoint of the general navigation system, a taxation of the colonial product on its exportation to another colonial port, while leaving the foreign product untaxed, was commercially unsound. Especially was this true at a time when the French supplies were expanding very rapidly. The effect was to drive the Americans into buying the cheaper French sugar. The act of 1733 merely equalized conditions by placing an import duty of five shillings a hundredweight upon foreign sugars imported into the colonies. This was identical with the old plantation duty on British sugar and removed the former discrimination against the British product.[56]

In general, the act of 1672 was considered a trade act and by 1760 was so generally accepted that it was not an object of special dislike and hence of systematic attempts at evasion as it produced no important sums of revenue in the continental colonies. Its very nature as an export duty tended to conceal its incidence from the northern colonies, where it was seen only in the somewhat enhanced cost of colonial products imported from the other colonies without setting up in their own ports annoying collection machinery. As time went on and people became accustomed to the higher prices produced by this act, all actual knowledge of the effect of such a law disappeared, and with it grounds for complaint. Such evasion as existed would have been confined largely to the tobacco and the sugar colonies, since most of the duties had to be collected there. The northern colonies were involved only in the case of reëxports of the enumerated products.

An examination of the alleged evidence of extensive colonial evasion of the trade and navigation laws discloses that they fall mainly into the following groups: (1) those that existed prior to 1700; (2) trading with the enemy in time of war; (3) attempts to evade customs taxes levied by Great Britain for revenue purposes, especially those on tea, molasses, and wine.

Conditions as they existed during the seventeenth century should not be presented as at all indicative of the practices or the attitude of the people who brought on the Revolution.[57] As historical information was very elementary at best and could not possibly have been the common property of very many, either in America or Great Britain, there needs to be specific evidence that the knowledge of the earlier practices was known to the revolutionary generation, or that the practices themselves continued. No sound evidence has been found that either condition existed. For that reason they will be excluded from further consideration in this study, and the discussion limited to conditions known to exist between 1760 and 1775, or to grievances specifically voiced during that time by the Americans and their friends.

Trading with the enemy in time of war has little to do with the navigation and trade ácts in general. A discussion of this properly belongs under a consideration of the operation of trading-with-the-enemy acts. War regulations, with their blockades, privateers, convoys, needs of fleets and armies and the consequent efforts of governments to bring about temporary changes in the course of trade, are no part of permanent trade practices. A very large part of the evidence usually presented deals with the trade with the French during the wars of the middle of the century. This has been called a smuggling trade in violation of the Navigation Acts;[58] but it consisted very largely of a sale of colonial commodities in their usual legitimate markets, most of which were not wanted in England and were not on the enumerated list. As these artificial conditions ended with the wars, they will be passed by as belonging to a different subject, and not a part of the irritation produced by the Navigation Acts themselves during the critical period of 1763-75. The leaders of the Revolution in no cases confused temporary irritations of the war regulations with the permanent trade and navigation system.

Molasses and Sugar

A very large part of the evidence concerning smuggling centers about the trade in molasses. This especially concerned Rhode Island, Massachusetts, New York, and Philadelphia, where most of the rum distilleries were located and for which molasses was the chief raw product. This evidence falls mainly within the period 1733-65.

The source of supply for molasses was the sugar islands in the West Indies. Americans at first had secured their chief supplies from the British colonies; but, about 1725, the sugar industry in the French islands began to be noticeably more efficient than the British, and, with the French discouragement of the manufacture of rum, molasses was a cheap raw product. The New England traders discovered both the supply and means of access to it. Prior to 1733, importation of molasses from this source was unrestricted by English laws so long as it went on in English vessels.

The act of 1733[59] sought to eliminate outside competition in the American colonial market and confine this trade to the products of the British sugar plantations by an import duty of six pence a gallon on the foreign product. This act was opposed by the New Englanders before its passage, but does not seem to have received especial attention when it was reënacted at successive intervals down to 1764.

This act is an anomaly among the vast number of trade and navigation acts. Its purpose was not to encourage the total trade of the British Empire. Trade laws were regularly enforced at the port of departure by putting the masters and owners of vessels under bond to complete a voyage according to the provisions of the law. This act employed taxation at the port of unloading for its enforcement, but provided no adequate plans for verifying the amounts due.

French molasses was a foreign manufactured product. Unlike other foreign products it reached its colonial market directly instead of through England. The carrying of non-enumerated goods to the French islands to exchange for molasses was legal in time of peace. It was legal to import molasses. The tax of six pence a gallon was the only requirement.

The trade was a direct advantage to the Americans as it supplied a needed market for their surplus goods. It was a direct advantage to producers and merchants in England because it greatly increased the capacity of the northern colonies to purchase British goods.

There was not enough molasses in the British sugar islands to supply the demand of the northern colonies. In addition the sugar growers were losing interest in selling molasses. There was more profit in distilling it into rum themselves, either in the West Indies or in the great English distilleries. It is even probable that the time came when the distillers in the British sugar islands found it profitable to use the cheap French molasses to supplement their own stock of raw materials.

The act was neither fish nor fowl. No one was interested in the act as a taxation measure. The British sugar growers were not interested in the collection of duties on foreign molasses either at their own ports or in the ports of other colonies. Many persons profited from the trade. Only customs officers were financially interested in the measure as a revenue producer, and this interest became personal.

The law never operated so badly as was predicted during the controversy in 1731-33. Just how much foreign molasses was imported can never be known because of two practices. Customs officials in the British West Indies were willing, for a personal consideration, to certify foreign molasses as British. This was done in a variety of ways. In some cases most of the molasses was on board when the vessel arrived at the British port, a few additional casks were purchased, and the entire cargo cleared as British. In other cases, the containers were set up at the British port, some filled with molasses and others with water, and the entire cargo was then cleared as British molasses. Later, French molasses was substituted for the water at a convenient port, and the entire cargo entered regularly at both West Indian and New England ports as of British origin. In many cases English sugar planters imported the French molasses secretly and sold it as English with certificates that it was produced on their plantations.

Such practices increased the official returns of molasses exported from the British plantations to the continental colonies. Officials called these practices "naturalization" of the foreign product. They gave the shipmaster a set of papers that was entirely regular, and thus freed him from all danger of interference at his home port, and hence constituted no formal evasion of the navigation laws. His bonds, clearances, cockets, etc., were all regular and in proper order to meet the most exacting customs regulations. Thus the very islands that were presumed to be protected by the Act of 1733 came to be directly interested in its evasion. Others besides local customs officers profited from the "naturalization" procedures.

As it was a long way from New England to the West Indies and it was difficult at best to compare exports from a West India port with corresponding entries of one in New England, it is probable that some of the clearance papers were left with the number of gallons of molasses to be filled in after they were approved by a West India customs officer. Some shipmasters probably deliberately forged their papers, although few would take that risk. Usually the complaisant attitude of the customhouse officials made such frauds unnecessary.

Another effective means of adjustment was in the northern colonial ports. The customs officers lived at these places, they knew conditions, many of them were themselves engaged in trade; they knew personally the importing merchants and shipmasters. They were interested in promoting the trade and prosperity of their own towns. They realized that six pence a gallon was an unreasonable import duty on molasses; that the act was never intended to produce a revenue; and that, like all other forms of taxation, it was subject to administrative regulation. Their usual practice seems to have been to make charges such that the total burden varied from one penny to half a penny per gallon upon the foreign product. In some few cases it may have amounted to even three pence a gallon.[60]

Undoubtedly there were many cases where the local customs officer accepted more for his own personal use than he recorded as collections for the government. There are cases where the governor himself was reported to have been a beneficiary of such arrangements and used the law as a means of adding to his own income. Bernard of Massachusetts was especially notorious in this respect; and Temple, the Surveyor General of the Customs, estimated that the governor received more from this source than from his regular salary. The collector at Salem was removed for corrupt practices in spite of the opposition of Bernard. Temple refers to this man as one of Bernard's "most valuable milch cows."

As settlements for less than the full amount of the duties were within the administrative powers of the customs officers, these practices were technically legal, although they amounted to compounding the violation of the law and a practical reduction of the duty to what the importer was willing to pay.[61]

The reduction of the duty from six pence to three pence per gallon in 1764, when this act was made permanent, was to break up the corruption in the customs service and make the charge conform to what merchants believed the trade would bear as well as to produce a revenue. The estimate of three pence turned out to be too high when rigidly enforced; and to meet the complaints that the tax was more than the African rum and slave trade could bear, the duty was lowered to one penny per gallon in 1766 and made uniform upon both foreign and British molasses.[62] With that final change it became a pure revenue measure and lost all resemblance to a trade or navigation act. From that period to the Revolution it seems to have been enforced with reasonable efficiency and was one of the chief sources of revenue of the American customs service.

The new duties on molasses quickly developed a change in the character of imports. There was no longer any need of smuggling French molasses into the British islands in order to secure certificates that it was of British origin. The British sugar planters lost their former profits from selling French molasses as their own production. As customs duties in American ports were the same for British and foreign molasses the trade quickly settled into its natural channels. Foreign molasses practically displaced British molasses in the colonial market. Imports listed as British shrank from 326,675 gallons in 1768 to 125,466 gallons in 1772. During the same years imports of foreign molasses increased from 2,824,060 gallons in 1768 to 4,878,794 gallons in 1772.[63]

With such quantities regularly imported there does not seem to have been much room for clandestine importations during these years. Harrington gives the impression that an illicit trade in molasses persisted at New York after 1767, but has only rumor to support her belief.[64] The detailed accounts of imports and exports preserved in the accounts of the Inspector General supply no foundation for such a conclusion. Had there been any material clandestine importation of molasses at New York it should have shown up in the form of increased exports of either rum or molasses or both. Instead the records reveal New York as a consistent heavy importer of both rum and molasses from other continental ports during these years.[65]

Instead of injuring the trade of the continental colonies with the sugar islands, the acts of 1764 and 1766 apparently had a favorable effect. Imports of molasses shifted to the foreign islands and imports of rum from the British islands increased. That meant greater markets for the produce of the continental colonies that was bartered for these products, a greater ability on the part of both groups of colonies to purchase goods from the home country and greater all-round prosperity. Only the revenue phase of the regulation was objectionable.

TEA

In the case of tea we have varying conditions. As a product of Asia, it was included in the general group of commodities that could be imported into England only in British ships. Furthermore its importation was monopolized by the East India Company, which alone had the legal right to trade east of the Cape of Good Hope.[66] Tea was one of the articles of consumption in England that was used for raising a revenue.

In 1660 the duty was five per cent on the values established at the time of importation, no specific value being set in the book of rates.[67] By acts granting additional subsidies in William's and Anne's reigns, this was increased to eleven and two-thirds per cent.[68]

In 1689 there was a duty of one shilling per pound added as an excise.[69] In 1695 another shilling a pound specific duty was added, with two shillings, six pence if the tea were foreign. A drawback of two-thirds of these additional duties was permitted upon exportation.[70] In 1711 another additional duty of two shillings per pound, with five shillings additional on foreign tea, was imposed, with a drawback of all of the new additional duties on exportation. If duties were paid in full on importation, a drawback of all the additional duties was allowed.[71] In 1723 the above additional specific duties were repealed as import duties, and an inland duty of four shillings per pound substituted,[72] the difference being that the East India Company did not have to advance any customs duties to cover these additional duties when the tea was imported, and they became due only when cleared from warehouses for consumption in England. By this arrangement the company avoided tying up capital in customs on tea awaiting sale in the warehouses.

If tea was exported directly from the warehouses, it did not have to pay the inland duty. In 1724 all importation into England of tea from foreign countries was forbidden.[73]

In 1745 the inland duty of four shillings per pound was repealed and an inland duty of one shilling per pound, plus twenty-five per cent of the selling price at the auction sales, was substituted. No drawbacks of these duties were permitted on exportation. Also the East India Company was permitted to import tea directly from Europe on licenses from the customs.[74] Three years later drawbacks were permitted if tea were exported to the colonies. It was thus freed from the inland duty, but it still had to pay the customs duties under the old acts.[75]

In 1767 all of the inland duties were taken off, and a complete drawback of all customs duties was permitted if the tea were exported to Ireland or America.[76] This act ran for five years, and on its expiration it was reënacted with a provision that three-fifths of the customs duties only should be drawn back on exportation.[77] The next year this was modified so as to permit the East India Company to export direct to America on license from the customs officers, without being subject to the payment of any of the customs duties.[78] Apparently tea bought of wholesalers in the ordinary course of business would still be subject to two-fifths of the old customs duties.

From the above account, it can be seen that there were times when tea bought in England was so burdened with taxation that its exportation to America was greatly discouraged. It was during such periods that most of the smuggling from foreign countries developed. At no time prior to 1767 was the probable saving of British customs duties by smuggling less than a shilling a pound, and on several occasions it was at least three shillings per pound. Any such artificial increase in prices, even if only the customs duties were added to the British price, could not but put a premium upon irregular trading, particularly by way of the Dutch ports in the West Indies, whence tea was imported practically free of duty.

The export of tea from Britain was almost exclusively a London trade, there being almost none from the outports or from Scotland.

Colonial imports entered mainly at Boston, New York, and Philadelphia. In the five years preceding the Townshend Revenue Act New York was the chief tea port of America, and in the next five years Boston became the colonial tea center. Importations at Philadelphia were erratic and are difficult to understand.

All of these ports show large increases in tea imports between 1763 and 1765, the total imports rising from 139,376 pounds in 1763 to 455,800 pounds in 1765 with an average for the five-year period (1763-67) of 328,125 pounds. The year of highest imports was 1768, the first year after the enactment of the colonial tea duty, and the year before the beginning of the nonimportation agreements.

In spite of the nonimportation agreements the average importations at these ports in the five years following the enactment of the colonial tax (1768-72) only dropped from 328,125 pounds to 295,876 pounds. This drop was confined to imports at New York and Philadelphia. The average imports at Boston actually increased during these years, rising from 110,471 for the first five-year period to an average of 179,169 pounds for the second five-year period. The above figures are for regularly cleared exports from England.[79] Actual arrivals at these ports can be checked after 1767 by the reports kept by the Commissioners of Customs. These tally very closely.

Tea is not a readily perishable product, and it is possible that stocks imported one year were carried over into the years when imports were small. Certainly all the agitation over the tea tax and the ceremonial signing of nonimportation agreements only reduced the total amount of tea available for consumption in the area north of Virginia in the five-year period after 1767 by 140,000 pounds from what had been available in the preceding five-year period.

English and American ports were so far apart and the customs management sufficiently different that it seems possible for ships to take on goods from the smugglers after clearing English ports, as was allegedly done in the case of molasses. We have the very careful records of arrivals in American ports kept by the American Customs Commissioners. These have been checked in the case of tea for the five years 1768-72. There is a fair agreement when one considers the length of time it took sailing vessels to cross the Atlantic except for the years of 1770 and 1771. The arrivals these years in Virginia, especially, are out of all proportion to the recorded exports but they may have been due to coastwise imports or to ships changing their course to avoid the nonimportation agreements in force at the northern ports. There were decreased arrivals at Boston and Rhode Island ports where most of the tea for New England was entered.[80]

There is no doubt that there was much smuggling of tea in British waters. Reported seizures of tea alone were reported as 103,289 pounds in 1765 and 139,810 pounds in 1787.[81] In fact smuggling was a most serious problem for the British during the decade before the Revolution. The value of confiscated smuggled goods sold at the several customhouses in England rose from £85,318 in 1765 to £141,300 in 1775 and £170,043 in 1776. It is possible that the prevalence of smuggling in England and the struggle against the practice led to the assumption that such practices were equally prevalent in America.[82]

It was during the period of high inland taxation of tea in Great Britain (1723-67) that the chief smuggling of tea in the colonies was developed. The American part of this trade centered at Boston and involved some of the leading merchants.[83]

The reduction of taxation in England automatically destroyed the profits in the colonial illicit trade, and it declined very greatly. Direct importations from England, properly entered at the colonial customhouses, became the regular practice and continued through the agitation against the Townshend Revenue Act and the East India Company. Even colonial inspection committees appointed by the nonimportation committees could not break up the direct importations from England; and the bringing of tea from there in his ships and entering it at the Boston customhouse is one of the main charges upon which John Hancock's contemporary reputation as a smuggler was founded. John Mein used the information he claimed to have secured direct from the customhouse to support his charges that Hancock and other Boston merchants were evading their own pledges to support the nonimportation agreements. The curious thing about this is that Hancock was charged, not with violating the Trade and Navigation Acts, but with importing in accordance with them.

There is little evidence that there was any extensive direct importation of tea from Holland or other sources in violation of the trade acts after 1765. There were rumors of such importations industriously circulated by the partisans of administration and by those who were seeking positions as agents of the East India Company in 1773.[84]

There may have been some illegal importations at New York and Philadelphia, but the presence of Dutch tea rests upon rumor only. There was only one seizure there by the newly vamped customs service; there were no such seizures at Boston reported in the public prints.[85]

Careful search of the newspapers reveals no advertisements of Dutch teas, or notices of their arrivals. On the other hand, the newspapers of every colony carry many advertisements of tea for sale, "just received from England in the latest ships." Frequently the name of ship and master are included in the advertisements,[86] and the customhouse reports show steady receipts and payment of duties even as late as 1774.[87] In fact, tea from England was coming in steadily and in sufficient quantities to make it a material source of revenue.[88] It was only with difficulty that this direct trade with England could be interrupted, and most of the tea riots and destruction of tea, aside from that at Boston, were aimed against the smaller importers who continued to import through regular channels from England as late as 1775.[89]

It is a curious commentary upon the theory of smuggling of tea from foreign sources on the eve of the Revolution that there were no known instances of such tea being found by the local committees at a time when they were seizing and destroying local supplies of tea, however small, and tea using of any kind was under the popular ban. On the other hand there were many cases of direct importations from England discovered and punished. Apparently the forces inducing men to trade within the navigation system were stronger than those leading them to break through it.

REFERENCES

CHAPTER 3

1. George E. Howard, *Preliminaries of the Revolution* (New York, 1906), p. 66.

2. 12 Charles II, c. 10.

3. To illustrate this point, below are sample lists from single issues of widely separated newspapers. These lists are relatively short; many are much longer.

CUSTOMHOUSE, SAVANNAH, GEORGIA

Entered Inward		Ship	Master	From
January	8	Sloop *Polly and Katie*	James Ward	St. Croix
	10	Brigatine *Peggy*	George Bridges	Philadelphia
	12	Schooner *Seahorse*	John Fridwell	Rhode Island
		Sloop *Polly*	Peter Taylor	Barbados
		Schooner *Molly*	John Gale	Salem and Marblehead
	13	Brigatine *Dona*	Isaac Cheeseman	London
		Sloop *Hope*	Charles Henry	South Carolina
	14	Brigatine *Britania*	John Roper	Jamaica

Entered Outward	Ship	Master	For
January 14	Brigatine *Annabell*	Francis Blake	St. Kitts
	Brigatine *Dolphin*	Josiah Crane	Grenada
	Brigatine *Happy Recovery*	G. Laverick	Cowes and Portsmouth
	Snow *Ann*	Daniel Thompson	Tortola
	Sloop *Sarah*	Alden Bass	Barbados
	Sloop *Betsy*	Nehemiah Skillins	Barbados
	Ship *Woolmanstone*	Benjamin Mason	Cowes
	Snow *Grenada*	Wm. Robinson	Liverpool
	Schooner *Britania*	Ebenezer Gorham	St. Kitts and Eustatia
	Brigatine *Betsy*	Richard Hosking	Antigua

Cleared		Ship	Master	For
January	10	Schooner *Grampus*	Charles Smyth	South Carolina
	12	Brigatine *Two Friends*	Stephen Parkinson	Jamaica

Georgia Gazette, January 14, 1767.

CUSTOMHOUSE, NEWPORT, RHODE ISLAND, October 17, 1768.

Inward Entries	Master	From
Sloop *Resolution*	Abraham Whipple	Philadelphia
Sloop *Betsy*	James Vial	Maryland

Outward Entries	Master	For
Sloop *Adventure*	George Champlin	Maryland
Sloop *Tom*	William Grinnell	Philadelphia
Brigatine *Diamond*	Richard Carpenter	West Florida
Sloop *Polly*	James Bourk	Georgia
Sloop *Pitt*	David Linsly	North Carolina
Sloop *Neptune*	Christopher Whipple	West Indies
Sloop *Bedford*	Robert Renny	North Carolina
Sloop *Polly*	Paul Folger	West Indies

Cleared for Departure	Master	For
Brigatine *Catherine*	Abraham Simmons	North Carolina
Schooner *Unity*	Daniel Blais	West Indies
Schooner *Jacob*	Benjamin Wright	Jamaica
Brigatine *Dare*	Benjamin Hicks	Jamaica
Brigatine *Betsy*	Benjamin Remington	Africa
Schooner *Hopewell*	Robert Gray	South Carolina
Brigatine *Little Sally*	Zachariah Allen	South Carolina
Sloop *Ranger*	George Mowald	Antigua

Newport Mercury, October 17, 1768.

4. John Montresor, *Journal* (New York, 1881), pp. 364 ff. Malachy Postlethwayt, writing in 1747, stated that sugar and molasses were imported into the colonies in ships "owned by foreigners." He does not state the number of ships engaged in this traffic, or the source of his information. *Britain's Commercial Interests Explained and Improved* (London, 1767), I, 486-87. The very complete reports from the customhouses for the years 1768-75 in the *Treasury Papers* in the Public Record Office in London do not reveal the visit of any foreign ships to American ports in a commercial way.

5. *The English Navigation Laws,* Chap. xix.

6. Postlethwayt, *op. cit.,* I, 401-18.

7. See Lord Sheffield (John Baker Holroyd), *Observations* (London, 1783), pp. 101-7. Lowell J. Ragatz points out that similar conditions were controlling factors in the sugar trade and operated so strongly as effectually to prevent direct shipments to the continent of Europe even after they were authorized by law. *Fall of the Planter Class in the British Caribbean* (New York, 1928), pp. 106-7.

8. David Macpherson, *Annals of Commerce* (London, 1805), III, 583.

9. *Ibid.,* III, *passim,* gives arrivals from year to year. Only one vessel was noted as being from America. The same source indicates that there was usually one vessel clearing from St. Petersburg for Boston each year. This probably carried hemp for the cordage industry. Besides, Russia was not a large importer of tobacco.

10. 3 George II, c. 28 and 4 George III, c. 27.

11. See David Macpherson, *Annals of Commerce* (London, 1805), III, 131, 200-209, 221.

12. 12 George II, c. 30. This privilege was granted only to ships built in Great Britain and was not open to colonial-built ships. It is one of the few instances where there was a discrimination against colonial shipping. David Macpherson (*Annals of Commerce*, III, 221) states that this right was only to ship south of Cape Finisterre, but the law (sec. 2) specifically states "to any foreign port of Europe." If vessels went south of Finisterre they did not have to touch at a port of England on the outward voyage (sec. 8). Macpherson was probably misled by this provision.

13. See the reports of ships arriving in Virginia from England or South Europe, either in ballast or with salt (*Virginia Gazette*, 1765-75). The interference with the very small westward cargoes of ships engaged in the Mediterranean trade is also one of the points made against the Sugar Act by the author of "An Essay on the Trade of the Northern Colonies," *Boston Evening Post*, February 6, 1764.

14. Lord Sheffield, *Observations* (London, 1783), pp. 53-54, 78-94; Timothy Pitkin, *Commerce of the United States* (Hartford, 1816), p. 156.

15. George E. Howard, *Preliminaries of the Revolution* (New York, 1906), p. 71; Wilbur C. Abbott, *New York in the American Revolution* (New York, 1929), pp. 35-36; Sydney G. Fisher, *Struggle for American Independence* (Philadelphia, 1908), I, 49-51, 67; George L. Beer, *The Old Colonial System* (New York, 1912), II, *passim*.

16. Lord Sheffield, *Observations on the Commerce of the United States*, Appendix IX. This table is quoted by Emory R. Johnson, *History of the Domestic and Foreign Commerce of the United States* (Washington, D. C., 1915), I, 89.

17. The only manufactured article advertised for sale prominently as imported from the continent of Europe was "Dutch fans" (hand machines for cleaning wheat) in the Pennsylvania papers, with an assurance that they had just been imported from Holland. Even these may have come through England.

18. Edward Channing, obviously quoting from manuscript records of the Commissioners of Customs, states that the recorded imports from England in a single year included 250,000 hats for men; 25,000 leghorn and chip hats for women; 321,942 yards of calico; 406,843 pounds of pewter ware; and many more articles. *History of the United States* (New York, 1912), III, 110-11. These quantities seem so ample for a population such as the continental colonies had as to leave relatively small demand for similar articles imported illicitly.

19. The fullest account of illicit trade in European goods is in V. D. Harrington, *The New York Merchant on the Eve of the Revolution* (New York, 1935), pp. 244-88. This lists an occasional vessel trading to Hamburg and Amsterdam. There is no attempt to indicate the relative proportion of this trade. The one ship of 155 tons to Amsterdam in 1764 looks pretty small compared with the 4,040 tons from Great Britain. *Ibid.*, p. 356. Even this foreign trade decreased after 1767.

20. 12 Anne, c. 16.

21. 4 George I, c. 27.

22. 8 George I, c. 15.

23. Section 1.

24. 4 George II, c. 29.

25. 15 George II, c. 29. Channing, *op. cit.*, III, 111, refers to "Irish bounty linens," but quotes figures from Adams Anderson, *Historical Deduction of the Origin of Commerce*, V, 197, whose account included other linens as well.

26. The exports and bounties on linens for three years are available. These are for England only. The Scotch exports were nearly as large.

	British Linen Yards Exported		Irish Linen Yards Exported	Bounty
1760	1,357,932	£ 8,487- 1-6	2,314,409	£14,465- 1- 1
1761	1,129,400	7,058-15-0	1,707,930	10,674- 1- 2
1762	1,729,902	10,806-16-6	2,792,613	17,453-16- 7
	4,217,234	£26,352-16-0	6,814,952	£42,592-18-10

(*Treasury* 1, Bundle 430, f. 282, Library of Congress, *Transcripts.*)

This totals an average import from England of more than three yards of linen for every man, woman, and child in America each year. This would seem to leave not much demand for illicitly secured foreign linens.

In 1774 there were imported into the port of New York alone 180,000 yards of Irish linen. Lord Sheffield, *Observations on the Commerce of the American States* (London, 1783), Table XII.

27. *Treasury* 64:252. Public Record Office, London.

28. *Customs* 14:1B. Public Record Office, London.

29. *Ibid.*

30. 18 George II, c. 24; 9 George II, c. 37.

31. *Treasury* 38:363. Public Record Office, London.

32. Sailcloth bounties, 1765 to 1774 inclusive, totaled £35,516, or an average of £3,500 per year. *Ibid.*

33. Gunpowder bounties totaled £14,400 for the ten years preceding the Revolution, or an average of £1,400 per year. *Ibid.*

34. Silk manufactures from 1765 to 1774 were paid a total export bounty on goods shipped to America of £78,035 or an average of £7,800 per year. *Ibid.*

35. Section 1.

36. 6 George III, c. 45.

37. 5 George III, c. 45.

38. Sydney G. Fisher, *Struggle for American Independence* (Philadelphia, 1908), I, 61, states that the Sugar Act "reduced by one half the duties which had been imposed on sugar and molasses by the 'old molasses act' of 1734." The molasses act cited as 6 George II, c. 13, levied a colonial import duty on foreign sugar of five shillings per hundredweight; while section 1 of the Sugar Act provided for colonial import duties on such sugar of one pound, two shillings, or twenty-two shillings per hundredweight, "over and above all other duties imposted by any former act of parliament." This would clearly indicate a total of one pound, seven shillings for the new duties, instead of the former five shillings, or a total of twenty-seven shillings per hundred-

weight, which is an increase in this duty of 440 per cent, instead of a decrease of one-half as stated by Fisher.

39. *Treasury* 64:390, Public Record Office, London.

40. Compiled from *Customs* 3:70-73; *Customs* 17:2 and from *Treasury* 38:363. The detailed results are as follows:

	Total Exports to the Colonies from Great Britain	Value of Foreign Goods Exported	Drawbacks
1770	£ 4,017,734	£ 781,851	£ 268,956
1771	6,110,698	1,189,141	409,064
1772	5,149,193	1,002,032	344,699
1773	4,041,561	786,835	270,560
1774	4,758,645	926,032	318,555
	£24,077,831	£4,685,891	£1,611,834

41. "We give the bounty on the importation of Indigo, and continue it upon exportation—enabling you, by the advantage of a double market to raise the price upon us afterwards.—

"Our own merchants are subject to duties on the importation of foreign commodities, but it is you who draw them back—so that they pay a tax and you receive a premium in this exchange of commodities."
Sir John Dalrymple, *Address of the People of Great Britain to the Inhabitants of America* (London, 1775), pp. 19-20.

42. *Colonial Office*, 324:10, p. 585.

43. Compiled from *Customs* 17:2. Exports of woolen goods to the various groups of colonies in 1773 were: New England £91,532; New York £51,387; Pennsylvania £118,699; Virginia and Maryland £104,827; the Carolinas £60,609. The total exports of British goods to these same colonies that year was £2,243,829.

44. *Boston Chronicle*, August, 1769 to February, 1770. A large part of his paper during this time was taken up with copies of manifests of ships' cargoes, presumably secured from the customhouse records. These were later republished by Mein in pamphlet form under the title, *A State of the Importations from Great Britain into the Port of Boston.*

This attack evoked much distrust and unfavorable criticism of the Boston merchants. The following sample is from the *Newport Mercury* for September 4, 1769. "The Boston news writers make John Hancock, Esq., one of the foremost of the patriots of Boston, and the strictest observer of the agreements for Non Importation. He should perhaps shine more conspicuously, and be less suspected in his character, if he did not keep a number of vessels running to London, and back, full freighted, getting rich by necessary freight on goods made contraband by the colonies."

Here is a charge of bad faith on Hancock's part, but there is no suggestion even that his ships were trading elsewhere than in legal channels. The offense, if any existed, was because they continued a legitimate trade during the non-importation agreements.

45. Thomas Hutchinson, *Diary and Letters* (Boston, 1884), I, 103. He asserts that Samuel Adams ordered the shipowners and consigners "at their

peril to cause the ships to be brought up to town." He uses this argument to justify himself for not having the ships detained outside the bar so that they could return to London, thus defending himself against the charge of neglect of duty made by Egerton Ryerson in *Loyalists of America and Their Times* (Toronto, 1880), p. 383.

46. *Historical View of the Domestic Economy of Great Britain and Ireland* (Edinburgh, 1812), p. 173. See also Lord Sheffield, *Observations* (London, 1784). Appendix, Tables XIII and XIV.

47. The form of Jefferson's argument is similar to that of Sir Matthew Decker in his *Essay on the Causes of the Decline of the Foreign Trade*, published in 1750. A copy of this pamphlet, slightly used, is in the Jefferson library. His copy is the Edinburgh reprint, which would indicate that he might have secured it prior to the Revolution, when the trade and commerce of northern Virginia were in the control of Scotch merchants.

48. George Chalmers, *Observations* (London, 1804), pp. 9-10.

49. *Ibid.*, p. 13.

50. 25 Charles II, c. 7, sec. 5.

51. 25 Charles II, c. 7.

52. These should not be confused with the "four and one-half per cent duties" collected by authority of the assemblies upon exports from Barbados, St. Christopher, Nevis, Montserrat, and Antigua, nor the "casual revenues" arising in the other colonies. See L. W. Labaree, *Royal Government in America* (New Haven, 1930), pp. 270-73.

53. The collections under 25 Charles II, c. 7, indicate that this law was at least partially enforced. We have available the collections for the fifteen years preceding 1764 in the following report made by the customs officials for the information of Grenville.

1749	£2,913	4	11½	1757	£1,832	9	7½
1750	860	10	8½	1758	997	18	1¼
1751	1,645	7	9½	1759	1,849	11	9½
1752	1,471	11	9¼	1760	1,165	0	1
1753	1,012	10	43/4	1761	381	0	6¼
1754	1,163	17	4¼	1762	704	9	5
1755	1,206	14	103/4	1763	1,321	19	1¼
1756	2,617	13	63/4	Total	£21,144	0	1

Customhouse, London, January 28, 1764. *Treasury* 1, bundle 430, f. 330, Fisher Transcripts (Library of Congress).

Edward Channing (*History of the United States*, III, 90, fn. 2) gives the collections for tobacco only, for 1767-75, as follows:

1767-69	£945	1770	£660	1773	£643
1769	539	1771	806	1774	1,533
		1772	320		

There is no explanation for the sudden expansion of collections in 1774. These figures are said to be from the accounts of Charles Stuart, *Declared Accounts*, Audit Office, *Customs*, bundle 844, roll 1137.

54. Lord Sheffield (John B. Holroyd), *Observations on the Commerce of the American States* (London, 1783), Table XII.

55. Vol. I, 72-73 (Philadelphia, 1775). This was published eight years before Sheffield's *Observations*.

56. 6 George II, c. 13.

57. All but three of the references to illegal trade listed in the index to the *New York Colonial Documents* are before 1701, and most of those given concern the period from 1688 to 1700 and are connected with piracy and other unsettled conditions.

58. The fullest discussion of this phase of the question is in George L. Beer, *British Colonial Policy*, 1754-65 (New York, 1907). Beer does not confuse this trade with a violation of the trade and navigation acts. Edward Channing (*History of the United States*, II, 566-67), does not specifically confuse the war measures with the trade and navigation acts, but gives his reader that impression. He states (p. 566): "For fifty years and more, in defiance of law, the continental colonists had traded with the French West India Islands; perhaps it was the fact that this commerce was always illegal that made it seem so heinous and unpatriotic in time of war as it really was. . . . This traffic was not only contrary to English law, but was also illegal under the statutes of Pennsylvania, New York, South Carolina, and other colonies." Yet the only British act he cites to support his statement is that of 1757 (30 George II, c. 9), which was specifically a war measure. Such statements are misleading. It certainly was not illegal during all this fifty years to export common food products, fish, and timber to the French islands and to receive in return both sugar and molasses. The Molasses Act of 1733 did not prohibit such trade but specifically legalized importation of the French products, provided they paid certain import duties.

59. 6 George II, c. 13.

60. For similar practices in England *see* Harper, *English Navigation Laws*, Chap. x.

61. On this point we have a variety of testimony: A Mr. Kelley testified before the House of Commons in 1766 that at New York, the compositions paid for molasses were from one-fourth to one-half penny a gallon and never higher than one dollar per 100 gallons; and that the price of molasses advanced after 1764. A Mr. Hale testified that imports into Boston were 9,000 hogsheads in 1763. *Treasury* 1, bundle 434, f. 55, Library of Congress, *Transcripts*.

We also have the letter from Jared Ingersoll to Thomas Whately, dated New Haven, July 6, 1764. "I am of the opinion that the foreign molasses will bear a duty of one penny half penny at most, the raw or brown sugar two shillings and six pence, and the clayed five shillings per cwt.—that there is not a single voyage of that sort planned with the remotest intention to pay the duty—was the duty lowered to where I have mentioned, the merchant would pay it (without compulsion) rather than run the risque of the custom-house office alone, and partly by reason of his having been used to pay a sum not much short of that." *Providence Gazette*, Nov. 8, 1766.

62. 6 George III, c. 52.

63. Report of the Inspector General, *Customs* 16:1, Public Record Office, London.

64. *New York Merchant on the Eve of the Revolution*, pp. 270-75.

65. *Customs* 16:1.

66. 9 and 10 William III, c. 44.

67. 12 Charles II, c. 4.

68. By 9 and 10 William III, c. 23, an additional subsidy was voted, which added five per cent; and by 2 and 3 Anne, c. 9, an additional one-third of a subsidy was granted, totaling eleven and two-thirds per cent on the value at the port. These duties remained in force until the Revolution. All drawbacks of customs duties in the later acts refer to these old basic duties.

69. 1 William and Mary, second session, c. 6.

70. 6 and 7 William III, c. 4.

71. 10 Anne, c. 26. The reference to additional duties is to these specific duties totaling four shillings per pound on East India tea.

72. 10 George I, c. 10.

73. This was accomplished by prohibiting importation of tea except from the place of its growth. As other laws limited the trade east of the Cape of Good Hope to the British East India Company, the effect was to make illegal all importations of foreign teas or the reimportation of exported British tea. 11 George I, c. 30, sec. 8.

74. 18 George II, c. 26.

75. 21 George II, c. 14.

76. 7 George III, c. 56. By the revenue act of the same year an American import duty was imposed, but the total effect of these two laws was to reduce considerably the old taxes on tea coming through England. This change is reflected in the average selling prices quoted in American newspapers after 1767. The revenue feature was retained.

77. 12 George III, c. 60.

78. 13 George III, c. 44.

79. The actual exports to these ports are listed below in pounds. Exports to areas between Nova Scotia and New York are listed as New England; practically, that meant Boston.

	1763	1764	1765	1766	1767	Totals
New England	37,225	142,214	175,030	118,482	79,406	552,357
New York	83,870	265,835	226,232	124,464	143,089	843,490
Philadelphia	18,281	41,949	54,538	60,796	69,216	244,780
	139,376	449,998	455,800	303,742	291,711	1,640,627

	1768	1769	1770	1771	1772	Totals
New England	291,899	86,004	85,935	280,825	151,184	895,847
New York	320,214	4,282	269	1,035	530	326,330
Philadelphia	174,853	81,729	......	495	128	257,205
	786,966	172,015	86,204	282,355	151,842	1,479,382

Compiled from *Customs* 3:63-72; and *Customs* 17:1-3, Public Record Office, London.

80. Comparison of Tea Exports from England and Arrivals at the Principal American Ports.

	New England		New York	
	Exports	Arrivals	Exports	Arrivals
1768	291,899	282,267	320,214	352,488
1769	86,004	111,134	4,282	16,986
1770	85,935	66,058	269	......
1771	280,825	283,638	1,035	344
1772	151,184	110,242	530	530
	895,847	853,339	326,330	370,348

	Philadelphia		Totals	
	Exports	Arrivals	Exports	Arrivals
1768	174,853	146,768	786,966	781,523
1769	81,729	112,159	172,015	240,279
1770	......	6,188	86,204	72,246
1771	495	......	282,355	283,982
1772	128	128	151,842	110,900
	257,205	265,243	1,479,382	1,488,930

Totals to America

	1768	1769	1770
Exports	902,936	245,502	178,006
Arrivals	870,794	317,598	478,551
	1771	1772	Totals
Exports	497,374	326,615	2,150,433
Arrivals	524,960	257,566	2,449,469

Compiled from *Customs* 3:68-73; *Customs* 17:1-3; *Customs* 16:1, Public Record Office, London.

81. *Treasury* 38:363, Public Record Office, London.

82. Report by Richardson, "Register of Seizures," 1779, *Ibid.*

83. See the series of letters on this point in S. A. Drake, *Tea Leaves* (Boston, 1884).

84. In the debates over the repeal of the Townshend Revenue Act in 1770, Thomas Pownall charged that the provisions affecting tea were operating in such a way as to cause the East India Company to encourage smuggling and discourage exportations to America, because it would have to make good the loss of the twenty-five per cent rebate of customs duties on the tea exported to the colonies. "If the Dutch do not get from Holland directly, or through their islands in the West Indies, supply the colonies entirely with this article, it becomes the interest of this British corporate merchant, circumstanced as matters stand by this agreement, to wish that the Dutch may do it entirely." Hansard, *Debates*, XVI, 865.

Isaac Barré also insisted that the three penny duty was interfering with the export of tea, and gave the value of tea exported to the colonies as £132,000 in 1768 and £44,000 in 1769. *Ibid.*, 783. Such estimates are obviously erroneous.

85. On this point consult A. M. Schlesinger, *The Colonial Merchants and the American Revolution* (New York, 1918), pp. 246-47. It is interesting to note that he accepts the smuggling rumors at these two ports at their full face value, especially after 1767.

86. Such advertisements may be found in nearly every newspaper in Amer-

ica during the years 1770-74. In some cases they do not disappear until 1775 and may be found in the Boston *Massachusetts Gazette* some time after the Tea Party.

87. Edward Channing (*History of the United States,* III, 90, fn.), gives these figures taken from Stuart's *Accounts,* Audit Office, Customs, bundle 844, roll 1137, as the duties collected on tea:

1767-69	£ 9,723	1772	£ 1,677
1769	8,189	1773	4,170
1770	3,413	1774	987
1771	4,596	Total	£32,755

There is a discrepancy between the figures in this table and those given in fn. 1, p. 128. The figures for the first column in the table on p. 90 seem to include other duties under the revenue act of 1767. These were repealed in 1770, which would account for the drop in receipts for that year. The remaining years are clearly for tea alone. These figures are net amounts and for only a part of the colonies. The total collections were considerably larger.

88. According to an article contributed from Boston under date of November 15, 1773, there had been the following regular importations of tea at Boston:

Year	Number of Chests	Number of Persons Importing		Number	Number of Persons Importing
1768	942	82	1771	890	103
1769	340	35	1772	375	70
1770	167	22	1773	378	61

Providence Gazette, November 20, 1773.

The significant things in this statement are the large number of importers and that tea was coming from Great Britain in large quantities. The records of exportations from England already cited corroborate this, as do the records of actual arrivals as recorded at the customhouses.

89. The famous case of Captain Chambers of Philadelphia is a good illustration. He had a separate cocket for his tea and for a time attempted to conceal its presence on board. His ship was returning from London (*Pennsylvania Gazette,* April 27, 1774). The *Peggy Stewart* is another case in point. Its tea was from England. In neither instance, apparently, was the tea East India property. All the recorded cases of tea importation in Virginia were in vessels from England with known orders of English goods on board. Here is one illustration from many available in the newspapers of the period.

In August, 1774, the Committee of Correspondence of Frederick County, Maryland, received word from a similar committee of Charles County that the brigantine *Mary Jane* had arrived in Wicomico from London with eleven chests of tea for various parties in Virginia and Maryland. Two chests were for Georgetown; one for Robert Peter, the other for John Ferguson, the factor of Finley and Company. Peter admitted that he had ordered the tea in December and relied "on the custom which had constantly prevailed in the province of Maryland since the partial repeal of the revenue act to justify his conduct." (*Maryland Gazette,* August 18, 1774.) This same committee caught Thomas

Richardson of Georgetown importing one hundred pounds of tea from Philadelphia, which he surrendered. He advanced no defense that it was Dutch *(Ibid.)*. These and many other incidents published in the newspapers during the year 1773-74 occur at a time when the Tories were watching for every opportunity to prove that the American patriotic party was operated mainly in the interests of smugglers. Any softness on the part of the committee toward Dutch tea would have been at once heralded throughout the Empire.

4

ATTITUDE OF LEADING AMERICANS

IN DETERMINING the extent to which the Navigation Acts were a contributing cause of the Revolutionary War, it is important to consult the writings and papers of the leading characters in the revolutionary movement. In most cases, all of their major contributions to the controversial literature of the period are known, and in addition most of their important official and private correspondence has been published.

The agitation for a popular revolution has to be carried on in the open. Secret plottings can have little to do with real issues; they are more likely to concern specific programs and individual responsibility for actions that might have important consequences to persons or their property, and might even involve their families or friends. Overt acts had to be committed, somebody had to assume leadership in doing them, and those who took risks had to be protected from immediate personal consequences. On the other hand, issues which divided men into political groups, and upon which individuals were willing to risk their all, had to be discussed in the open and in ways that could be understood by the masses whose support was essential to the success of the cause.

Consequently the attitude of Americans on the basic trade and navigation regulations had to be stated clearly over and over again in the mass of controversial literature that preceded hostilities. We propose to examine that attitude in some detail.

ATTITUDE OF NEW ENGLAND

As the center of the earlier agitation was believed to be in New England, and especially in Massachusetts, we shall begin with the two most prominent figures in the literature of that agitation, John and Samuel Adams. The records left by these two men are quite different. Samuel Adams was the political worker, the man of the people, the man who knew individuals and their peculiarities, who sensed the arguments that had the widest appeal and used them. He was probably the most active contributor to local newspapers of any American of his period. As no other individual, he realized the extent to which this vehicle could be used to reach the public, not only in Boston, but everywhere in colonial America and in England as well.

Few of his contributions bear his own signature; many of them represent the combined labors of himself and his revolutionary associates in Boston. Frequently the articles take the form of instructions, addresses to the governor, resolutions, petitions, memorials, etc. In this form they were copied from the Boston newspapers into nearly every newspaper and magazine in America and widely reproduced in newspapers and magazines in Great Britain. The more important of these papers were also printed in pamphlet or broadside form for wider circulation and more permanent reference. In the crucial years from 1768 to 1775 this material emanating from Boston became the political bible of the Revolution. The ideas were not those of Samuel Adams but those of the group for which he wrote.

Adams apparently had discovered that articles signed by an individual with his own name had little weight, because they invited personal attack and tended to obscure real issues. The use of fictitious names also had its limitations. Such material was discounted as propaganda, as the device was largely used by political factions who employed writers to supply desired articles for the press. Many newspapers refused to print such writings and would not copy them from other papers except upon request of some of their patrons. On the other hand, the official form given to the arguments thrown out by the Hancock-Adams group gave them a character which insured them a place on the most prominent news page of every paper and at the same time, by concealing Adams' connection with them, made personal attacks upon him and his associates impossible. In this way attention was attracted to issues instead of individuals.

Along with this mass of official or semi-official material, there came from the pen of Samuel Adams a stream of short articles which were called "scurrilous" by General Gage and others of the official class. Most of them were published in the *Boston Gazette* under a variety of signatures, all fictitious. Between 1768 and 1772 a total of sixty-seven of these contributions appeared under the names of "Vindex," "Candidus," and "Poplicola." Most of these deal with local incidents, personalities, and current political happenings and were obviously written chiefly for consumption in Boston and Massachusetts.[1]

The surprising thing in this mass of material prepared and published in the chief commercial city of the colonies is to find so few attacks upon the commercial system and none upon the Navigation Acts specifically. A few of the more important references to the mercantile situation are given in the following pages, arranged in the order in which they appeared.

In the instructions to the representatives from Boston, chosen in 1764, there is the following: "It is the trade of the colonys, that renders them beneficial to the Mother Country: Our Trade, as it is now, and always has been conducted, centers in Great Britain, and in return for her manufactures affords her more ready cash, beyond any comparison, than can be expected by the most sanguine promoters of these extraordinary methods."[2]

In discussing the inequity of the Stamp Act in a letter to John Smith, he says: "You are sensible Sir, that her policy has been to oblige the colonys to carry the chief of their produce there and to take off her manufactures in return; and as they must conform to her price, both in buying and selling, one would think the advantage she reaps by their trade sufficient."[3]

The same sentiment appears in the instructions sent to Denys de Berdt, colonial agent for Massachusetts,[4] and in the continued correspondence with him.[5] These contain the usual statement of the effects of the Navigation Acts; that they compelled the Americans to buy their manufactures and European goods through British merchants; that the enumeration of certain products forced them to be sold in Great Britain, frequently upon a glutted market; that these regulations compelled them to pay more for what they bought and permitted them to receive less for what they had to sell, than would be the case if these laws were not in force; that such laws operated as an indirect tax upon the colonists. But nowhere does one find a request that the system be changed. Objection is made only to imposing taxes in addition to those already existing.[6]

Among the numerous papers prepared by Samuel Adams is the "Letter to Shelburne," sent by the Massachusetts House of Representatives in 1768, protesting against the Townshend Revenue Act. This was released for publication as soon as it had been delivered and is as much a letter to the British and American public as it is to Secretary Shelburne. Although Adams composed the letter, his name is nowhere publicly connected with it. As it reached almost the entire newspaper-reading public in both Great Britain and America, what it contains is relatively important for an understanding of the arguments used in formulating commonly held opinions.[7] After a detailed statement of the economic burden of the Navigation Acts the letter says:

"The House is not, at this time, complaining of this policy of the mother state; but beg your Lordships impartial and candid consideration, whether it is not grievous to the colonies to be additionally taxed upon the commodities of Great Britain here, and to be solely charged with the defending and securing his Majesty's colonies."[8] The same sentiment in an even more elaborate form appears in the letter to the Commissioners of the Treasury.[9] A year later in a letter signed "Shippen," he referred to the enforcement of the provisions of the Sugar Act. "They felt themselves happy, till new acts, equally unconstitutional were made, and severities imposed upon trade, unknown even at the time of the stamp act."[10]

In 1772, in one of his controversial articles, Adams says: "It has not been made a question, that I know of, whether the parliament hath a right to make laws for the regulation of the trade of the colonies. *Power* she undoubtedly has to enforce her acts of trade; . . . if the trade of the colonies is *protected* by the British navy, there may possibly be from them inferred a just right in the parliament of Great Britain to restrain them from carrying on their trade to the injury of the trade of Great Britain." But this is very different from a power to pass laws for the sole purpose of raising revenue. "In one case it may be the wisdom of the Colonies, under present circumstances to acquiesce in *reasonable* restrictions . . ." but it was their duty to resist taxation, because it meant their enslavement.[11]

In the list of infringements of colonial rights, adopted by Boston at the time of instituting the provincial committees of correspondence, we find a condemnation of the Commissioners of Customs and their operations, of the revenue acts, swarms of officers, search warrants, and trials in courts of vice-admiralty; but there is no condemnation of the old Navigation Acts. In section nine, however, they complain specifically of the restriction upon slitting mills, hat manufactures, and the transportation of domestic wool; but these are made a part of a constitutional argument that such measures were internal regulations, and hence a violation of the powers of government granted by the charter.[12] As this paper was prepared for popular consumption in the rural towns of Massachusetts, it may be looked upon as something of a feeler. That part of the list of grievances that refers to colonial manufactures does not seem to have met with any important popular response; hence it was not strongly insisted upon in the future.

John Adams' published works, consisting of personal letters, public papers, and his diary, show an almost total absence of any attack upon the Navigation Acts. His notes on the discussions in the first Continental Congress also reveal few of the delegates favoring any such attack. On September 8, 1774, his diary has a note that Colonel Lee, in the committee for stating grievances of the colonies, said that the Navigation Acts were a "capital violation" of the theoretical rights of the colonies, based upon nature, the British constitution, colonial charters, and immemorial usage.[13] Adams is not clear as to what phase of the matter was under consideration.

His own attitude is possibly best stated in his long constitutional controversy with Daniel Leonard,[14] who wrote under the name of "Massachusettensis," while Adams used the name of "Novanglus." These articles are outstanding, complete statements of the conservative Tory and revolutionary attitudes on the eve of the Revolution and were undoubtedly read in all of the northern colonies. Adams used an elaborate historical argument that parliamentary power did not always exist; that the first general legislation affecting the colonies was the Navigation Act; that this was protested by Massachusetts, but finally expressly ratified; that Virginia also denied its validity and was finally given an express promise by the king that the new measure should not be used for taxation purposes; and that all taxes, except those collected in England, should be imposed by the local assembly.[15] Then he adds:

We have by our own express consent, contracted to observe the Navigation Act, and by our implied consent, by long usage and uninterrupted acquiescence, have submitted to the other acts of trade, however grievous some of them may be. This may be compared to a treaty of commerce, by which those distinct states are cemented together in perpetual league and amity. And if any further ratifications of this part or treaty are necessary, the colonies would readily enter into them, provided their other liberties were inviolate.[16]

There are also references to the Navigation Acts in the series of letters to William Tudor in 1818; but, as these were written from memory and more than half a century after the events, they are of doubtful value as a record of just what James Otis said, although they indicate clearly that he did not attack the acts as trade measures so long as they were not perverted to revenue purposes.[17] Governor Stephen Hopkins of Rhode Island was another outstanding leader of New England thought. In his pamphlet controversy with Martin Howard he says:

Although each of the colonies has a legislature . . . to take care of its interests, and provide for its peace and internal government, yet there are many things of a more general nature quite out of the reach of these particular legislatures, which it is necessary should be regulated, ordered and governed. One of this kind is, the commerce of the whole British empire, taken collectively, and that of each kingdom and colony in it, as it makes a part of the whole. . . .[18]

James Otis was one of the earliest revolutionary leaders. His *Rights of the British Colonies,* published in 1764, covers a good deal of ground and is so obscure in its form of statement that one cannot always be sure that he understands what Otis had in mind. In discussing the commercial relations of the colonies and the rest of the Empire, he points out that the colonists did not have the full rights of Englishmen resident in England; yet he says the Navigation Act "is a good act, so are all that exclude foreign manufactures from the plantations."[19] He seems to have approved of excluding European manufactures from the colonies, but insisted upon a right to trade with other colonies. Apparently some phases of the navigation system were displeasing to him, but his treatise cannot anywhere be said to be an attack upon the Navigation Acts. His main thesis was based upon the theory that Parliament was the supreme legislature for the Empire and could enact any laws for the common good.[20] It unquestionably was an attack upon taxation by Parliament, admiralty courts, and the unwise customs machinery of the Sugar Act of 1764.

Another early pamphlet, *A Dissertation on the Canon and the Feudal Law,* supposed to have been written by Jeremiah Gridley of Massachusetts, points out certain evils of the existing constitutional system by which a small body of influential West India planters, English merchants, or manufacturers could secure legislation in their own interest, at the expense and against the wishes of the whole body of English citizens in the colonies. He specifically complains of the wine, oil, and fruits provisions of the Sugar Act; the Hat Act; and the laws restricting iron and steel manufacture. A part of his argument is based upon the theory of natural rights. While this pamphlet calls in question the general constitutional system and certain acts that appeared to be locally burdensome, there was no attack upon the basic laws of the navigation system, and especially no suggestion that foreign shipping should be permitted to compete in the general trade of the Empire.[21]

Oxenbridge Thatcher of Massachusetts also attacked the Sugar Act in a pamphlet. He insisted that the northern colonies were the losers commercially by the annexations because Canada, while it was a part of France, had been excluded from trade with the British West Indies; but that trade was now open to her, and, as Canada produced goods similar to those of New England, she would compete directly for the West India trade.

Then he pointed out the new provisions in the Sugar Act that would burden trade: the admiralty courts and the provisions by which officers of the navy were given powers of customs officers. Such men, not experienced in trade and law, he believed were wholly unfit for such duties, as they would make wholly unwarranted seizures because they did not know trade customs and long-standing legal practices. Especially did he object to the provisions exempting customs officers from all personal responsibility for illegal seizures with their consequent expense and burden to the shipowners. He argued that this act would hurt England, because "everybody knows that the greatest part of the trade of Great Britain is with her colonies";[22] but nowhere did he attack the Navigation Acts themselves.

Edward Bancroft, writing in 1769, took an attitude similar to that of Dickinson, who will be discussed later. He did not oppose regulation of commerce, provided there were no taxes connected with it. He favored prohibition of a trade that was injurious to the mother country. As for manufacturing, he believed that the colonies should be free to carry on such enterprises of that kind as they found advantageous, but that England could rightfully prohibit the exportation of such manufactures if she found herself injured by them. He denied that the earlier trade laws were taxation measures, insisting that they were purely regulative and hence gave no precedents for the later taxation schemes.[23]

A "gentleman in Newport," writing to a correspondent in Philadelphia in the early part of 1768, assumed that the parliamentary right to regulate trade was practically unquestioned. He says:

The parliament of Great Britain, it is acknowledged have a right to regulate the trade of the whole British empire, but impositions for the regulation of trade, and taxes for levying money on the colonies are distinct propositions, and do not by any means involve each other. . . . In regulating the trade of the colonies, great attention ought to be exercised, and the consequences of such regulation should be deliberately considered. Rather than to violate the rights of the colonies, it is to the interest of Great Britain in her regulation of trade to grant them the greatest indulgence, for commerce delights and flourishes in a free air.[24] He admits that the late restrictions had been burdensome, and "not only incompatible with the interest of Great Britain, but utterly inconsistent with the liberty of the colonies.

MIDDLE COLONIES

In the middle group of colonies the outstanding leaders in the discussion which gradually formed public opinion in favor of the Revolution were John Dickinson and Benjamin Franklin of Pennsylvania and Daniel Dulany of Maryland. An examination of their public utterances reveals their own attitude toward the Navigation Acts and also that of the more radical elements in the population of that section. Joseph Galloway and Samuel Seabury are the best representative spokesmen of the conservative, Tory element of Pennsylvania and New York, and Jonathan Boucher for similar elements of the population of Maryland and Virginia.

Franklin does not often discuss the Navigation Acts. The fullest reference to them is in his account of the negotiations aimed at conciliation, in which he was engaged just before his departure from England in 1775. In recounting what he said in his first and last interviews with Chatham, who remarked that there was an opinion in England that "America aimed at setting up for itself as an *independent* state; or, at least, to get rid of the *Navigation* Acts,"[25] Franklin records:

I assured him, that, having more than once travelled almost from one end of the continent to the other, and kept a great variety of company, eating, drinking, and conversing with them freely, I never heard in any conversation from any person, drunk or sober, the least expression of a wish for separation, or hint that such a thing would be advantageous to America. And as to the Navigation Act, the main, material part of it, that of carrying on trade in British or plantation bottoms, excluding foreign ships from our ports, and navigating with three quarters British seamen, was as acceptable to us as it could be to Britain. That we were even not against regulations of the general commerce by Parliament, provided such regulations were *bona fide* for the benefit of the *whole empire,* not for the small advantage of one part to the great injury of another, such as the obliging our ships to call in England with our wine and fruit, from Portugal or Spain; the restraints on our manufactures, in the woolen and hat making branches, the prohibiting of slitting mills, steel works, &c. He allowed, that some amendment might be made in those acts; but said those relating to slitting mills, trip hammers, and steel works, were agreed to by our agents, in a compromise on the opposition made here to abating the duty.[26]

Just before leaving England in 1775, Franklin was drawn into informal negotiations by men closely connected with the ministry and induced to write out a set of seventeen propositions which he believed would lead to a permanent union. These are especially important, because we have not only the points, but also Franklin's notes for discussing them and the reaction of men in touch with the ministry upon each one. Four of these deal with trade and navigation:

3. The Acts of Navigation to be all reënacted in the colonies.
4. A naval officer, appointed by the crown, to reside in each colony, to see that those acts are observed.
5. All acts restraining manufactures in the colonies to be reconsidered.
6. All duties arising on the acts for regulating trade with the colonies, to be for the public use of the respective colonies, and paid into their treasuries. The collectors and custom-house officers to be appointed by each governor, and not sent from England.[27]

On the 3rd and 4th Articles I observ'd, we were frequently charg'd with views of abolishing the Navigation Act. That in truth, those parts of it which were of most importance to Britain, as tending to increase its naval strength, viz. those restraining the trade to be carried on only in ships belonging to British subjects, navigated by at least ¾ British or colony seamen &c. were as acceptable to us as they could be to Britain, since we wish'd to employ our own ships in preference to foreigners, and had no desire to see foreign ships enter our ports. That indeed the obliging us to land some of our commodities in England before we could carry them to foreign markets, and forbidding our importation of some goods directly from foreign countries, we thought a hardship, and a greater loss to us than gain to Britain, and therefore proper to be repeal'd. But as Britain had deem'd it an equivalent for her protection, we had never apply'd, or propos'd to apply, for such a repeal. And if they must be continu'd, I thought it best (since the power of Parliament to make them was now disputed), that they should be reënacted in all the colonies, which would demonstrate their consent to them. . . . The gentlemen were satisfy'd with these reasons and approv'd the 3rd and 4th Articles.[28]

The 5th they apprehended would meet with difficulty. They said, that restraining manufacturers in the colonies was a favorite here; and therefore they wish'd that article to be omitted, as the proposing it would alarm and hinder perhaps the considering and granting others of more importance. But, as I insisted on the equity of allowing all subject in every country to make the most of their natural advantages, they desired I would at least alter the last word from *repealed* to *reconsidered*, which I comply'd with.[29]

The attitude reflected in these letters is essentially the same as that in Franklin's letter to Joseph Galloway at about the same time dealing with plans for a permanent union, which Franklin believed might be of as much disadvantage as advantage.[30] He again proposed the repeal of all laws restraining manufactures, and the reënactment by Parliament and the colonial legislatures of the main navigation acts, giving the necessary duties arising from the operation of such laws to the colony where they were collected, and providing that the customs officers should be appointed by the governors. "Then the business will be cheaper and better done, and the misunderstandings between the two countries, now created and fomented by the unprincipled wretches generally appointed from England, be entirely prevented."[31]

Finally we have a paper prepared by Franklin to be read at the head of the army when Washington took command. It was not so used and was first published in the *London Public Advertiser*, July 18, 1777. It was entitled "Vindication and Offer from Congress to Parliament."[32]

"Forasmuch as the enemies of America in the Parliament of Great Britain, to render us odious to the nation, and give an ill impression of us in the minds of other European powers, have represented us as unjust and ungrateful in the highest degree; asserting, on every occasion, that the colonies refuse to contribute to their own protection, and to the common defense of the nation; that they aim at independence; that they intend an abolition of the Navigation Acts. . . ."[33]

"The charge against us, *that we refuse to contribute to our own protection,* appears from the above to be groundless; but we farther declare it to be absolutely false"; it was well known that the colonies had voted money to aid in carrying on wars. "But, as Britain has enjoyed a most gainful monopoly of our commerce"; and as the colonies have paid their own civil expenses, this had been considered an equivalent for aid in time of peace. On reconciliation the colonies would continue their former practice of granting aids in time of war; "but whenever she shall think fit to abolish her monopoly, and give us the same privileges of trade as Scotland received at the union, and allow us a free commerce with all the rest of the world; we shall willingly agree (and we doubt not it will be ratified by our constituents) to *give and pay* into the sinking fund [one hundred thousand pounds] sterling per annum for the term of one hundred years; which duly, faithfully, and inviolably applied to that purpose, is demonstrably more than sufficient to extinguish *all her present national* debt; since it will in that time amount, at legal British interest, to more than [two hundred and thirty millions of pounds].

"But if Britain does not think fit to accept that proposition, we, in order to remove her groundless jealousies, *that we aim at independence, and an abolition of the Navigation Act,* (which hath in truth never been our intention,) and to avoid all future disputes about the right of making that and other acts for regulating our commerce, do hereby declare ourselves ready and willing to enter into a *covenant with Britain,* that she shall fully possess, enjoy, and exercise that right, for an hundred years to come; the same being *bona fide* used for the common benefit; and in case of such agreement, that every Assembly be advised by us to confirm it solemnly by laws of their own, which once made, cannot be repealed without the assent of the crown."[34]

John Dickinson probably exerted a greater influence upon American public opinion than any other man, even Samuel Adams. Dickinson did his writing over his own name, while Adams made his major contribution in the mass of public papers that poured from Boston and Massachusetts political bodies. Hence

Adams' personal responsibility for his writing was far less well known than was Dickinson's.

Dickinson first came into prominence during the Stamp Act controversy with his pamphlet, *The Regulations Respecting the British Colonies on the Continent of America Considered, in a Letter from a Gentleman in Philadelphia to his Friend in London,* which was first printed by Bradford in Philadelphia in 1765 and at once reprinted with a slightly changed title by Almon in London.

After describing in some detail the commercial system and the burdens it imposed upon the great agricultural colonies, he says: "However under all these restraints and some others that have been imposed upon us, we have not till lately been unhappy. Our spirits were not depressed. We apprehended no design formed against our liberty."[35] Then he shows how the new regulations under the Sugar Act tended to limit their markets, and how the Stamp Act would deprive the country of specie and make times harder. Then he takes up the case of Florida, where the Navigation Acts had recently been put in operation.

Sure no one considers *Florida* in the same light with *these colonies* and thinks that no vessels should be permitted to trade there, but British shipping. This would be to apply the acts of navigation to purposes directly opposite to the spirit of them. They were intended to preserve an intercourse between the *Mother country* and her *colonies,* and thus to cultivate a mutual affection; to promote the interest of both, by an exchange of their most valuable productions for her manufactures; thereby to increase the shipping of both; and thus render them capable of affording aid to each other. Which of these purposes is answered by prohibiting a commerce, that can be no other way carried on? That is by forbidding the Spaniards to bring their wealth for us to Flordia.[36]

His *Letters of a Pennsylvania Farmer* appeared in 1768 at the height of the agitation caused by the Townshend Acts. They were first published as a series of twelve letters by William Goddard in the *Pennsylvania Chronicle,* as he says against the solemn and profane objections of his partners who considered them "too inflammatory for that latitude."[37] From the *Chronicle* they were copied into nearly every newspaper in America,[38] into several British news-papers, and were speedily printed in pamphlet form by numerous local printers in America and England, besides being reprinted in several foreign editions.

Probably no other document of the pre-revolutionary period was read by more people than *The Farmer's Letters*. Their effect upon revolutionary thought was very great, consequently what they said about the Navigation Acts is important. Dickinson's atti-tude is best stated in his second letter in which he says:

The Parliament unquestionably possesses a legal authority to *regu-late* the trade of Great Britain, and all her colonies. Such an authority is essential to the relation between a mother country and her colo-nies; and necessary for the common good of all. . . . We are but parts of a *whole;* and therefore there must exist a power somewhere, to pre-side, and preserve the connection in due order. This power is lodged in the parliament; and we are as much dependent on Great Britain as a perfectly free people can be on another.

I have looked over every *statute* relating to these colonies, from their first settlement to this time; and I find every one of them founded on this principle, till the *Stamp Act* administration. *All before,* are calcu-lated to regulate trade, and preserve or promote a mutually beneficial intercourse between the several constituent parts of the empire; and though many of them imposed duties on trade, yet those duties were always imposed *with design* to restrain the commerce of one part, that was injurious to another, and thus promote the general welfare.[39]

Concerning manufactures he says: "Great Britain has prohibited the manufacture of iron and steel in these colonies, without any objection to her *right* of doing it. The like right she must have to prohibit any other manufacture among us. Thus she is pos-sessed of an undisputed *precedent* on that point."[40]

In 1774 in *A New Essay,* designed as a set of instructions to the delegates from Pennsylvania to the First Continental Congress, after discussing the tax and repressive measures and suggesting concessions to be asked for, he adds:

In case of obtaining these terms, it is our opinion, that it will be reasonable for the colonies to engage their obedience to the acts of navigation, and to every other act of parliament declared to have force, at this time, in the colonies, other than those above mentioned, and to confirm such statutes by acts of the several assemblies. . . .

As to the regulation of trade . . . we are of opinion, that by making some few amendments, the commerce of the colonies might be settled on a firm establishment, advantageous to Great Britain and them, requiring and subject to no future alterations, without mutual consent. We desire to have this point considered by the congress; and such measures taken, as they may judge proper.[41]

The Tory writers insisted that Dickinson's admission of parliamentary power to regulate commerce involved a recognition of her general powers of legislation. Dickinson refuted this in his *Essay* of 1774, maintaining that Parliament had the power to regulate trade legally, "not as the supreme legislature of these colonies, but as the supreme legislature and full representative of the parent state, and the only judge between her and her children in commercial interests, which the nature of the case, in the process of their growth admitted. It has been urged with great vehemence . . . that a power of regulation is a power of legislation, and a power of legislation, if constitutional must be universal and supreme in the utmost sense of the words. It is therefore concluded that the colonists by acknowledging the power of the regulation, have acknowledged every other power."[42] This he denied, and pointed out that regulation of trade was largely a crown function, carried out by treaties, agreements, etc.; that it was absolute in no sense; and that it was customary to go to Parliament only when the regulation involved revenue legislation. Then he added:

"The power of regulation appears to us to have been pure in its principles, simple in its operation, and salutory in its effects. But for some time past we have observed with pain, that it hath been turned to other purposes, than it was originally designed for, and retaining its title both became an engine of intolerable oppressions and grievous taxations."[43]

The Reverend Jacob Duché, the chaplain of the First Continental Congress and certainly a most conservative man and one who must have known intimately the political opinions of leading Philadelphia politicians, wrote: "We wish not to interfere with that commercial system, which they have hitherto pursued. We do not wish to possess . . . [the luxuries of the East]. . . . We only wish, that what we have, we may be able to call our own."[44] If there had been any general hostility to the Navigation Acts, he should have known of it in a commercial city like Philadelphia, especially with so many well-to-do merchants in his congregation.

Lord Stirling, the senior officer in the Revolutionary army from New Jersey, a prominent landowner, and a man with extensive personal acquaintance in England, has left considerable portions of his correspondence. This reflects no hostility to the Navigation Acts. On the contrary, the only item that refers particularly to them advises the still further development of the commercial policy that would enable the Americans to expand their production of raw materials. At the same time that he suggests the use of bounties and other means of encouraging the development of the iron, hemp, and wine industries, he advises legislation to discourage the flow of American capital into industries directly competitive with those already established in England. As one who had found experimenting with the wine industry both expensive and unsuccessful, he personally desired a British bounty on American production.[45]

Southern Colonies

In the southern group of colonies the active leaders in the paper controversy were Thomas Jefferson, Patrick Henry, R. C. Nichols, and Arthur Lee of Virginia; William Henry Drayton and Henry Laurens of South Carolina; and John Jacob Zubly of Georgia. George Washington, while an outstanding leader, took no part in the newspaper and pamphlet war between 1765 and 1775, and his published writings do not reveal that he ever expressed an opinion on the subject of the Navigation Acts. The same seems to be true of Patrick Henry. He was an orator and not a pamphleteer. Such writings of his as have come down to us do not indicate that he considered the Navigation Acts a part of the controversy and worthy of his serious attention.

Jefferson's attitude is best stated in his *Summary View of the Rights of British America,* written in 1774 to serve as a set of instructions for the Virginia delegates to the first Continental Congress. This does not include any attack upon the Navigation Acts and trade laws. In his *Autobiography,* written many years later, he

says that from the beginning he thought the only tenable position
was

that the relations between Great Britain and these colonies was ex-
actly the same as that of England and Scotland, after the accession of
James, and until the union, and the same as her present relations with
Hanover, having the same executive chief, but no other necessary political connection; and that our emigration from England to this country gave her no more rights over us, than the emigrations of the Danes
and Saxons gave to the present authorities of their mother country
over England. In this doctrine, however, I had never been able to get
any one to agree with me but Mr. Wythe.[46] He concurred in it from
the first dawn of the question, what was the political relation between
us and England? Our other patriots, Randolph, the Lees, Nicholas,
Pendleton, stopped at the half way house of John Dickinson, who
admitted that England had a right to regulate our commerce and to
lay duties on it for the purposes of regulation but not of raising a
revenue.[47]

Here is an unusually clear summary of prevailing opinion
among the Virginia political leaders.

Jefferson's attitude is also stated in the notes he made in 1786
on Soule's history of the Revolution. Speaking of the Navigation
Acts, he wrote: "We had been so long in the habit of seeing them
consider us merely as objects for the extension of their commerce,
and of submitting to every duty or regulation imposed with that
view, that we have ceased to complain of them. But when they
proposed to consider us as objects of *taxation*, all the states took
alarm."

After referring to the general acceptance of Dickinson's views,
he proceeded to point out how the questioning of the power of
Parliament to legislate would in theory invalidate the Navigation
Acts.

The *Navigation Act*, therefore, becomes a proper subject of treaty between the two nations. Or if Great Britain does not choose to have its
basis questioned, let us go on as we have done. Let no new shackles be
imposed and we will continue to submit to the old. We will consider
the restrictions on our commerce, now actually existing, as compensations, yielded by us for the protection and privileges we actually enjoy,
only trusting that if Great Britain on a revisal of these restrictions, is
sensible that some of them are useless to her and oppressive to us, she

will repeal them, . . . Place us in the condition we were when the king came to the throne, let us rest so, and we will be satisfied. This was the ground on which all the States very soon found themselves rallied, and that there was no other that could be defended.[48]

During the Stamp Act agitation, Richard Bland stated fully the historical relationship between England and Virginia, and the controversy over the Navigation Act in the reign of Charles II. On the basis of theory he could see no reason why an Englishman in Virginia should be less free to carry on trade than a similar subject in England. He did not, however, present the trade laws in themselves as a grievance. Such objection as he conceived could be raised to the Navigation Acts would have to be based upon theoretical grounds rather than on their practical workings; and even then it would seem to be a theoretical objection only to the enumeration clauses of the acts. But nowhere did he suggest a theoretical right for foreigners to compete in the shipping industry.[49] We have the testimony of Jefferson, already cited, which states that Bland finally accepted the Dickinson point of view on commercial regulations.

So far as Virginia is concerned, we have additional evidence. R. C. Nichols was treasurer of Virginia and in that capacity probably came into direct contact with all of the prominent men of the colony. In a pamphlet on the eve of the Revolution he says, speaking of the Sugar Act and the Townshend Acts, they were "acquiesced in, as they carried the appearance of advantages to the colonies and bore the semblance of regulations of commerce."[50] Here is an admission that any law that appeared to be purely regulatory encountered practically no opposition in Virginia. James Wilson, another prominent Virginian, a physician—a profession that brought him into the most intimate personal relationships with leading families where he must have heard political issues discussed in the most confidential terms—wrote that some of the politicians were theoretical free traders.[51] Instead of reflecting any hostility to the Navigation Acts, he proposed a solution of the constitutional difficulty that had grown out of the attempt of Parliament to secure a revenue under the form of trade regulation, by vesting regulation of trade in the crown instead of Parliament.

This he believed would preserve the essential values of common imperial control and at the same time eliminate all future confusion of the taxing power, which was vested exclusively in the legislative branch of government, with general commercial regulations.[52]

Richard Bland based his arguments largely upon the theoretical laws of nature. His discussion is confined almost entirely to the constitutional questions involved, and he does not at any point claim that the old commercial system or the Navigation Acts were grievous.[53]

Arthur Lee was about as radical as any American in listing the specific trade regulations and restrictions that the Americans looked upon as burdensome. He included in his list of objectionable restrictions those that applied to steel, hats, wines, slitting mills, logwood, and woolens; but he did not include the basic regulations affecting shipping and European goods. Logwood is the only item in his list that was even touched by the enumeration clauses of the trade acts.[54]

Daniel Dulany was the ablest political writer in Maryland. His pamphlet, *Consideration on the Propriety of Imposing Taxes in the British Colonies for the Purpose of Raising a Revenue by Act of Parliament*, published in 1765, had a wide circulation. He admitted fully the right of Parliament to regulate trade, but drew a sharp distinction between laws that were regulative and those that were intended to raise a revenue.[55]

On the negative side we also have Jonathan Boucher, who was widely acquainted with Virginia and Maryland leaders. He was the tutor of Mrs. Washington's son, young Custis, and hence intimately known to George Washington. He was very influential in Maryland politics and not infrequently drafted laws and other important papers for the legislature.[56] He was also a relatively prolific writer, and after leaving America published a history of the rise of the rebellion.[57] In recounting the revolutionary complaints, he nowhere included attacks upon the Navigation Acts or the general commercial system. Had there been any such active undercurrent of opposition to them he would have known it; and, for reasons that will appear later, he would have been interested in giving it the widest possible publicity. His silence on this point is pretty clear evidence that no such opposition existed in the Potomac area. Instead of treating the trade and navigation laws as burdensome to the colonies, he ascribed the wealth and prosperity of America to British laws.[58]

William Henry Drayton and Henry Laurens of South Carolina do not disclose that they considered the Navigation Acts in any way involved in the controversy. Laurens was bitterly opposed to the abuses of the customs officers and admiralty courts under the acts of 1764 and 1767, but did not protest against the general commercial system.[59] Drayton, who wrote extensively under the name of "Freeman," did not list the Navigation Acts in his specific enumeration of objectionable acts of Parliament, although he assailed admiralty courts, writs of assistance, corrupt customs officers, placemen sent from England, and the other features of the Grenville-Townshend system.[60]

J. J. Zubly was the only important political writer in Georgia. His *Humble Inquiry* is probably the clearest analysis of the taxation and constitutional controversy that can be found among the hundreds of pamphlets produced by the Stamp Act. No writer stated the issue more clearly than Zubly, that taxation of Americans by Parliament could not be admitted; yet throughout the pamphlet there is not a suspicion that he believed the commercial system was one of the points at issue, or that the Americans desired to be free from it.[61] His attitude is important because Georgia had little shipping of her own and her exportable products were largely enumerated in the older trade regulations.

WHIGS AND TORIES

The controversy between the Whigs and Tories in 1774-75 brought to light differences of opinion and led to a testing of the popularity, if not the validity, of the arguments commonly used. There were three provinces only in which this difference took the form of extensive public discussion in print.

The first of these was Massachusetts, where the controversy was carried on first in the newspapers, and later this newspaper material was reprinted in pamphlet form. John Mein had made himself the head of this controversy on the Tory side during the nonimportation agitation (1769-70), but sacrificed a good business in an unpopular cause.[62]

In the months immediately preceding the outbreak of hostilities, Daniel Leonard came to the defense of the Tories in a series of letters to the *Massachusetts Gazette* under the pseudonym of "Massachusettensis." For many years Judge Jonathan Sewall was credited with the authorship of these letters, which are especially important because they seem to present the point of view of an entire group rather than that of a single individual. John Adams answered them under the name of "Novanglus." They ran through the Boston papers during the closing days of 1774 and the early months of 1775, until they were terminated by the beginning of hostilities at Lexington and Concord.

Each writer assembled the arguments for his side of the controversy in a masterful manner and each showed that he had kept fully abreast of the controversial literature of the past ten years. Leonard, or "Massachusettensis," wrote with all of the horrors of a civil war staring him in the face; consequently his letters have a ring of honesty and seriousness about them that is frequently lacking in the pamphlets and political pieces of the day.

On the matter of trade and navigation he was explicit. Speaking of the situation prior to 1765 he says:

Acts of Parliament for regulating our internal polity were familiar. We had paid postage agreeable to act of parliament, for establishing a post-office, duties imposed for regulating trade, and even for raising a revenue to the crown without questioning the right, though we closely adverted to the rate or quantum. We knew that in all those acts of government, the good of the whole had been consulted, and whenever through want of information any thing grievous had been ordained, we were sure of obtaining redress by a proper representation of it. We were happy in our subordination.[63]

In his letter of January 2, 1775, Leonard showed that regulations of trade were necessary for a large empire and that they could only be enforced by customs officers.[64] In his letter of February 20, he conceded that the revolutionary group of Americans admitted the right of Parliament to legislate "for the purpose of regulating trade,"[65] thus granting that the Americans had not been attacking the navigation and trade policy.

In his next letter he proceeded to show that Parliament had long exercised taxation powers and that many of the acts of trade accepted by the revolutionary party were revenue measures, including 25 Charles II, c. 9 and many others.[66] This argument is elaborate and seems designed to drive his opponents into abandoning their objection to revenue laws or else openly opposing the entire regulation of trade and commerce.

His letter of March 20 is devoted to showing that the acts of trade were equitable, that they promoted the general good, and that, if they seemed to restrain and burden the colonies, other provisions involved similar restraints and burdens upon England. He made much of the bounties, drawbacks, and other expensive encouragements given American industry.[67] Thus he presented a line of argument that was intended to render unpopular any later attack upon the navigation and trade acts and would also counteract the current complaints of the burdens imposed by the acts of 1764 and 1767.

Among Leonard's most ungenerous statements was the assertion that the revolutionary leaders were connected with and were promoting the interest of smugglers. He charged: "A smuggler and a Whig are as cousin Germans, the offspring of two sisters, avarice and ambition. They had been playing into each other's hands for a long time. The smuggler received protection from the Whig, and he in his turn received support from the smuggler."[68] To which Adams answered: "Some years ago, the smugglers might be pretty equally divided between the whigs and the tories. Since that time, they have almost all married into the tory families, for the sake of dispensations and indulgences. If I were to let myself into secret history, I could tell very diverting stories of smuggling tories in New York and Boston. Massachusettensis is quarreling with some of his best friends."[69]

The Tories in general undertook to show: (1) that the American Whigs were chiefly interested in smuggling, or that their leaders were from that group and their measures were designed to further the gains of the illicit trader; (2) that it was not so much the paltry taxation that was involved, but the evasion of the Navigation Acts as a whole that was desired; or (3) that there was no possible line of demarcation between regulation of trade and revenue and other legislation; (4) that consequently when Americans claimed an exemption from general legislation, they were aiming at complete independence. Their position can best be understood by extracts from some of their stock arguments.

Isaac Wilkins contented himself with an attack upon the members of the first Continental Congress because they spent their time "condemning the acts of Parliament intended to prevent smuggling and illicit trade."[70] Here he deliberately confused the enforcement of revenue measures with commercial regulations, obviously intending to give the impression that the Americans were trying to aid and abet the smuggling trade.[71]

In New York the Tories had an active newspaper publisher in James Rivington, who was amply supplied with funds and who developed the foremost Torry press in America. He not only published numerous Tory articles, but from his press there poured a steady stream of Tory pamphlets, most of them probably definitely subsidized by the British government. Samuel Seabury, under the pseudonym of "A. W." and "Farmer," was the most prolific writer, ably assisted by Joseph Galloway, who wrote anonymously at first and openly later, when he became an *émigré*. Galloway properly belongs with Philadelphia instead of New York, although most of his pamphlets are published from the latter city.

Seabury based his attack upon the revolutionary policy on practical grounds. He was opposed to the whole program of commercial pressure upon England organized by the Americans, because he believed it would result in injury to the colonies. While he indulged in many unfair charges against the Whig party, including their alleged connection with the smuggling interests, and asserted that the New Englanders were engaged in a plot to bring about a complete separation from England, he did not claim that they were opposed to the Navigation Acts and were putting forward other claims to conceal their real purpose.

He especially attacked the whole program of the Continental Congress as unsound. He elaborated upon England's commercial position and her dependence upon manufacturing, and emphasized the importance to her of the colonial trade. He clinched his argument with the assertion: "These considerations establish the right of the British parliament to regulate the commerce of the whole empire, beyond the possibility of contradiction, a denial of it would be a denial of a right in the British empire to preserve itself." He even defended the policy of raising a revenue by taxation upon colonial commerce to help pay the costs of the navy that defended it.[72]

Isaac Hunt emphasized the point that the trade of England with the colonies was very important and that there was no expectation that she would grant the demands of the colonies. "It is so easy to believe," he says, "Great Britain will not tamely give up her right of regulating the trade of the colonies, which she has planted, raised, supported and protected at a vast expense of blood and treasure, nor will she suffer the profits of that trade to fall into the hands of rival nations."[73] He nowhere charged the American Whigs with playing the game of the smugglers, but he assumed that the policy adopted involved a conflict over trade and that taxation and trade regulation were closely akin.

John Drinker[74] was less restrained, but he did not claim that the Whigs were attempting to break through the Navigation Acts. He did charge, however, that much of the restraint upon trade had been enacted because of the activity of the smugglers.[75] Then he went on to insist that smugglers were not respected in England, but had undue political influence in America, although the prejudice against smuggling in Philadelphia was so strong that many people would not buy the smuggled tea; and that, because of this prejudice, considerable quantities of English tea were brought there from Boston with certificates that the duty was paid—which tea was eagerly bought.[76] He also insisted that there was one religious denomination in the city that made the non-purchase of illicitly imported articles a matter of faith. He recognized no constitutional controversy and asserted that the opposition to the tea measures was due to the threat the East India Company made to the smugglers of tea.[77]

Writing in 1780, Galloway, in exile, claimed that the opposition to the tea measures came from the Congregationalists, the Presbyterians, and the smugglers, but that the clamors of the latter did not have much weight with the people.[78] As this was written in England, published there, and obviously intended to appeal to a British audience, it should not be given very much weight as evidence of the attitude of contemporary American opinion.

The arguments of the Tories in the middle colonies were not permitted to go unchallenged. Dickinson effectually answered Galloway. Alexander Hamilton won his first claim to national distinction by attempting to answer Seabury. Like John Adams, Dickinson and Hamilton could not be charged with smuggling or with undue connection with the commercial interests. The position of Adams and Dickinson has been adequately stated.

Hamilton did not deny Seabury's argument of the importance of England's commercial relations with the colonies, but insisted that all the advantages claimed by Seabury could be secured along with harmonious feelings between England and America if the regulations did not include a revenue.[79] Thus Hamilton accepted and defended the orthodox principle of Dickinson and the majority of the American Whigs.

A short quotation will make this clear.

But it is granted, that Great Britain has a right to regulate the trade of the empire. The Congress has acknowledged it, so far as concerned their constitution. You infer from them, that all parts of the empire must be subject to her. They need only be, so far subject, as is necessary for the end proposed, that is the regulation of their trade. If you require any further subjection, you require *means* that are disproportionate to the *end,* which is unreasonable, and not at all allowable.

With respect to the justice of submitting to impositions, on our trade, for the purpose of raising revenue, to support the Navy, by which it is protected, I answer that the exclusive regulation of our commerce, for her own advantage, is a sufficient return to Great Britain, for protecting it. By this means, a vast accession of wealth is annually thrown into her coffers.[80]

This is a clear admission of the right of regulation so long as it is in no way connected with the raising of a revenue without the consent of those who had to pay it.

Thomas Hutchinson of Massachusetts was a historian and a

careful observer. He should be classed with the Tories—certainly he was opposed to the revolutionists and supported the regulatory and coercive program. He shows that he correctly understood the issues raised by the Americans, and nowhere does he claim that the Navigation Acts themselves were an issue. Writing of the agitation in 1769 he says:

Although acts for taxes were pronounced null, yet the general authority over the colonies had not been denied. . . . The supremacy of parliament was generally admitted and in many cases was considered useful, as in preventing fishing on the Newfoundland banks before April. It was also allowed that one great end of settling the colonies was the benefit which would arise from this commerce, and it seems reasonable to submit to a 'due' regulation on it, but the power reserved of judging when the regulation was 'undue' destroyed the whole concession.[81]

The attempts to enforce acts against the illicit traders, he says, had a tendency to stir up an opposition to the authority of Parliament and accelerate the declaration of independence. But this was during the period of taxation, and he was discussing illicit trade in terms of the efforts to evade the revenue measures rather than the Navigation Acts.

WHIG MERCHANTS

As evidence of the attitude of Americans toward the Navigation Acts, we have the private papers of prominent merchants who were also Whigs. The index to the published *Letters and Diary of John Rowe* does not include any of the following items: Navigation Acts, acts of trade, smuggling, illegal trade. While he was prominently identified with events and his letters show that he understood the issues involved, they nowhere intimate that the regulation of trade, except for revenue purposes, was an issue of the time.

A careful search of the great unpublished collection of the Orme commercial papers in Essex Institute at Salem, Massachusetts, does not reveal any active correspondence concerning the evils of the Navigation Acts; nor do the letters reveal any direct evidence that this house was interested in smuggling. The one pertinent item that came to light was an instruction to a captain of one of his ships that he was to be expressly careful not to violate the trade laws or in any way lay his ship open to possible seizure.[82] This item is significant. The instruction was confidential, was never intended for publication, is one of the few that have come down to us, and reveals the principles under which the important house of Orme conducted its business.

The *Letter Books of John Watts* reveal a similar situation. We have letters such as the one to Moses Franks of December 22, 1765,[83] in which he condemns taxation by Parliament, admiralty courts, trials without juries, the sending of ships to Halifax for trial, and the too-numerous placemen sent over from England; but there is no general condemnation of the commercial system as a whole and no specific denunciation of the old Navigation Acts.

The most extensive and detailed complaint against trade regulations is that drawn up by the Boston merchants in 1769. This deals specifically with the provisions of the Sugar Act—with its taxation of molasses and sugar, and the regulations affecting the shipment of lumber and the importation of wines and fruits from southern Europe. The chief point in this argument is that the fisheries and commerce, including shipbuilding, would be adversely affected by such regulations. The specific burdens upon trade that were objected to are those imposed in taxation measures enacted after 1763.[84]

RESOLUTIONS OF AMERICAN POLITICAL GROUPS

Between 1765 and 1775 apparently every town, county, and colony in America adopted resolutions on the issues involved in the controversy with the home country. These were widely circulated through the newspapers, and there are literally hundreds of them still preserved in this source. There is a surprising similarity in the content of such resolutions in all of the colonies from New Hampshire to Georgia. An examination of large numbers of these has failed to reveal a single one in which the commercial system in general was attacked, and none that even suggested a repeal of the Navigation Acts.

About as near as any came to assailing the commercial relations with England are statements similar to that of the town of Pomfren, county of Windham, Connecticut, in connection with the Stamp Act controversy. "That we have ever unmolestedly enjoyed (except some grievous acts of trade &c.) our just rights and privileges. . . ."[85] The expression "some grievous acts of trade," taken in context with similar phrases of the time, obviously refers to the Sugar Act of 1764 and not to the earlier acts of trade. Possibly they included the whole of the sugar and molasses regulations as objectionable, which would add the act of 1733 to their list of "grievous acts." They may have been intended to include the regulations affecting hats, wool, and iron and steel manufacturing, as did many other sets of resolutions; but they evidently did not intend to attack the commercial system as a whole.

Timothy Ruggles of Massachusetts, the president of the Stamp Act Congress, was opposed to the action of that body and particularly out of sympathy with the boycott movement in connection with the Townshend Revenue Act. He offered a set of resolutions in the Massachusetts House of Representatives which was rejected, the third of which is significant as it indicates the attitude of a conservative minority. This resolution stated that the colonies should at all times refrain from setting up manufactures which might be detrimental to the mother country.[86] The fact that this resolution was rejected, along with others that condemned the popular policy of subsituting home manufactures for British imports, may have been due to a popular undercurrent of feeling against such restrictions as existed on colonial manufacturing; but it seems more probable that it was because of popular faith in a temporary boycott as the surest way of securing a repeal of the laws.

Not only did the individual colonies, in their official proceedings, refrain from attacking or complaining of the Navigation Acts, but they sometimes went out of their way to approve them. An example is the action of the Assembly of Jamaica, December 28, 1774.

That your petitioners fully sensible of the great advantages that have arisen from the regulations of trade in general, prior to the year 1760, as well to Great Britain and her colonies, as to your petitioners in particular, and being anxiously desirous of increasing the good effects of these laws, as well as to remove an obstacle which is new in our Government, and could not have existed on the principles of our constitution, as it hath arisen from colonization, we do declare for ourselves and the good people of this island, that we freely consent to the operation of such Acts of the British Parliament, as are limited to the regulation of our external commerce only, and the sole object of which, is the mutual advantage of Great Britain and her colonies.[87]

Jamaica was one of the colonies most directly affected by the shipping clauses and also by the enumerated-products clauses of the Navigation Acts. If any colony had cause to condemn them, she had. Yet she approved them and based her complaint upon taxation, and not upon trade regulation. This action of Jamaica was not something that was secret, but was widely known on the continent, as is evidenced by its publication in a Philadelphia newspaper.

Finally, as a test of the most widely held opinions among the revolutionary leaders, we have their formal statements of reasons for their actions. The resolutions of the Stamp Act Congress are entirely silent on the matter of trade regulations in general, and there are no phrases that can be interpreted as even a remote denunciation of the Navigation Acts. Clauses IX and XI of these resolutions clearly apply to the Sugar Act of 1764, and Clause X states the common colonial argument that they were paying taxes indirectly because of the Navigation Acts. There are no other references to either trade or commerce.

The First Continental Congress met on the eve of the Revolution. A certain number of acts were singled out for protest, all of them enacted in the reign of George III. They were: 4 George III, ch. 15 and ch. 34; 5 George III, ch. 25; 6 George III, ch. 52; 7 George III, ch. 41 and ch. 46; 8 George III, ch. 22; 12 George III, ch. 24; the four repressive acts against Massachusetts; and the Quebec Act. None of the older trade or navigation acts was considered so objectionable as to be singled out for specific attack. The above acts were condemned unanimously by the Congress.

The fourth resolution, which alone refers to the old commercial system, specifically commends it. The exact words are:

But from the necessity of the case, and a regard to the mutual interest of both countries, we cheerfully consent to the operation of such acts of the British parliament, as are bona fide, restrained to the regulation of our external commerce, for the purpose of securing the commercial advantages of the whole empire to the mother country, and the commercial benefits of its respective members; excluding every idea of taxation internal or external, for raising a revenue on the subject, in America without their consent.[88]

This resolution was not adopted unanimously; but the fact that even a majority of the colonies as late as 1774 specifically approved the navigation and trade system in general is significant. If the old commercial system had been a common source of irritation, it surely would have been revealed in this body of revolutionary thinkers.

The "Declaration of Causes for Taking up Arms" and the "Petition to the King" in 1775 do not include any reference to the commercial system as a source of grievance. There is a brief reference to it in the "Report on Lord North's Conciliatory Resolution":

We are of opinion it is not just that the colonies should be required to oblige themselves to other contributions, while Great Britain possesses a monopoly of their trade. This of itself lays them under heavy contribution. To demand, therefore, additional aids in the form of a tax, is to demand the double of their equal proportion; if we are to contribute equally with the other parts of the empire, let us equally with them enjoy free commerce with the entire world. But while the restrictions on our trade shut to us the resources of wealth, is it just we should bear all other burthens equally with those to whom every resource is open?[89]

The final draft quoted above is not materially different from the original draft. Phraseology is improved, but there is no change in the fundamental ideas.[90] This is not a complaint against the old commercial system, but the familiar argument that it constituted in itself a taxation system through which the colonies indirectly contributed to the support of the imperial government, and that therefore they were not tax dodgers. It is the same argument advanced by Franklin that, if direct taxation should be supplied by the colonies, the indirect taxation by way of trade restrictions should be removed.

Finally, we have the Declaration of Independence, drawn by Jefferson. In this there is again no mention of, or reference to, the Navigation Acts. The charge that King and Parliament had conspired together to pass unconstitutional laws "for cutting off our trade with all parts of the world" obviously referred to the Boston Port Bill and the New England Restraining Act, and not to the earlier acts regulating trade. The absence of all reference to the latter contributes additional evidence that Americans in general did not look upon the old commercial system as a grievance.

Thus in America we find none of the prominent Whigs publicly attacking the trade and navigation acts. Over and over again they assert their satisfaction with conditions as they were prior to 1764 and their willingness to submit to all regulations prior to 1774, if attempts to raise a revenue for expenditure by the crown were eliminated.

During the ten years from 1765 to 1775, there were many political pamphlets published in America; and those that even assume that elimination of the Navigation Acts was a motive on the part of the revolutionists can be counted almost on the fingers of one hand. Without exception these came from the pens of Tory writers: some office holders, some secretly in the pay of the ministerial party, some probably honest opponents. The argument that the Americans were trying to evade the trade regulations seems to have been put forth as a charge of bad faith against the republicans, and also for the purpose of alarming the large commercial interests in England who formed the bulk of the American political supporters in the home country.

The great mass of American writers on both sides of the question realized that the issues involved were constitutional; that they concerned, first of all, the basic right of the colonists to govern themselves; second, the problems of mutual relationships between different parts of a rapidly growing empire; and third, the use of American government positions and incomes as a part of the corrupt spoilsmen's politics of England. Attempts to identify the American Whig movement with a petty group of illicit traders in a few of the seaport towns was plainly a part of the desperate partisan tactics of only the most unscrupulous writers.

The only phase of the mercantile system that received even scanty criticism was that embodied in the wool, hat, and iron acts. Even this scanty criticism never cited any specific hardships from the operation of these acts. It seemed to be based upon a fear that future regulations might include imperial administrative and enforcement machinery that would interfere directly with local enterprise and local government. They wanted no more such agencies as the Commissioners of Customs.

With the three-year agitation in favor of American manufactures that accompanied the nonimportation agreements against British products that were taxed under the Townshend Revenue Act, one would expect much more frequent reference to this part of the British system. The few individuals who used it were in a position to know of the loose talk in England during the nonimportation agitation that Americans should be prevented from manufacturing goods for their own market. They probably feared that this loose talk might produce legislation intended to carry out such a policy. The argument was too obscure and of immediate interest to too few people to have mass appeal. As an independence trial balloon it was a dud.

ARGUMENTS FOR INDEPENDENCE

Closely connected with the controversy between Whigs and Tories was some formal propaganda for independence. A few Americans delved into the history of the relations between the colonies and the home country, studied the historical development of the main controversy, and developed formal arguments to combat the British propaganda and convince their fellow countrymen of the wisdom of the American cause. Such material is of great historical importance in revealing what arguments had the widest popular appeal at the time.

If the movement for independence was to succeed it had to be sold to the great masses of the American people, especially in those areas where loyalism was strong. If the Navigation Acts or the mercantile system were common sources of irritation in America these salesmen of the Revolution could not have failed to know it and make the maximum use of it.

William Henry Drayton of South Carolina was one of the most important leaders in this field because of the service he rendered in his own colony. Commencing with the passage of the repressive acts in 1774 Drayton used his position as judge of the Superior Court of the colony to explain the issues to the people of South Carolina. The device which he used was a formal address to the grand jury of each county when he entered it to hold court. The southern custom of making the opening of court an occasion for the assembling of large numbers of people from all sections of the county made such addresses very important. No Tory opponent had a similar opportunity to reach audiences of that kind.

Drayton's addresses were prepared with great care and were as free from errors of fact as he could make them. Practically all of them were printed in the *South Carolina Gazette,* where they served the same purpose in spreading the Revolution in the southern colonies that the resolutions and other formal constitutional discussions in the Boston town meetings and the Massachusetts legislature did in the northern colonies.[91]

In only one of these addresses, that for April 23, 1776, did he include any material reference to the commercial relations with England. This address should be classed as a formal effort to sell the idea of independence. In it he went into the historic foundation of our differences with Great Britain in great detail. He gave eleven specific instances in which he believed the British government had made "the most arbitrary attempts to enslave America." Number seven in this list reads "by restricting the trade and commerce of America."[92]

In his detailed comparison of the work of the government under Congress with the old government he referred to the British prohibition of slitting mills and their encouragement by Congress. "The British authority discouraged our attempting to manufacture for our own consumption" while the new government encouraged the manufacture of many things. "Upon the whole, it has been the policy of the British authority to oblige us to supply our wants at their market, which is the dearest in the known world, and to cramp and confine our trade so as to be subservient to their commerce, our real interest being ever out of the question. . . .

On the other hand, the new constitution is wisely adapted to enable us to trade with foreign nations, and thereby supply our wants at the cheapest markets."[93]

Even this mild statement apparently failed to meet with sufficient popular approval to warrant its repetition in later addresses. As a trial balloon it had failed. The people of South Carolina were not interested in arguments along that line. Drayton does not again resort to it.

William Livingston rendered a service similar to that of Drayton. As revolutionary governor of New Jersey he also had to deal with a large number of very lukewarm supporters of independence and many open loyalists. His main opportunity to reach his people was through his addresses to the state legislature. We know the main arguments he used from his address in 1777. His verbal denunciations of the British for their tyranny and oppressions are far from temperate; but in recounting all the infamies he believed they had committed, he never once referred to the trade and navigation laws. He even went so far as to assert that all of the alleged oppressions could have been endured for another hundred years had it not been for the policy of taxation.[94]

Had Livingston believed an attack upon the commercial system would have won adherents he certainly would have used it. He and his state were in a most critical position and no argument was overlooked that would win support. As a prominent merchant he had his own experiences with the system and must have known intimately the public attitude toward the old regulations. The fact that he did not refer to them as a grievance is significant.

Thomas Paine was one of the most effective political pamphleteers of the Revolution. His appeal was to the army and to the people of the Middle and New England states. He knew how to use fighting language and how to rouse the spirit of resistance.

Had he discovered any general dislike of the old commercial system and the navigation laws on the ground that they were injurious, he would have made use of it. Instead he referred only to the past prosperity of the colonies, and showed that their growing wealth was feared by the home country, that New England had the greatest naval-building facilities of any country in the world, and that England had no just ground for complaint against the provinces. He appealed to the hopes of Americans that under an independent government of their own, the profits from a free trade would exceed those from a controlled and regulated one.[95] But nowhere in his reported addresses and writings did he seek to hold up commercial relations prior to 1764 as intolerable.

Every report we have of the arguments used to sell independence to the masses of Americans shows that there was no popular basic discontent with the trade and navigation laws that could be appealed to. There were a few people interested in manufacturing and trade who disliked certain restrictions that were a part of the old system, but their numbers were too few to include their grievances in the mass appeals. The one argument that had wide appeal was that the relations with the home country were happy prior to the revenue legislation beginning in 1764. Apparently complaints of the strictly mercantile classes lost all appeal as speakers moved back from the principal port cities. Attacking the old commercial system was not an effective way to win Tory sympathizers to the cause of independence.

CONTEMPORARY AMERICAN HISTORIES

The contemporary history emphasizes the arguments and animosities that were most prevalent at the time. If the Navigation Acts were considered an active or a contributing cause of the separation from the home country, we should expect the contemporary writers to elaborate that grievance. What is the evidence?

The earliest American history of the Revolution was prepared by William Gordon and published in 1788.[96] Gordon was a dissenting English minister who came to America during the disturbances and was pastor of the church at Jamaica Plain, near Boston. He was not only a spectator at close range during the entire Revolution, but he had opportunities to know personally the leaders in the revolt—especially the New England group.

His account is replete with local incidents and happenings but is entirely negative so far as any discussion of the Navigation Acts is concerned. Apparently he never heard them complained of as a grievance during his stay in America. The nearest approach to a reference to them is in the discussion of the unfair British charges that the Americans were aiming at independence.

The colonies might object to some acts passed respecting them, particularly . . . the act prohibiting the cutting down of pitch and tar trees, not being within a fence or enclosure. . . . The act prohibiting the exportation of hats made in the colonies, even from one colony to another. . . . The act for the more easy recovery of debts in his majesty's plantations and colonies in America, which made houses, lands, negroes, and other real estate assets for the payment of debts. . . . But whatever objections were made to the above acts, no general measure was adopted to obtain their repeal. They continued in being. . . .[97]

The first history of the Revolution written by an American and published in the United States was by David Ramsay of South Carolina. Ramsay was not only a contemporary, but he was in a position to know the inside secrets of the revolutionary party. He was a member of Congress, a member of the committee on foreign relations, and states that he had access to the entire records of Congress in writing his history. Consequently we have here a man who met the revolutionary leaders constantly, both in public and in private, and who by his long years of service at the capital came into direct contact with even the most concealed of American political plans. Few were in a better position to state the American view of the origin of the quarrel and he could have had no reason to conceal or misrepresent the most hidden motives. He writes:

The sad story of colonial oppression commenced in the year 1764. Great Britain, then, adopted new regulations, respecting the colonies, which, after disturbing the ancient harmony of the two countries for about twelve years, terminated in a dismemberment of the empire.
These consisted in restricting their former commerce, but more especially in subjecting them to taxation, by the British Parliament. By adhering to the spirit of her Navigation Act, in the course of a century, the trade of Great Britain had increased far beyond the expectation of her most sanguine sons, but by rigidly enforcing the strict letter of the same, in a different situation of public affairs, effects, directly the reverse, were produced.
Though all the colonists disrelished, and many, from the pressure of actual sufferings, complained of the British restrictions on their manufactures and commerce, yet a great majority were disposed to

submit to both. Most of them acknowledged that the exercise of these powers was incident to the sovereignty of the mother country, especially when guarded by the implied contract that they were only to be used for the common benefit of the empire. It was generally allowed, that as the planting of colonies was designed not to erect an independent government, but to extend the old one, the Parent State had a right to restrain their trade in every way, which conduced to the common emolument.

They for the most part considered the Mother Country as authorized to name ports and nations, to which alone their merchandize should be carried, and with which alone they should trade, but the novel claim of taxing them without their consent, was universally reprobated, as contrary to their natural, chartered and constitutional rights . . . the claim of taxation on one side, and the refusal of it on the other, was the very hinge upon which the revolution turned.[98]

Ramsay was also an important contributor to the history of South Carolina which was one of the colonies most affected by the shipping clauses in the Navigation Acts and by the provisions dealing with enumerated products. His position as a prominent member of Charleston's leading families, a son-in-law of Henry Laurens, and a representative of his province throughout the Revolution put him in a position to speak with authority concerning opinion in his own colony on the eve of the struggle with the home country.

In discussing conditions in his own state he says:

No instance can be produced where the relative connection, between a colony and the parent state was more likely to last. In none was there a stronger bond of union from a reciprocity of benefits, or a fainter prospect of contention from the interference of their respective pursuits. The colony consumed an immensity of British manufactures, which she could neither make for herself nor purchase elsewhere on equal terms in her valuable native commodities. The exchange of the one for the other, was a basis of profitable commerce. Carolina, satisfied with her political condition, did not covet independence. It was forced upon her as the only means of extrication from the grasp of tyranny, exerted to enforce novel claims of the mother country, subversive of liberty and happiness.[99]

In this there is reflected no evidence of any complaint against the Navigation Acts nor even against the commercial system.

The next American history of the Revolution that came from the presses of our own country appeared in 1805 and was written by Mrs. Mercy Warren, a member of two of New England's most active revolutionary families. Mrs. Warren was a sister of James Otis, the wife of Governor Warren, and a sister-in-law to Dr. Joseph Warren, who was killed at the battle of Bunker Hill. She was thus closely identified with two of the most active leaders of revolutionary agitation in New England, and was in a unique position to have heard the endless constitutional and political controversy analyzed. If Americans anywhere found the Navigation Acts burdensome and were plotting against them, one would expect to find evidence of it in commercial New England, and especially within the homes of the leading patriots where real issues must have been discussed openly.

If Mrs. Warren found any evidence of that kind, she did not reveal it. Her history does not even mention the Navigation Acts as such. She did, however, understand the misrepresentation of America by the official classes.

They represented the mercantile body in America as a set of smugglers, forever breaking over the laws of trade and of society; the people in general as factious, turbulent, and aiming at independence; the legislatures in the several provinces as marked with the same spirit; and government everywhere in so lax a state, that the civil authority was insufficient to prevent the fatal effects of popular discontent.[100]

It is obvious that the contemporary historians who lived through the revolutionary struggles, participated in its discussions, knew intimately the most prominent leaders, and wrote enduring accounts of the great events of which they were a part were not themselves conscious of any general dissatisfaction with the old trade and navigation system. So far as they were concerned that issue did not enter into the controversy with the mother country in any material way.

The entire mass of contemporary literature reveals no appeal to basic free trade theories. Adam Smith did not publish his *Wealth of Nations* until 1776. His theories acquired adherents in America very slowly. The idea that the basic mercantile practices of the eighteenth century were wrong was not a part of the thinking of the Revolutionary leaders, but was a concept developed by a later generation of writers.

REFERENCES

CHAPTER 4

1. Harry A. Cushing, *Writings of Samuel Adams* (New York, 1904-6), I, II.

2. *Ibid.*, I, 4.

3. Boston, December 19, 1765. *Ibid.*, p. 42.

4. Instructions of the House of Representatives, Boston, December 20, 1765. *Ibid.*, pp. 62-63.

5. *Ibid.*, pp. 113-14.

6. Instructions of the House of Representatives, Boston, December 20, 1765. *Ibid.*, pp. 142-44, 158-59.

7. This letter is dated January 15, 1768. Copies of it may also be found in a great variety of contemporary sources, as it was printed in nearly all the colonial and some English newspapers, also in several pamphlets. It is in the *Georgia Gazette* for June 1, 1768; the *New York Mercury* for April 4, 1768; the *New York Journal* for March 31, 1768; the *South Carolina Gazette* for May 2, 1768; the *Boston Gazette* for March 21, 1768.

8. Harry A. Cushing, *Writings of Samuel Adams*, I, 158-59.

9. February 17, 1768. *Ibid.*, p. 194. This obtained about the same publicity as did the "letter to Shelburne," and copies may be found in the same places.

10. Published in the *Boston Gazette*, January 30, 1769; reprinted in the *Writings of Samuel Adams*, I, 297-306.

11. Article signed "Candidus," first published in the *Boston Gazette*, January 27, 1772; reprinted in *Writings of Samuel Adams*, II, 322-26.

12. *Ibid.*, 359-69.

13. Charles Francis Adams, *The Works of John Adams* (Boston, 1850-56), II, 370.

14. Adams supposed this writer to be Jonathan Sewall. *Ibid.*, IV, 5-10.

15. *Ibid.*, "Novanglus," No. 7. Published in *Boston Gazette* in 1774, also printed separately in pamphlet form under the title *Novanglus and Massachusettensis*. The edition of 1819 credits Jonathan Sewall on the title page with the authorship of the Massachusettensis essays.

16. *Works*, IV, 113-14.

17. *Ibid.*, X, 314-59.

18. *The Grievances of the American Colonies Candidly Examined* (London,

1766), p. 19. This was originally printed in Providence in 1765 under the title *The Rights of the Colonies Examined.*

19. James Otis, *Rights of the British Colonies Asserted and Proved* (Boston, 1764), p. 54.

20. *Ibid.*, p. 33.

21. Thomas Hollis, *The True Sentiments of America* (Dublin, 1769), pp. 115-17.

22. *Sentiments of a British American* (Boston, 1764), p. 13.

23. Edward Bancroft, *Remarks on the Review of the Controversy Between Great Britain and Her Colonies* (London, 1769), pp. 4, 46, 68, 123-24. Bancroft was a native of Massachusetts, but was residing in England at the time this pamphlet was published. He later became a Tory, but was considered sufficiently American to be employed by Franklin in the American secret service. *Dictionary of American Biography*, I, 563.

24. *Pennsylvania Gazette*, April 7, 1768.

25. Jared Sparks, *The Works of Benjamin Franklin*, V, 6; A. H. Smyth, *Writings of Benjamin Franklin*, VI, 322-23.

26. Sparks, *op. cit.*, V, 6-7; Smyth, *op. cit.*, VI, 323.

27. Sparks, *op. cit.*, V, 12; Smyth, *op. cit.*, VI, 328-29.

28. Sparks, *op. cit.*, V, 15-16; Smyth, *op. cit.*, VI, 331-32.

29. Sparks, *op. cit.*, V, 17; Smyth, *op. cit.*, VI, p. 333.

30. "When I consider the extream corruption prevalent among all Orders of Men in this old rotten State, and the glorious publick Virtue so predominant in our rising Country, I cannot but apprehend more Mischief than Benefit from a closer Union. I fear they will drag us after them in all the plundering Wars which their desperate Circumstances, Injustice, and Rapacity, may prompt them to undertake; and their wide-wasting Prodigality and Profusion is a Gulph that will swallow up every Aid we may distress ourselves to afford them.

"Here Numberless and needless Places, enormous Salaries, Pensions, Perquisites, Bribes, groundless Quarrels, foolish Expeditions, false Accounts or no Accounts, Contracts and Jobbs, devour all Revenue and produce continual Necessity in the Midst of natural Plenty." Franklin to Joseph Galloway, London, February 25, 1775. Smyth, *op. cit.*, VI, 311-12.

31. *Ibid.*, VI, 313.

32. *Ibid.*, pp. 412-19. Apparently this was drawn up in a committee of Congress, but does not appear on their minutes. See note, *ibid.*, p. 412.

33. *Ibid.*, p. 413.

34. Smyth, *Writings of Franklin*, VI, 417-18.

35. John Dickinson, *The Late Regulations*, etc. (Philadelphia, 1765), p. 7.

36. *Ibid.*, p. 37.

37. "The *Farmer's Letters* appeared in the *Chronicle, supposed* to be written by the ingenious *Mr. Dickinson,* a gentleman, whom at that time I had never seen. Here the ignorance of *Mr. Wharton* and the envy of Mr. Galloway and the wickedness of both united were clearly manifested. They were angry, they fretted, they swore and *affirmed,* that they were too inflammatory for this lattitude. While Mr. Galloway, exclaimed with a countenance expressive of the deepest envy, that they were '*damned ridiculous! mere stuff! fustian! altogether stupid and inconsistent!* . . . *only a compilation by* Dickinson and

Thomson!' The very *sagacious* and *deep-read* Mr. *Wharton*, with a great deal of solemn dump and grimace in his look, signified that 'Friend Goddard was very *impudent* in introducing such pieces into our *Chronicle* at such a time.' . . . I *presumed* to reason with them, and assured them that the letters were very agreeable to the people, and for my part, I thought they deserved the serious attention of all *North America*. Mr. *Galloway* ridiculed my notions about liberty and the rights of mankind, and observed that the people in *America* were mad—they knew not what they wanted—and indeed were incapable of judging on such matters—that such factious pieces would answer for the select-men of *Boston* and the mob meetings of *Rhode Island*, but he was sure they would soon be despised here, *Pennsylvanians* (a few hot-headed people excepted) being of a different make, of more solidity, none of *your* damned republican breed—but loyal to the King, and friends to Monarchy. . . . I formed my own opinions of the men . . . and still continued . . . to publish the letters. The *Farmer's Letters* grew more and more admired, and these *gentlemen* then judged it dangerous *openly* to declaim against them, or vilify their supposed author. . . . I could here call forth a series of letters dated *Virginia*, but wrote in *Philadelphia*, now deposited in a certain desk, designed for a complete answer to the *Farmer's Letters*. . . ." William Goddard, *The Partnership, Or the History Of the Rise and Progress of the Pennsylvania Chronicle*, etc. (Philadelphia, 1770), p. 16.

38. Tyler says that all but four of the twenty-five papers in America printed these letters. *Literary History of the American Revolution*, I, 237.

39. *Letters from a Pennsylvania Farmer*, pp. 7-8.

40. *Ibid.*, p. 15.

41. John Dickinson, *A New Essay on the Constitutional Power of Great Britain over the Colonies in America with Resolves of Committees for the Province of Pennsylvania and their Instructions to their Representatives in Assembly* (Philadelphia, 1774), pp. 18-27.

42. Paul Leicester Ford, *The Writings of John Dickinson* (Philadelphia, 1895), I, 401.

43. *Ibid.*, p. 415.

44. Jacob Duché, *The Duty of Standing Fast in our Spiritual and Temporal Liberties* (Philadelphia, 1775), pp. 15-16.

45. Letter from the Earl of Stirling to the Earl of Shelburne, August 6, 1763. William A. Duer, *The Life of William Alexander, Earl of Stirling* (New York, 1847), pp. 74-77.

46. George Wythe of Williamsburg, Jefferson's instructor in law and later professor of law at William and Mary College.

47. Thomas Jefferson, "Autobiography," Paul Leicester Ford, *Writings of Thomas Jefferson*, I,8, Memorial Edition, I, 11-12.

48. *Writings of Thomas Jefferson*, Memorial Edition, XVII, 126-28.

49. Richard Bland, *An Inquiry Into the Rights of the British Colonies* (Williamsburg, 1766), pp. 20-26.

50. R. C. Nichols, *Considerations on the Present State of Virginia* (Williamsburg, 1774), pp. 9-12.

51. James Wilson, *Considerations on the Nature and the Extent of the Legislative Authority of the British Parliament* (anonymous at the time), p. 35.

52. "But if the Commerce of the British Empire must be regulated by a

general superintending power, capable of exerting its influence over every part of it, why may not this power be entrusted to the King, as a part of the Royal prerogative? By making treaties, which it is his prerogative to make, he directs the Trade of Great Britain with the other States of Europe; and his treaties with those states have, when considered with regard to his subjects, all the binding force of Laws upon them. Where is the absurdity of supposing him vested with the same right to regulate the Commerce of the distinct parts of the dominions with one another, which he has to regulate their Commerce with foreign States. . . .

"If the power of regulating trade be, as I am apt to believe it to be, vested by the principles of the constitution, in the Crown, this good effect will flow from the doctrine; A perpetual distinction will be kept between that power and a power of laying impositions on Trade." *Ibid.*, pp. 34-35.

53. *An Inquiry into the Rights of the British Colonies, Intended as an Answer to the "Regulations Lately Made Concerning the Colonies and the Taxes Imposed Upon Them Considered,"* in a *Letter Addressed to the Author of that Pamphlet* (Williamsburg, 1766).

54. Arthur Lee, *An Appeal to the Justice and Interest of the People of Great Britain in the Present Disputes with America* (London, 1774), p. 50. *the British Colonies for the Purpose of a Revenue, By Act of Parliament* (New York, 1765), p. 22.

56. Jonathan Boucher, *Reminiscences of an American Loyalist* (Boston, 1925), pp. 59, 92-93.

57. Jonathan Boucher, *A View of the Causes and Consequences of the American Revolution in Thirteen Discourses Preached in North America Between the Years 1763-1775* (London, 1797).

58. *Ibid.*, p. 39.

59. Henry Laurens, *Some General Observations on American Customhouse Officers and Courts of Vice-Admiralty* (Charleston, 1769).

60. *A Letter from Freeman of South Carolina to the Deputies of North America Assembled in the High Court of Congress at Philadelphia* (Charleston, 1774), pp. 11-15.

61. J. J. Zubly, *An Humble Inquiry into the Nature of the Dependency of the American Colonies* (Savannah, 1767).

62. Mein was one of a group of newspapermen who acted as political, paid henchmen for the dominant political group. People in Massachusetts suspected that he was in government pay but did not have positive proof. The proof is in his letters after his failure in Boston which are preserved in the *Treasury Papers,* London. He was rewarded for his American services by a royal pension of £200 a year. *Correspondence of King George III,* (Fortesone, ed. London, 1928), V, 468.

63. Letter of December 19, 1774. *Novanglus and Massachusettensis* (Boston, 1819), p. 147.

64. *Ibid.*, p. 160.

65. *Ibid.*, p. 197.

66. *Ibid.*, p. 199-201.

67. *Ibid.*, pp. 213-17.

68. *Ibid.*, p. 161.

69. *Ibid.*, p. 69.

70. Isaac Wilkins, *An Alarm to the Legislature of the Province of New York Occasioned by the Present Political Disturbances of Pennsylvania* (New York, 1775), pp. 11-12.

71. This argument is further elaborated in another of his pamphlets. *Observations on the Late Popular Measures Proposed to the Serious Considerations of the Sober Inhabitants of Pennsylvania* (New York, 1775), pp. 11-12.

72. Samuel Seabury, *A View of the Controversy Between Great Britain and Her Colonies,* etc. (New York, 1774), pp. 15-23.

73. Isaac Hunt, *The Political Family, or a Discourse Pointing out the Reciprocal Advantages which Flow from an Uninterrupted Union Between Great Britain and America* (Philadelphia, 1775), p. 13.

74. *Observations on the Late Popular Measures Offered to the Serious Consideration of the Sober Inhabitants of Pennsylvania* (Philadelphia, 1774).

75. "It is an opinion but too justly founded that the unrestrained course of this dishonest dealing hath excited the politicians of Britain to meditate on the most effectual means to shackle American trade, and to lay even *internal burthens* on American backs." *Ibid.*, p. 9.

76. *Ibid.*, pp. 11-12. He says: "This is a fact so well understood, that to insist further on the verity of it, might seem unnecessary, if not impertinent." Fn. p. 12.

77. *Ibid.*, p. 3. Leonard, in his letter of January 2, 1775, makes a similar implication (*Novanglus and Massachusettensis,* pp. 160-61). This contention on the part of the American Tories is interesting in view of the assertions in debates on the repressive acts of 1774, by prominent members of the House of Commons who had been friendly to America, that the main encouragement of smuggling had come from the East India Company itself. Hansard, *Debates,* XVI, 865.

78. "There was another description of men whose interest was affected by it: these were the smuggling merchants in the seaport towns, who in defiance of law and the most sacred of all obligations, an oath, had long been in the practice of importing tea from St. Eustatia, and Holland." Joseph Galloway, *Historical and Political Reflecting on the Rise and Progress of the American Rebellion* (London, 1780), pp. 57-59.

"The people in general suspected the independent views of the republicans; they saw the interested motives of the smugglers; and they knew the regulations were beneficial to themselves." *Ibid.*, p. 58.

The very form of the charge shows that the smugglers were not in good esteem, or the argument would not have been used. The towns in which the illicit traders were said to be the strongest are among the towns where the Revolution had to be put over with the support of the back country.

79. "It seems to me not impossible, that our trade may be so regulated, as to prevent the discord and animosity, at the prospect of which you are so terrified, without the least assistance from a revenue." Alexander Hamilton, *The Farmer Refuted, or a More Impartial and Comprehensive View of the Dispute Between Great Britain and the Colonies, Intended as an Answer to the Letter from A. W. Farmer, Entitled A View of the Controversy, etc.* (New York, 1775), pp. 48-49.

80. *Ibid.,* pp. 40-41.

81. Thomas Hutchinson, *History of the Colony of Massachusetts Bay* (Boston, 1795-1828). III. 265.

82.   "Salem, New England, Dec. 9,
                                                                        1771.

Mr. George Chapman.

You being Master of our Schooner Molly now ready to sail, Our Orders are that you proceed [to] Maryland or Virginia . . . and which of them you shall think you can do best at, there proceed to, and make Report and entry according to law . . . be very careful that you break no Acts of Trade neither must you suffer any Tobacco or any other goods to be brought home in our Schooner that will in the least Expose her to a seizure, . . .

                                                      Your,
                                                    Friends and Employers
                                                    Joseph Henfield
                                                    Tim Orme"

"The above is a true copy of my order Rec. from my Employers.
                                                    George Chapman"

Timothy Orme Manuscripts, Letters, XII.

83. John Watts, *Letter Book,* p. 407.

84. Merchants of Boston, *Observations on Several Acts of Parliament* (Boston, 1769), pp. 2-6.

85. *Newport Mercury,* January 13, 1766. The present spelling of the name of this town is Pomfret.

86. *Pennsylvania Chronicle,* March 28, 1768.

87. *Pennsylvania Gazette,* Supplement, March 1, 1775.

88. Copy in William Macdonald, *Select Charters,* pp. 357-61.

89. Copies in *Ibid.,* Numbers 76, 77, 78.

90. Cf. *Some Papers Laid Before the Continental Congress* (Library of Congress, 1907). pp. 55-65.

91. The addresses for April 23 and October 15, 1776, and for October 21, 1777, are reprinted in Hezekiah Niles, *Principles and Acts of the Revolution in America* (Baltimore, 1822).

92. *Ibid.,* p. 73.

93. *Ibid.,* p. 78.

94. *Ibid.,* pp. 270-72.

95. Thomas Paine, *Political Writings* (1839) I, 34-49-51, 179-80, 209.

96. William Gordon, *History of the Rise, Progress, and Establishment of the Independence of the United States of America* (London, 1788). Although Gordon made too free use of the material prepared by Burke for the *Annual Register,* his history is entitled to be classed as a contemporary American account.

97. *Ibid.,* I, 107-9.

98. David Ramsay, *The History of the American Revolution* (Philadelphia, 1789), I, 47-49.

99. David Ramsay, *A History of the Revolution in South Carolina* (Charleston, 1784), I, 220.

100. Mercy Warren, *History of the Rise, Progress and Termination of the American Revolution,* etc. (Boston, 1805), I, 39-40.

5

THE EMPIRE AFTER A CENTURY UNDER THE NAVIGATION ACT

I N 1763 the British Empire was just completing a century of experience with the Navigation Act. Even the most ardent advocate of free trade must admit that the system had worked. It was not perfect. No system of state regulation of economic enterprise is. Every colonial power had regulations of some kind designed to confine the trade of the colonies to the home country. But England's regulations were different from the others. Under these the British Empire had prospered while that of every other power had declined.

In 1660 there were six rather weak colonies on the continent: Virginia and Maryland in the south and Massachusetts, Connecticut, Rhode Island, and New Hampshire in the north. The total English population on the continent did not exceed 80,000. At no place were settlements one hundred miles from the coast and in most places they were hardly more than twenty-five miles. Four other nations disputed England's hold on the eastern coast of North America: Spain, Holland, Sweden, and France.

In the West Indies, England held: Barbados, Antigua, St. Christopher, Nevis, Anguilla, Montserrat, and Jamaica. These were the rich sugar islands. In addition there was Bermuda off the coast of Virginia.

By 1763 the British colonies in America had expanded into an almost continuous chain from the Arctic Circle to the Equator.

The original six of 1660 had grown to nineteen and included Hudson Bay, Newfoundland, Nova Scotia, Quebec, New Hampshire, Massachusetts, Rhode Island, Connecticut, New York, New Jersey, Pennsylvania, Delaware, Maryland, Virginia, North Carolina, South Carolina, Georgia, East Florida, and West Florida. France, Holland, Sweden, and Spain had been eliminated from the continent east of the Mississippi. The main settlements were expanding beyond the Alleghenies and advanced outposts were at Detroit, Vincennes, and Ft. Chartres, approximately a thousand miles inland from the coast.

In addition there had been some expansion of the sugar islands by the settlement or acquisition of the Bahamas, Tortola, St. Vincent, Dominica, and Grenada and the Grenadines. In the whole Caribbean area Spain retained only Cuba, Puerto Rico and one-half of the island of Santo Domingo. France held only one-half of the same island and Martinique, Guadeloupe, Marigalante, and Desirade. Outside of America England had acquired control of all India and important colonies on the west coast of Africa.[1]

The English merchant, the colonist and warrior had built up in a century an overseas empire that was one of the wonders of history.[2] Such growth does not just happen. There are reasons why England in so short a time had been able to develop the mightiest colonial empire in the world. Among these are the navigation and trade policies as they were developed up to 1764.

France and Spain had sought to preserve a loyal nationalism in their colonies by preventing the migration to them of dissenting elements. None but Catholics of proved orthodoxy were accepted as prospective settlers. Political dissenters might be killed, imprisoned, or forced to flee the country, but they could not go to the colonies. National religious and political unity in the colonies was insured and central control by the home government maintained. Their colonies represented a high degree of "economic and political planning," but such planning was subject to the frailties of wisdom, understanding, and economic interest of the few at the seat of power.

In contrast, the English colonial Empire just grew. One-third of the period from 1660 to 1763 has been called the period of "salutary neglect."[3] It should be called the period of "glorious free development." Here was planning of a different order. Instead of a few at the seat of government doing the planning, thousands of free men were planning their own homes, their own farms, their own occupations, their own towns, their own forms of government; establishing their own markets; and developing and exploiting for their own use the resources of a vast continent.

There was no planned migration of the approved orthodox to the English colonies. Anybody could go to America who could secure the transportation either by paying his way or by mortgaging his labor for a period of years to those who would supply transportation. Possibly that was the origin of the great American institution of installment buying.

William Penn was even permitted to advertise the advantages of his cheap land to distressed people on the continent and invite thousands of German peasants and skilled artisans to come to America to improve their economic and political condition and help develop the country. Jews driven from Spain by religious persecution settled in the British sugar islands. French Huguenots, compelled to leave their country or renounce their faith, were welcomed in South Carolina and the towns of other colonies. Scotch Highlanders and Scotch-Irish by the thousands migrated to the land of plenty and economic opportunity.[4]

Every economic, social, and political element in Britain that was not wanted at home was free to go to the colonies and sometimes even assisted or required to do so. Agricultural workers on the farms of northern England, pushed off the land by the steady progress of the enclosure movement, acquired land and new homes of their own in the rapidly growing middle and southern colonies.[5]

France and Spain in their colonial empires had to deal only with native populations. England had to rule foreign elements of European origin. There were some French and some Spanish in the conquered West Indies sugar islands and both Dutch and Swedish elements in New York and Delaware. These elements were not expelled but absorbed.

The French and Spanish colonies had no taint of foreign elements. The British colonial Empire in America was built upon the principle of free enterprise and equal treatment for immigrants from any country. By 1764 it was already the great "melting pot" for the peoples of Western Europe—a reputation that was to continue and to grow for another hundred and fifty years.

As a result of the policy just described the vast colonial empire, stretching from Hudson Bay on the north to Honduras on the south, had the utmost variation in industries, occupations, character of population, religion, and political and social institutions. The list included fur trading in Hudson Bay and Canada, fishing in Nova Scotia and Newfoundland, varied industries and shipping in New England, food supplies in the Middle Colonies, tobacco in Virginia and Maryland, naval stores and wood products in North Carolina, rice and indigo in South Carolina and Georgia, sugar and its by-products in the West Indies, and dyewoods from Honduras.

In form of government they were just as varied: almost complete self-government in the larger colonies on the continent: crown colonies with almost no self-government in Hudson Bay, Canada, the Floridas, and some of the West Indies. In twelve of the colonies on the continent governors and other colonial officials were paid by taxes raised and expended by the colonial assemblies. In five others on the continent—Canada, Nova Scotia, Georgia, East Florida, and West Florida such officials were paid by parliamentary appropriations from funds raised by Britain. In most of the colonies the principle applied that the sole power of taxation was vested in the local colonial assembly. In some of the West Indies there was taxation by Parliament in the form of export duties on their main products, known as the "Plantation Duties."[6]

In religion there was the widest possible variation. Canada was solidly Catholic with that religion supported by public taxation. In New England the prevailing religion was Puritan Congregationalism. There were many Quakers in Pennsylvania, Delaware, and New Jersey. Presbyterians were numerous in the back country of the Middle Colonies and as far south as South Carolina. The coastal regions of the southern colonies and the West Indies were almost solidly Church of England.

There were practically no Negro slaves in the more northern

colonies, a few in New England and the Middle Colonies, and increasing numbers in the tobacco and rice-growing areas. In some of the sugar colonies Negro slaves exceeded the white population ten to one.[7]

What kept such diverse colonial governments from disintegrating? It was not force, because there were very few British troops anywhere on the continent before 1754 and these were ostensibly to guard against Indian outbreaks. After 1763 troops were retained to hold the conquered provinces of Canada, the Floridas, and the West Indies. Not until 1768 were British armed forces ever assigned the task of enforcing royal authority in a British colony and then in a province that had been the spear point in all the wars that England had waged against France for control of the continent.

The forces which bind an empire together are numerous and varied. The things all of the colonies had in common were loyalty to the same king; except in Canada, a common language and a common system of legal institutions; and, without exception, equal commercial rights in the far-flung Empire.

Regardless of where they lived they had a right to take their ships and their products to any other port of the Empire west of the Cape of Good Hope and there exchange them for such goods as they desired, subject to whatever local regulations as applied to other English ships. They were free to produce for their own needs any article they could make with their own resources. They were protected from all competition from foreign ships while engaged in trade within the Empire. Their sailors were English just the same as if they resided in England. They had assured markets for their products somewhere within the Empire or in areas tributary to that Empire either economically or politically. A common navy protected their commerce from pirates in time of peace and privateers in time of war.

One of our most careful students of colonial conditions in the West Indies sums up the situation as follows:

Exploitation of the British Caribbean during the eighteenth century involved three primary forms of commerce—intercourse with Africa, with the mainland colonies of North America, and with Great Britain.

The first of these rested on the planters' need for a steady supply of laborers to open new lands and to replace slaves which did not maintain their numbers. The other two were based upon meeting the differing wants of complimentary production areas.

These several kinds of inter-empire trade were coördinate, and together they long formed one of the most nearly perfect commercial systems of modern times. They were open only to British subjects and were governed by numerous regulations mirroring contemporary mercantilist doctrines. But such limitations served the West Indies well, for they enabled them to procure supplies at lowest figures, to market their products at top prices and to thus build up immense fortunes.[8]

The assured permanency of the economic relations between various parts of the Empire promoted growth. Colonials could embark on profitable industries knowing that conditions of credit, markets, and shipping would not change suddenly. The assured large and growing colonial markets encouraged industrial development in England on a scale that did not exist in any other European power. Stability is the basic element in the growth of wealth. Both colonials and Englishmen were developing real wealth on a scale seen nowhere else in the world.

In 1763 all of the British colonies were prosperous and expanding rapidly in population with the exception of the older sugar colonies. In spite of extensive special legislation in their behalf they were decadent and losing population. This condition was not due to external economic regulations—these were all favorable—but to internal conditions which favored the development of a few large plantations owned by absentee planters and run by slave labor. As the island areas were limited, this engrossing of the land by a few owners left little room for an expanding population of poor but industrious free laborers. These had to seek better opportunities on the new sugar islands or in the larger colonies on the continent.[9]

No such condition existed in the colonies on the mainland. There were rich rice, indigo, and tobacco planters with vast holding of real estate, but none of these planters resided in England. In spite of their large holdings there was still unlimited opportunity for free laborers to secure homes and lands in the limitless western part of the colonies.

Nowhere else in the world was a European population expanding so rapidly as it was in the British colonies on the continent during the period from 1660 to 1763. Estimates of population at earlier periods are vague. In 1660 there were only two important areas of English population on the continent—Virginia and Maryland and New England. Population of the latter was estimated at 80,000 in 1689 and at 400,000 in 1760. In the Middle Colonies there were not more than 40,000 in 1689 and ten times that number in 1760. The whole region south of Pennsylvania had less than 90,000 in 1689, and in 1760 there were 700,000. The region south of Virginia increased in population forty times between 1689 and 1760.[10]

For the entire continent the most careful estimates agree that the population was doubling in less than twenty-five years. Assuming that it was twenty-five, 10,000 Englishmen arriving in America in 1675 would have been 160,000 by 1775, while 10,000 Englishmen remaining in England would have totaled only about 20,000 on the same date. The population of England was about 5,000,000 in 1760, but overseas there was an additional 1,500,000 that was soon to exceed England herself, in numbers.

Such a story of real progress is without parallel in modern history. In 1660 England was just recovering from a long period of civil war. Her royal family was in the secret pay of the King of France, the dominant military power on the continent. By 1760 England had stripped France of her colonial empire, destroyed her navy, and left her rapidly approaching bankruptcy and revolution. England, with a far smaller population than France, had in one hundred years forced the larger power in 1763 to sign a treaty more humiliating than was required of any other large nation prior to 1919.

No small part of the amazing development of English power was due to the operation of the navigation and trade policies as applied to the colonial Empire. The commodity clauses of the Navigation Acts had made England the chief distributor of goods from the Far East as well as the vital products from America. The shipping regulations, along with special protection given to the fishing and whaling industry, had given England by 1760 the greatest merchant marine in the world and a reservoir of sailors nearly equal to the combined numbers of seamen in all the other nations of western Europe.

The reserve sea power of England had been enormously increased by the encouragement of colonial trade, colonial shipping, and colonial shipbuilding. The encouragement of agriculture and the migration of English settlers had given her control of the vital sinews of empire. Tobacco, rice, sugar, wheat, fish, indigo, iron, timber, and naval stores proved more valuable than gold and silver, the chief exports of the Spanish colonies, or furs from those of France.

When war came, the resources to build new ships and sailors to man them were in British hands. Her colonial populations could not only feed themselves but could supply food in almost unlimited quantities for other areas. In contrast, the Spanish empire supplied no surplus food and France did not have a single colony that could supply its own food.[11] Neither France nor Spain had colonial shipbuilding industries or colonial reservoirs of sailors to add to their home resources. England had: and in time of war the highways of commerce quickly passed into her hands.

The trade acts had steadily fostered English domestic production of textiles and other industrial goods for export. The rapidly expanding colonial market could have been supplied with goods from foreign sources. Instead, bounties, drawbacks and preferential tariffs were steadily operating to shift colonial consumption to articles of English manufacture and divert the colonists from the use of similar articles of European production.

The profits from the colonial trade supplied English producers and merchants with the liquid capital to expand British production. Thus England was strengthened and the very basis for competition by powers on the continent undermined. They steadily lost access to the growing American market by way of England, they were excluded from the direct trade, and English bounties, drawbacks, and increasing efficiency steadily clipped the profits from an earlier trade through illicit channels.

There was a clause in one of the earliest Navigation Acts that has escaped notice, but was most important. All merchants and factors doing business in the British colonies had to be *bona fide* British subjects.[12] Thus Holland, France, and other trading countries had no native agents in the British colonies to promote the use of exports. Had they been permitted such factors they could have built up a market for their own manufactures and could have used the profits of such a trade to finance its delivery through illegal channels.

The merchants and factors were the bankers of the time. These were all British and only British capital could reap the rewards that came from developing a region of unlimited resources, such as America, and supplying its growing demands for manufactured goods.

It is no mystery that the industrial revolution as well as the agricultural revolutions developed first in England. British textile manufactures had the fly shuttle after 1733 and the spinning-jenny and roller spinning before the close of the Revolution. The application of steam power to drive the new machinery, the "atomic bomb" of the eighteenth century, followed in a few years. The capital to finance these new inventions had come from earnings of British producers and merchants in the years before 1775, and the efficiency of the new machines enabled English producers to undersell competitors and hold the American market long years after the Revolution.

The acid test of loyalty is whether individuals are willing to sacrifice for a cause. The real test of whether a hundred years of the trade and navigation acts had made the Americans disloyal to the Empire came in 1754 with the outbreak of the final struggle for control of North America.

Three previous wars involving the colonies since 1689 had arisen over European questions in which colonials had only remote interests. This war originated in America by the action of Virginia in attempting to protect her title to the Ohio Valley. It was Virginia troops, supported by Virginia money, that formed the advance guard of British Empire beyond the mountains. The struggle thus precipitated soon developed into the first of a series of world conflicts. The resources developed by a hundred years of British colonial policy proved decisive.

From the colonial and British shipyards came new ships faster than France could capture them. From the port of New York alone one hundred twenty-eight privateers were fitted out.[13] Little Rhode Island supplied half as many more. Many more came from other colonial ports. This swarm of armed vessels, supported by the heavily armed ships of the British navy, literally swept the western ocean clear of French, and later Spanish, merchant vessels, and at the same time maintained fairly normal trade between various parts of the colonial Empire.

Nor were the colonies lacking in supplying armed forces for the larger military expeditions. Forbes used mainly provincial troops to capture Fort Duquesne. For the campaign of 1758 more than 20,000 provincial troops were supplied, besides volunteers for the regiments of Royal Americans and sailors for the navy. New England alone supplied 15,000 men each year for the campaigns of 1758, 1759, and 1760. There was no draft in England, but there was in Massachusetts and Connecticut, where all able-bodied males were enrolled in the local militia and forces for the war were supplied by drafts upon the organized local companies and men so drafted were compelled to serve. For these years Massachusetts kept 7,500 men in the field and Connecticut, 5,000. These quotas were much higher in proportion to population than was demanded of England herself.[14]

Nor were the colonies lax in raising funds for the struggle. Massachusetts advanced a total of $1,500,000 or more. Both she and Connecticut levied excessive taxes on real property and in addition heavy excise taxes. Massachusetts even resorted to a stamp tax and a poll tax on every male over sixteen of nineteen shillings each. Other colonies responded according to their abilities. The southern colonies supplied fewer men in proportion to their population than did New England, but they had the slave problem to deal with and the menace of a serious Indian war on their own frontiers to meet.

When Spain entered the war British West Indian troops seized the French island of Martinique and a combined expedition of British regulars and colonial troops captured Havana. One thousand men for this expedition were supplied voluntarily by Connecticut and it was a Connecticut officer who was second in command of the expedition.[15]

Measured by the acid test of war the colonies were unquestionably loyal in the struggle from 1754 to 1763. It was not New England's war. The main battlefront in Canada in 1757 was further from New England, measured in time, than Canada was from Europe in 1914. Havana, Cuba was further from Connecticut by the same measure in 1762 than Australia and New Zealand were from North Africa and Singapore in 1941. In spite of the distance and their lack of a direct interest in the causes of the war, Massachusetts and Connecticut contributed in men and money to the success of the imperial cause on a scale fully comparable to that of the British dominions in recent wars.

Whoever seeks to connect the Navigation Acts with the American discontent which led to the Revolution must start with the fact, proved by the acid test of war, that a century of experience under these laws had produced a colonial population that was as militantly loyal as that of England, and possibly more so. This situation is the more impressive because New England, the group of colonies that has been assumed to have been most adversely affected by the Navigation Acts, was the section that was most ardent in fighting the battles of the Empire that imposed the regulations.

Obviously New England had prospered in the first hundred years of the navigation system or she could not have put forth the effort she did, and in a few years extinguish the relatively heavy war debt she incurred because of her loyalty.

A careful search of the contemporary writings of the period has not revealed a single expression by an American that can be called disloyal to the Empire. In all cases they date the beginning of objectionable legislation which threatened their freedom and industry with 1764.

For one hundred years the trade and navigation system had provided the most important cement of empire. How this cement was dissolved in ten short years by a changed policy is discussed in the next section.

REFERENCES

CHAPTER 5

1. Francis Parkman, *Montcalm and Wolfe* (Boston, 1884), II, Chap. xxxi. Frank W. Pitman, *Development of the British West Indies* (New Haven, 1917), Chap. xiv.

2. Lawrence M. Larson, *History of England and the British Commonwealth* (New York, 1932), p. 566.

3. Evarts B. Greene, *Provincial America* (New York, 1905), p. 174.

4. *Ibid.*, Chap. xiv; Edward Channing, *History of the United States* (New York, 1908), II, Chaps. iv, xiii, xiv.

5. L. M. Larson, *History of England and the British Commonwealth* (New York, 1924), Chap. xx.

6. Frank W. Pitman, *Development of the British West Indies* (New Haven, 1927), pp. 166-76.

7. Evarts B. Greene, *Provincial America*, Chap. xviii; Edward Channing, *History of the United States*, II, Chap. xv; Curtis P. Nettels, *Roots of American Civilization* (New York, 1938), Chap. xviii; Frank W. Pitman, *Development of the British West Indies*, Chap. i; Lowell J. Ragatz, *Fall of the Planter Class in the British Caribbean* (New York, 1928), Chap. i.

8. Lowell J. Ragatz, *op. cit.*, p. 81.

9. *Ibid.*, Chaps. i-iv.

10. E. B. Greene, *Provincial America*, pp. 258-59, 281, 314-15.

11. Edward Channing, *History of the United States*, II, 566.

12. Charles II, c. 18, ii. The penalty was forfeiture of all their goods.

13. Virginia D. Harrington, *The New York Merchant on the Eve of the Revolution* (New York, 1935), pp. 303-7; Irving B. Richman, *Rhode Island* (Boston, 1905), p. 105.

14. Francis Parkman, *Montcalm and Wolfe,* II, 88-89. According to Governor Pownall of Massachusetts, her war debt in 1758 was already £366,698 sterling and that taxes to meet the war expenses had been levied in Boston amounting to 13s-2d per pound of income, or 60 per cent.

15. Alexander Johnston, *Connecticut, A Study of a Commonwealth* (Boston, 1887), p. 258.

PART II

*DISSOLVING THE CEMENT
OF EMPIRE*

6

NEW LEADERS AND NEW POLICIES

Now there arose up a new king over Egypt, which knew not Joseph.
—*Exodus*, I:8.

WHOEVER seeks to explain the American Revolution must start with the proved loyalty of all the colonies in 1763 and their general satisfaction with the commercial system which bound the Empire together. Americans themselves dated the beginning of oppressive policies with 1764.[1]

What we have to explain is how new policies, inaugurated that year, changed the century-old commercial system from a force that had produced imperial unity into one that caused disunity in one short decade.

FINANCIAL DIFFICULTIES

England in 1763 faced problems not unlike those that confronted her at the close of World War II. A great war had been won. Physical control of vast new areas was in her hands. A new debt of embarrassing proportions had been accumulated. The costs of defense of the enlarged dominions imposed budgetary problems of the most serious nature. Taxes were oppressively high and should be reduced, but interest on the debt and existing costs of government could not be met with less income. Lowering governmental costs involved reductions in funds for the army, navy, a lot of new officers, pensions, spoilsmen who gathered about the new royal family, and in the sums used for political corruption. England had more commitments at home and abroad than she had money to support. Either some commitments had to be given up or additional sources of income found.

IMPERIAL REORGANIZATION

In 1763 England was without effective political leadership. The King had displaced Pitt and there was no other man in public life who commanded the confidence of the entire country to fill his place. In this situation George Grenville was charged with the responsibility of bringing in legislation to meet the financial difficulties. Had his problem been purely matters of revenue his task might have been simple. They were complicated by new demands for imperial reorganization that had been promoted during the war, not unlike the dreams of world unity that developed in the United States during World War II.

These demands centered in government circles made up of officeholders at home and in the colonies, including King George III and his closest advisers. This group desired changes in the political organization of the colonies that would create in each of them a government that could be controlled from London. To make this effective it was necessary to have a colonial revenue, at the disposal of the Ministry, which could be used to support executive, administrative, and judicial officers in the colonies who would be appointed by and be completely subservient to those who ruled the home government.

Grenville, Townshend, and the other new political leaders knew the extent to which real political power in the larger colonies had passed into the hands of the legislative assemblies. They saw the gradual evolution of a colonial government in which the governor had little more real power than kings had in England for the past fifty years. They feared that continued development along such lines would terminate in actual political and commercial independence. They did not realize that loyalty to the Empire was most intense in those colonies in which real government was most completely in the hands of popular leaders chosen at free elections.[2]

The program desired by King George III and his governmental

party amounted to a proposed constitutional revolution in the Empire which precipitated questions and discussions as serious as those facing England in 1688. It will be sufficient to state that they ran through most of the controversial legislation of the decade and were ultimately settled by force.

BRITISH MERCHANTS

In addition to the government party there was another group with a definite colonial policy. This included the merchants; manufacturers; shipowners; banking, financial, and insurance interests; and the large numbers of workers dependent upon these for employment. We shall call this group the British merchants.

The merchants and their political supporters had been in major control of the government for the century preceding 1764. They believed firmly in the importance of trade in developing the wealth and the political strength of the Empire. The growth of the colonies, their loyalty, and the expansion of markets for British goods in America were proof to them of the soundness of their policy. They too were imperialists, but in a very different sense from the governmental party. They favored the trade and navigation acts as the bulwark of British colonial prosperity and instinctively opposed any policy that would burden that trade.

The merchants were heavily committed financially to continued American prosperity.[3] Many of their fortunes had been made in handling colonial sugar, rice, indigo, tobacco, naval stores, and other products. Their ships served American trade. They had advanced millions of pounds to buy land, supply slaves, and otherwise stock the great colonial plantations. Others had invested vast fortunes in warehouses and other means of marketing colonial products. Manufacturers in many cases had developed their business wholly to supply the colonial market. All were deeply concerned with maintaining the *status quo* with the colonies. Whatever injured America injured them. Their own prosperity was dependent upon continued colonial prosperity.[4]

Through their constant communication with their American factors, agents, and customers the merchants knew American conditions better than did any other group of Englishmen. In every issue that affected colonial trade they were the friends of America. They were suspicious of or hostile to the new schemes of the governmental party for colonial reorganization, because if they resulted in alienating America they would also be injured. The representation of the merchants and manufacturing groups in Parliament was far less than their numbers and wealth justified; therefore, to protect their interests and direct policies, they had to have the support of other groups that were represented.

LANDED GENTRY

The landed gentry had more votes in Parliament than any other group. Any ministry had to have their support to remain in power. They knew little about America and had no colonial program of their own. They had favored the merchant's program so long as it produced revenue from customs duties, gave employment to the workers, and kept the poor rates down. They were seriously embarrassed by the increased land taxes incident to the recent colonial war and feared the consequence to their future welfare of the large national debt. They owned much of the land that controlled the votes in the "rotten boroughs," and secured part of their income through the sale of seats in the Commons. In the past such payments had been supplied by the merchants while in power. After 1764 the paymaster became King George III or his friends. The money came from taxes the same as other expenses.

The promise of the governmental party to secure a revenue from America appealed to the landed gentry as just and reasonable. The debt had been largely due to a war in behalf of the colonies. The new costs for army and navy were for the protection of the colonies. They were prosperous and able to pay for their own protection. The landed gentry were loyal to the crown and were disposed to look upon colonial opposition to the ministerial program as something closely akin to treason.

By the judicious distribution of offices, the use of money directly and indirectly, the purchase of seats, and the careful buying of votes in contested elections the governmental party was able to secure and to hold the support of the landed gentry during the crucial years from 1764 to 1779.[5]

Higher Clergy

The higher clergy regularly followed the political program of the group in power because appointments and preferments were secured that way. Their support was important because they supplied some votes and considerable popular influence that could be used to offset that of the merchants. Promises of an extension of the English episcopal system to America especially appealed to them. If such an extension could be secured, it would create a growing number of new jobs and increase the chances of preferment for the younger clergy. The opposition of the Americans to the new governmental program was believed to center in areas dominated by American dissenting clergy. In some cases colonial opposition was ascribed to the erroneous ideas that had been disseminated by local religious leaders.

Some of the British clergy seemed to have been greatly enamored with the suggestion that the extension of the English episcopal system to the colonies would provide a loyal clergy that would soon teach Americans the errors of their political views.[6] It was much like the temptation held forth to win the support of American educators to the extreme war policies in the late war—end all danger of renewed Fascism by reëducating the Germans, Italians, and Japanese—of course with higher salaries for the educators than they received at home. It was a wonderful opportunity for patriots.

By such arguments and hopes the governmental party retained the support of the higher clergy for its program of imperial reorganization and thus made the question of an American bishop an issue related to that of securing a colonial revenue by a basic change in the century-old commercial system.[7]

Triumph of the Governmental Faction

Every political group, once installed in office, seeks to remain in power as long as possible. The governmental party was no exception to the general rule. It was more ruthless than its predecessors in consolidating political power in its own hands and crushing opposition to its colonial policy. The rule in England and America was "reward friends and punish enemies."

Steadily the influence of the merchants was undermined. Some lost lucrative government contracts which were transferred to persons who supported the governmental party. In other cases merchants with large commitments, like Trecothic of London, were attacked through their business connections in the colonies.[8] The rapid expansion of the Scotch tobacco business at Glasgow after 1760 reduced the proportion of colonial tobacco handled by the merchants at London, Bristol, and the other outports.

The old trading centers were the strongholds of the British merchants and the centers of opposition to the colonial policy of the governmental party. The Glasgow merchants and their factors in America were loyal supporters of the governmental party. Some merchants and manufacturers believed the assertions of the king and his friends that the object of the new colonial program was to secure the colonies permanently in commercial dependence upon England.

In 1765-66 the merchants had been able in a few months to mobilize public opposition strong enough to force the repeal of the Stamp Act upon a hostile administration.[9] It took them three years to secure the repeal of the anti-trade features of the Townshend Revenue Act of 1767. They were entirely powerless to prevent the passage of the Repressive Acts of 1774.

Such, in brief, was the political background for Grenville's fateful decision to create an American revenue. He was himself no enemy of America. He knew his finance and was honestly attempting to put England's financial house in order. Since England was raising her major revenue by taxing the trade that passed through her ports, it was natural that he should think first of similar devices to raise a colonial revenue.

The trouble was that his decision involved a revolution in the century-old trade and navigation system. It had been instituted to divert trade into English channels, to develop English colonies, to build up demands for English goods, and to increase English shipping. The system was expensive, but the nation as a whole and the Empire had prospered under the policy. It had meant regulation for the purpose of promoting trade. Grenville's policy meant regulation for producing revenue. The test of the success of the old policy had been whether the regulations promoted imperial trade. The test of success of the new policy was the amount of revenue it would produce.

Grenville was not seeking to make the *old system* yield a revenue. He was destroying it and substituting a different policy. Protection had supplied the common economic interest that had been the cement of empire. The new policy of taking what the traffic would bear dissolved that cement. The old policy had been one of colonial development. The new policy became a policy of exploitation of America for the personal profit of a ruling minority of "king's friends" who were seeking to use the resources of America to retain power in England.

An incidental but not unimportant part of the new program was to extend to America the party spoils system which had grown up in England. This would enable the group in power to use the increased number of well-paid jobs in America to reward party supporters. Such a program inevitably drew America into party controversies in England. Royal officials had to be ministerial supporters. Attacks upon them and their policies were interpreted in England as attacks upon the government. American opposition had to seek support from the political opposition in England. It could not get a hearing from those in power.

Political rewards in England and the possible pickings from the new revenue system in the colonies were not sufficient to satisfy the avarice of all the followers of George III. Some looked back to the precedents of Charles II and the Restoration, when America had been used to supply estates to Penn, Clarendon, and other favorites. The America of George III might also be similarly used to create great new landed estates. The Floridas, Canada, and the interior of the continent offered almost unlimited opportunities to reward the faithful.

The richest lands were in the Ohio Valley, where hardy spirits from North Carolina, Virginia, and Pennsylvania were already staking out their claims. For a century Americans had been left to their own devices to conquer the wilderness, deal with the

Indians, and occupy the back country. In the past the story had been chiefly one of hardship. Now that fortunes were in sight, the ruling clique in London saw an opportunity to push the colonials aside, deprive them of their claims, and themselves take over the fortunes that were passing into the hands of leading American families. Men thus threatened with dispossession did not like the program. It was an easy way to change their former loyalty to the Empire into an attitude of hostility toward the ruling ministry.

Alvord and others have studied this phase of the problem and have uncovered so much evidence that it appears almost as a major cause of the Revolution.[10] It was important because it coincided in time with similar attacks upon the fortunes of American merchants and shippers under the guise of the revenue acts. It gave the shipping interests of the coast and backwoodsmen similar grievances in common. Morgan's Riflemen and the Sons of Liberty spoke the same language. The economic cement of empire of both groups was being eroded by the new spirit of exploitation that ruled in London.

War Against Commerce Goes On

The defeat of the French armed forces in Canada did not end hostilities in America. The navy had embarked upon a form of total war against foreign commerce that gradually developed into a war against colonial commerce.

During the war with France England put into operation a number of trading with the enemy acts. To begin with, these had been based upon laws enacted long before the discovery of America and seizures under them were ultimately held illegal by the courts so far as they applied to America. New laws were enacted which did extend to the colonies. The task of enforcing the regulations was given to the navy. The enemy with which trade was forbidden was France from 1756 to 1761, and Spain from 1762-63. The main theater of operations was the island possessions of these countries in the Caribbean. The trade to be intercepted was not that of enemy states or neutrals, but chiefly that from the British American colonies on the continent.

For a century this trade had been developing with the open or tacit approval of the home government. The foreign islands in the Caribbean were the best available market for surplus British colonial fish, food, horses, timber, and other colonial products. Such trade was not contrary to the British Navigation Acts. It did not reduce exports of British manufactures but increased them. Through that trade British merchants not only increased their exports to their own colonial markets, but acquired access to French and Spanish colonial markets that could not be reached directly. In addition the possibility of repayment of millions of pounds due from American merchants depended in part upon the profits from this trade.

Americans did not consider their traffic to the Caribbean as in any way disloyal. It was the same trade they had carried on in time of peace. It was the regular main outlet for many of their colonial products. The profit from this trade supplied the chief, and in some cases the only, means by which they could continue to buy British goods and pay the heavy taxes by which they supported the war effort.

As the laws governing seizures at sea are based upon where vessels are found and the papers they carry, new hazards were opened to colonial traders. British naval officers were unfamiliar with trade customs and applied the letter of the regulations given to them. The result was that the British navy suddenly became a greater menace to ordinary colonial commerce than were French vessels. Beer has assembled the main evidence and it needs no further elaboration here.[11]

With the coming of peace the greatly enlarged navy was continued in its wartime job of policing British commerce.[12] As the crews received one half the net proceeds of all seizures; it was profitable for them to seize colonial ships on purely technical grounds. Trials were in the admiralty courts, the burden of proof of innocence was upon the owner of the seized vessel. Costs were assessed against the owner even in case of acquittal; the owner had to give a heavy bond before he could file a claim to his own vessel; and there was no practical way a naval officer in the colonies could be sued for wrongful seizures. Thus the navy was shifted from its proper function of protecting colonial commerce to a position of open warfare upon that commerce. Legislation after 1763 increased the technical grounds for seizures and opened new opportunities for naval action against colonial shipping. Thus the warfare that was begun against France in 1756 was continued with varying degrees of vigor against British colonial commerce until the outbreak of open hostilities in 1775.

The chief sufferers from this continued warfare upon American commerce were those most heavily engaged in inter-colonial trade, and commerce with the Caribbean. Vessels engaged in the direct trade to Great Britain or the Mediterranean were less likely to fall foul of purely technical regulations. Geographically this meant the warfare was mainly against the trade of the northern colonies and much less against the trade of the sugar, rice, indigo, and tobacco colonies.

REFERENCES

CHAPTER 6

1. Eleventh Resolution, *Declaration and Resolves of the First Continental Congress,* October 14, 1774.

2. O. M. Dickerson, *American Colonial Government* (Cleveland, 1912), Chap. iv; George L. Beer, *British Colonial Policy, 1754-1765* (New York, 1907), Chaps. 9-11.

3. Henry Cruger, Jr. in a letter to his father, dated Bristol, February 14, 1766, stated that the merchants had proved to the House of Commons that the American debt owed British merchants at that time totaled £5,000,-000. A few days later he wrote Aaron Lopez of Providence, Rhode Island, that he owed Cruger at that time £10,784. This was a large sum to be owed by a relatively small trader. "Commerce of Rhode Island," Massachusetts Historical Society, *Collections,* Seventh Series, IX, 139-43, 151-57.

4. Dora Mae Clark in *British Opinion and the American Revolution* (New Haven, 1930), Chaps. ii-iv, has given the best summary of the attitude of British merchants as a group.

5. *Ibid.,* Chap. v.

6. *Ibid.,* pp. 182-85. See also letter of Henry Cruger, Jr. to his father, Bristol, February 14, 1766. "Commerce of Rhode Island," Massachusetts Historical Society, *Collections,* Seventh Series, IX, 139-43.

7. Miss Clark in her study of public opinion in England found contemporary evidence that the issue of an American bishop was not one of "purely colonial origin" as claimed by J. T. Adams, *Revolutionary New England, 1691-1776,* p. 359. *Op. cit.,* p. 184.

8. This is discussed, *infra,* Chap. ix.

9. Henry Cruger, Jr. in a letter to his father, February 14, 1766, describes in detail how the Bristol and other merchants put over the repeals, not permitting a single order from an American merchant for goods to be sent to the manufacturers until they joined in petitions for the repeal of the Stamp Act. "Commerce of Rhode Island," Massachusetts Historical Society, *Collections,* Seventh Series, IX, 145.

10. Clarence W. Alvord, *The Mississippi Valley in British Politics* (Cleveland, 1917).

11. George L. Beer, *British Colonial Policy, 1754-1765* (New York, 1907), Chaps. v-vii.

12. 3 George III, c. 22, sec. viii. See also the discussion in Beer, *op. cit.,* Chap. xi.

THE SUGAR ACT

THE Sugar Act of 1764 was the first of the new measures planned to reorganize the colonial Empire. It has generally been discussed as merely the first in a series of unpopular taxation measures. It was far more than a tax-raising law. Its other detailed sections were intended to provide a constitutional revision of the entire colonial system. The taxation clauses excited the most immediate attention and the discussion concerning them has tended to obscure the other, more fundamental provisions.

The articles selected for taxation were: (1) foreign sugars and molasses; (2) Madeira and other wines imported directly from their places of growth; (3) wines from Spain, Portugal, and other points imported from England; (4) foreign coffee and indigo; (5) foreign silks, silk mixtures, calicoes, linens, lawns, and cambrics imported from England; (6) British-grown coffee and pimento exported from any British colony.[1]

SUGAR AND MOLASSES

The duties on sugar and molasses were considered an extension of the Molasses Act of 1733 and sections five and six made the modified act perpetual. The rate on foreign molasses was reduced from six pence a gallon to three pence. The New England traders continued to protest that the new rate was so high as to seriously handicap the trade to Africa and the West Indies. To meet this objection the rate was lowered in 1766 to one penny a gallon and made uniform on all molasses, whether British or foreign.

This effectually ended all contention that the measure was a trade act to encourage the British sugar industry. It ended the commercial argument that the tax would burden the rum trade by unduly raising prices of molasses. It also ended the smuggling trade in molasses on the continent as it was no longer profitable for the trader to pay customs officers for certifying false entries or to buy molasses from West Indian planters who had imported it from the French islands and certified it as of British production.

It has been customary to discuss the Sugar Act as a measure aimed at the prosperity of the northern colonies, using the arguments of Israel Maudit, agent for Rhode Island, as the chief evidence. His arguments, and those of other agents, were assumptions as to how the act might work and not statements of how it operated in practice. Probably no one, even the agents themselves, took such arguments seriously. It is difficult to see how anyone could believe that cutting existing tariff rates by half, forcing pilfering customs officers to surrender a part of their takings to the treasury, and ending the practice of the West Indian planters of certifying French molasses as British, could totally wreck the New England fishing industry. While higher prices for molasses might hamper some of the former trade, it could not possibly destroy all of it.[2]

The law was passed. None of the threatened calamities occurred. Fish were still caught, cured, and marketed in the old channels. Molasses continued to be imported in large quantities, mostly from foreign sources.[3]

The constitutional argument remained, that it was taxation without the approval of the governed. This merged with constitutional arguments against other taxes and does not again appear as popular clamor against the molasses duty which remained as one of the major sources of revenue to the Revolution.

The tax on foreign raw sugar was unchanged, while that on refined sugar was increased. These clauses are reminiscent of the older trade acts as they operated as protective tariffs in favor of the British sugar grower and English refiners. Large quantities of brown sugar continued to be imported, but only a little more than half the quantities imported were of British production.[4] Foreign refined sugar practically disappeared from the list of imports.

The export duties on British coffee and pimento were entirely contrary to the older principles of trade legislation. They raised a small revenue but their effect was to burden British trade and discourage the use of articles of British growth. They resemble the 4½ per cent export duties levied under older laws in the West Indies. More than one half of the colonial imports of coffee centered at Philadelphia,[5] which port was also the largest colonial market for pimento.[6] While these are stated in the law as export duties, in practice they were collected at the colonial port of importation, as were the other duties.[7]

The import duty on foreign silks, calicoes, linens, lawns, and cambrics was either an effort to discourage the use of such articles or a rather obvious sop to the English manufacturers of competing articles. As a revenue measure it was wholly unimportant and was changed to an English export duty two years later. Its appearance in the law is best explained as a bid for votes from certain manufacturing interests.

It has been customary to blame the Sugar Act to the greed of the West India sugar planters, especially those resident in England and with seats in the House of Commons. That they supported the bill is certain, but an analysis of the bill fails to show that they received unusual benefits from the act.

The only apparent advantage accruing to the sugar planters from the acts of 1764 and 1766 was a legal monopoly of the rum trade to the other colonies. This monopoly they already had in fact and could have retained without additional legislation. This is proved by what happened after the Revolution, when they had to compete with the rest of the world for the American market. More than ninety per cent of the American rum imports for 1789-90 came from the British sugar islands.[8] For this doubtful advantage they had to forfeit any preference for their molasses as against foreign molasses in the vast colonial market; to be satisfied with their existing legal advantage in the sale of raw sugar to the continent; to submit to export duties on their pimento and coffee except when shipped to England; to submit to all of the new taxes imposed by the act; and, worst of all, to face the elaborate new enforcement provisions which seriously threatened their past profits from "naturalizing" foreign sugar and molasses—that is, secretly importing it into the sugar islands, moving it to their plantations, and then certifying it as of their own production.[9]

It is probable that the Sugar Act was as great a disadvantage to the economy of the sugar islands as it was to that of the continental colonies. They received enough apparent advantages to insure their parliamentary support of the measure, but one must look for the origin of the measure to far more powerful forces than those directed by the sugar planters.

WINE

All of the wine used in America was of foreign origin; consequently, there could be no pretence that a tax on its importation had any relation to protecting or encouraging a British industry.

Second only to molasses, the tax on wine was the most productive of all the new duties imposed by the Sugar Act.

Prior to 1764 most of the wine used in America had been imported directly from the Azores and southern Europe. Wine from this area had always been free for such direct importation. The large number of ships carrying food products to the Mediterranean had found their only return cargoes either salt or wine and a few minor articles such as lemons, olive oil, currants, raisins, etc. Merchants claimed that the small earnings derived from these cargoes constituted the only profits from the fish trade to the Mediterranean.[10]

The importation of wine and salt was legal, but the other articles, being the products of Europe, were imported in violation of the Navigation Act. As the quantities were small, the custom of permitting a traffic of such long standing, and as no injury to the trade of the Empire could be shown, there was no expectation that it would be disturbed. New regulations in the Sugar Act subjected shipowners to grave hazards in following the old customs.

The Sugar Act imposed entirely new duties of £7 per tun on all wine from southern Europe, imported directly, and ten shillings a tun upon similar wine imported by way of England.

Wines other than French exported from England were entitled to a drawback of all duties paid in England except seventy shillings a tun.[11] Vessels engaged in the Mediterranean trade could choose between sailing directly for America and paying £7 a tun on their cargoes of wine; or stopping at a British port, unloading and reloading everything but salt and wine, paying a duty of seventy shillings a tun on any wine on board and paying an additional duty of ten shillings a tun in America.

The difference in duty between a direct voyage to America with wine and one by way of a British port, was £3 for a tun of 252 gallons.[12] The cost of stopping at the British port, the expense of loading and unloading, and the delays, probably amounted to about £3 on every tun of wine carried. Thus the cost of a voyage directly to the Mediterranean or one by way of England was approximately the same. The imports and the amount of duties collected indicate that most ships continued to sail directly for America and pay the £7 a tun.[13]

In addition to the desire for revenue there may have been some of the older concepts of the trade laws involved in planning the wine duties. British wine merchants would profit from any increase in wine purchases in England. The difference in tax was three pounds in favor of importing wines from England. There was always a shortage of freight for ships sailing from England to America. Additional wine shipments would supply additional freight. Shipowners and wine merchants who hoped to profit from the increased business could supply a few additional votes for the bill. The administration was seeking political support for its program.

The tax on wine fell very unevenly upon the American colonies. The wine trade was concentrated at a few major ports. As the duties had to be paid in specie this had a tendency to make coin scarce at the wine ports, because whatever was paid in duties was withdrawn from circulation, transmitted to the account of the English government, and expended frequently at other points. In any case it was removed from the usual channels of local trade.

The ports of New York, Philadelphia, and Charleston carried

on an extensive trade to southern Europe and received in return large quantities of wine. Prior to 1764 an important reëxport trade in wine was developing at the chief American wine ports. New York customhouse records show that in 1763 more than 1,200 pipes of wine were imported, of which approximately one-fifth was reëxported to Quebec, other colonies, the West Indies, and even to England, Scotland, and Ireland. The other wine ports carried on a similar export business.

The new duty of £7 a tun practically terminated the American distributing trade in wine and transferred much of it to the British wine merchants who were favored by the lower English duty. Exports of wine from New York shrank from over 250 pipes in 1763 to a little more than seven pipes in 1769.[14]

The new duties also had the effect of curtailing the colonial consumption of wine. Total wine imports at New York dropped to less than half those recorded in 1763.[15] It is probable that the new wine duties had a more serious affect upon the total course of colonial trade than did the much more widely discussed changes in the duty on molasses. After 1764 the trade in molasses continued to flow in the same trade channels as before and increased in volume. Wine not only decreased in total amount imported, but shifted to new trade channels.

The actual effects of the new wine duties upon the course of the wine trade are hard to estimate. We have the British records of exports to the colonies, and the records kept by the American Customs Commissioners of imports received at the various ports. The large British exports are divided about equally between Port wine and Spanish wine. Apparently this was all recorded as Port by the American customs officials, as they recorded but two kinds of wine imports—Madeira and Port. The American records show an increase in the amount of Port imported after 1768 and a decline in the quantity of Madeira.[16] This may indicate a gradual shift to England as a source of supply, or a rising taste for Port and Spanish wines due to the presence of military and naval personnel. Quebec drank mostly Port and the southern planters preferred Madeira.

Imports indicate that some people in Boston preferred Port and others Madeira with a strong tendency toward Port in the later years.

The popular impression that Boston was the chief center of the American wine trade is based upon the undue emphasis given the Captain Malcolm and similar incidents in the standard accounts, and a tendency to treat the Revolution as an episode in Massachusetts history. Boston, in fact, was relatively unimportant as a wine port.

The leading market for wines from England was Quebec. According to the American customs reports more than half of all the Port wine imported by America from 1768 to 1772 went to that port. The British records of exports to America in 1773 show that nearly two-thirds of all the Spanish wine exported to America went to Canada.[17] The second largest market for wines from England was Philadelphia, followed closely by New York. Boston was fourth and furnished a market for a little less than eight per cent of the British wine exports to the colonies.[18]

The American figures for the five years from 1768 through 1772 tell a similar story. During these years the records show a total importation of 7,749 tuns of wine. More than ninety per cent went to the major ports of six colonies. Canada was first, Philadelphia second, New York third, and Boston sixth.

Was there a different story when it came to Madeira wine? Only slightly: New York was the chief port of direct importation, Philadelphia was second, Charleston, South Carolina, third, and Boston fifth. Instead of being the chief wine center of America, Boston has a record of importing during the five years less than half as much Madeira wine as Charleston.[19] This difference cannot be explained on the theory of smuggling at Boston. During the years 1768-72 there was enforcement at that port, if anywhere. The army was there, that was headquarters for naval forces engaged in policing American trade, and the Customs Commissioners were there.

It is obvious that wine imports were much more influenced by the general course of trade than they were by import duties. Returning ships brought cargoes from their best markets on the outward voyage. In 1772 there was three times the tonnage of ships cleared from Charleston, South Carolina, for southern Europe as from Boston, and approximately twice the tonnage from southern Europe entered Charleston as entered Boston.[20] Philadelphia had nearly twice as many tons of shipping clear for southern Europe that year as did Boston, New York, and Charleston combined. The returning tonnage that year from south Europe showed a total of 8,415 tons entering Philadelphia and only 4,778 tons at the other three ports combined. The wine imports from South Europe came with the returning ships.

NEW REGULATIONS FOR COMMERCE

The Sugar Act has usually been discussed as a taxation measure. Six of its sections concerned new taxes but more than forty additional sections were devoted to a revision of the customs and commerce regulations which amounted to a constitutional revolution in the relations of the colonies to the home country. Such clauses attracted little immediate attention for two reasons: immediate attention and discussion centered on what happened to sugar and molasses and the other clauses came into use slowly and hence attracted no immediate attention. It is doubtful if the entire Sugar Act was even published in the colonies as was the Stamp Act. Certainly few Americans had any comprehension of the vital provisions of the measure at the time of its passage.

The provisions in the last forty-odd sections were not included for immediate use, but were there for the purpose of changing the old system to the new system that was being planned. They became a vital part of the later revenue and enforcement legislation.

Cockets were now required to be carried by all ships found beyond more than two leagues—seven miles—of the coast.[21] Such documents had to include a complete list of the cargo, description of each package, its contents, by whom shipped, and its destination. A fee was charged by the customs officers for their issuance. Penalty for not having such a cocket, or for having on board goods not covered by the cockets was confiscation of such goods.

The two leagues rule affected all coastwise traffic, which had formerly been subject only to local control. No master of a sailing vessel going from one port to another, even in the same colony, could be sure that his ship would not be further out from land than seven miles. Most indentations of the coast were more than fourteen miles in width. Rocks, reefs, bars, and other hazards forced masters of small vessels to steer wide of them. Wind and tide could quickly drift any sailing vessel beyond the two-league limit. In case of doubt it was the eye of the officer of the revenue boat that estimated the distance from shore.

The number of enumerated products was increased by the addition of coffee, pimento, whale fins, raw silk, hides, skins, pot and pearl ashes.[22] This section followed the general lines of the older trade and navigation acts. As there was little market for these articles developed outside of the British Empire, enumeration involved no new economic stresses. It did increase the number of enumerated products to the place where few ships would be able to complete a cargo without including some article that was enumerated. This clause thus had the effect of forcing every master of a vessel to give bond for enumerated products.

Iron and lumber were not enumerated but were separately listed as articles which should be covered by special bonds. Had they been enumerated they would have been covered by the general bond required for all enumerated products. Instead two new bonds were required not to land any such articles in any part of Europe other than Great Britain.[23] This provision cut off a considerable direct trade in lumber to South Europe and diverted it to England. Its most serious results, however, were its effect upon purely local shipping. Iron and wood in some form made up a part of the cargo found on board practically every colonial vessel.

In addition a new bond had to be given for non-enumerated goods on condition that no foreign molasses that it might have on board or later take on board, should be landed outside the Empire.[24] Again this provision applied without distinction as to size of vessels and whether they were even capable of reaching a foreign destination. Even if they had no molasses of foreign origin on board, and had no intention of loading any, they had to give bond under this section.

The Sugar Act thus forced each master of a vessel to give three additional bonds for each clearance from an American colonial port from Quebec to Honduras. This made a total of four bonds—one for enumerated products, one for non-enumerated, one for iron, and one for lumber.

The sections requiring these additional bonds all contained clauses specifying that such bonds should be given *before* such goods were placed on board, and the sections requiring bonds before loading applied to all vessels and not merely to those engaged in trans-ocean trade.[25] Section twenty-nine also required that a "sufferance or warrant" should be obtained before any goods were placed on board. This section, together with the bonding provisions, made the law incapable of literal compliance in many parts of America.

Most of the smaller vessels loaded all or parts of their cargoes at plantations or small villages many miles from the nearest customhouse. Farmers brought in their produce when they could. Warehouses at loading points were frequently nonexistent. Goods had to be put under cover and the ship was usually the only available shelter.

Under the law, the master of each vessel was presumed to make a special trip to the customhouse and secure a permit or give bond every time a farmer drove up with produce, leaving the goods exposed to the elements until he could return with the proper papers. Such a trip might require days to complete and would have to be repeated every time a new batch of produce was offered. Securing a cargo for ships of even moderate size required weeks, and no master of a vessel engaged in the plantation trade could possibly know in advance what products, and in what amounts, he could secure to freight his vessel. That could only be known when final negotiations for cargoes had been completed.

The universal custom had been for vessels to load as best they could, then proceed to the nearest customhouse, give bonds, and comply with other clearance regulations. There was neither fraud or suspicion of fraud in the regular practice. After 1764, following the regular trade custom became a crime punishable by forfeiture of ship and cargo. This was no idle threat, as will be shown later.

It was only at the large ports where there were docks, warehouses, and general trade facilities near the customhouse that the bonding provisions could generally be complied with.

Section twenty-nine of the Sugar Act changed radically the former legal relations of the colonies to the home country. Had the British government been successful in putting this section into operation it could have created centralized controls as powerful as those later established under the Constitution.

Prior to 1764 only ocean-going trade had been subject to parliamentary regulation. Coastwise trade had been left pretty much alone, except so far as enumerated products were concerned, and then only when shipped from one colony to another. There had been no attempts to extend imperial control over inland waterways. All regulations had been conceived in terms of trade from one ocean port to another. Trade among and to the West Indies was destined to retain that character.

Markedly different trade conditions were developing on the continent. Here colonies were expanding westward with indefinite boundaries. Coastwise shipping was increasing and expanding both along the coast and into inland waterways. Interior water communications were being developed and supplemented by inland roads and highways. Freight wagons were coming into common use in many sections. Real inter-colonial commerce across land boundaries was developing in some areas closely akin to our modern interstate commerce.

Section twenty-nine sought to establish imperial customs and admiralty jurisdiction over this developing inter-colonial commerce. The loose wording of the statute appeared in the customs manuals as a requirement that no goods could be loaded or shipped in any manner from one colony to another without a cocket and other papers issued by a customs officer the same as was required for shipments by sea. As will be shown later, customs officers ultimately appeared on inland freight roads and made a determined effort to apply this provision to purely inland transportation.

Other sections regulated the loading of vessels in England for the colonies,[26] and colonial trade with Ireland. Still other sections set up elaborate machinery to deal with alleged violations; placed the burden of proof of innocence upon the master or owner of any vessel charged with violating some one of the numerous regulations;[27] required the defendant to pay the costs of the suit against him even when he proved he was innocent of any violation of the law;[28] and provided that, before the owner of a vessel charged with some violation could even appear in court to claim his vessel, he had to give bond for £60 to cover costs of the suit against his ship.[29]

An extensive system of admiralty courts had just been created with jurisdiction over trade, revenue, and ordinary admiralty cases and operating under a system of law different from that used in the local colonial courts. Here was an obvious effort to create a set of imperial courts with an independent imperial judiciary somewhat like that later created by the United States under the Constitution. The old admiralty courts dealt only with offenses on the high seas or at least cases involving high seas commerce. The new courts were intended to deal with all offenses against imperial commercial and revenue laws. Section forty-one of the Sugar Act provided specifically that all cases involving violation of the trade, navigation, customs, or revenue laws were to be tried in the admiralty courts. Thus offenses against imperial law were to be tried in an independent system of imperial courts.

The Navigation Acts had operated successfully for one hundred years without the new provisions described above. They are present in this new law, not to enforce the navigation system and interrupt forbidden trade outside the imperial commercial system; but to lay the legal foundation for the changed colonial Empire that was being planned and to provide fat pickings for the army of placemen that was soon to be sent to the colonies.

A final provision that must never be overlooked was the legal details for disposing of vessels, goods, and other property seized under this and other laws. One-third went to the person who informed against the ship or individuals connected with it; one-third to the governor where the seizure was made; and one-third to the imperial treasury.[30] Such a system would support an army of political favorites, unsalaried snoopers, and "swarms of officers" sent over to prey upon colonial commerce. Suits against individuals were authorized to three times the highest value of the goods allegedly involved, to be divided the same way.

IMPORTANCE AS A REVENUE MEASURE

The Sugar Act has been greatly underrated as a tax measure. Usually writers have passed it over with some general statements. A part of the difficulty has been the nature of the records and their availability. The Sugar Act applied to all of the American colonies, including the West Indies. The records most frequently consulted, those of the Customs Commissioners created in 1767, include returns only from the seventeen colonies on the continent and Bahama, Bermuda, and Newfoundland.

The Customs Commissioners had an Inspector General and a Treasurer. The former kept detailed records of the movement of commerce at each port, including separate lists of the importation and exportation of all articles subject to duty, and the total duties from all sources collected at each port. The Treasurer recorded sums that reached his hands which in most cases were net amounts after the costs of collection had been deducted. Americans were interested in the gross amount taken from them and not in the net amount that finally reached the British exchequer.

Channing, who has printed the only detailed returns from the tax laws, used the accounts of the Treasurer.[31] These figures vary widely from the reports of gross receipts in the Treasury Papers in London.[32] For instance, Channing gives the total receipts from all parliamentary taxes on America in 1769 as £33,914, while the gross receipts were reported in London as £42,787; for 1773 Channing found £32,635, and the London report shows £47,669. It is impossible to reconcile the London figures with those used by Channing. Apparently the two accounts include different items.

So far as the continental colonies are concerned the Inspector General's reports of the articles imported each year at every port and the total duties paid on them appears the most accurate statement of what Americans actually paid. Using these records we have the results shown in the following table.

TABLE 9. COLLECTIONS UNDER THE SUGAR ACT OF 1764 AS MODIFIED IN 1766. REPORTED BY THE INSPECTOR GENERAL[33]

	1768	1769	1770	1771	1772
Molasses @ 1d per gal.	£11,927	£18,488	£15,103	£15,806	£20,328
Sugar, foreign, brown @ 5s per cwt.	4,145	12,836	8,759	5,269	14,055
Coffee, British @ 7s per cwt.	937	1,425	1,418	818	1,461
Madeira wine from Azores @ £7 per tun	7,000	6,510	5,341	4,872	6,055
Port wine from England @ 10s per tun	254	433	108	240	417
Pimento, British @ ½d per lb.	99	107	72	80	159
Indigo, foreign @ 6d per lb.	28	139	109	1	95
TOTAL—Sugar Act	£24,390	£39,938	£30,910	£27,086	£42,570
TOTAL—All duties	36,706	43,578	39,799	34,801	46,225

From the above table it is clear that for the five years covered by this report, collections under the Sugar Act amounted to eighty-two per cent of all sums exacted from the Americans by parliamentary taxation and amounted to more than ninety per cent in 1772. The London figures for 1773-74 show an even higher ratio. Adding to the above data the statement of collections discovered by Beer for 1765-67,[34] we have a total for the eleven years of the life of the Sugar Act of a little more than £295,000, not including minor export duties on the new list of enumerated products added in 1764, nor confiscations that will be discussed later. Neither does it include the fees required to transact business at the customhouses.

The Sugar Act was not only the first of the taxation measures, but it was the most burdensome of all. The total exactions under it of approximately £30,000 a year is a small tax upon a total population of more than two millions of Americans (in 1770) as pointed out by some writers, but it did not operate that way.

More than seventy per cent of all sums collected from the continental colonies under the Sugar Act fell upon the trade of only five ports in four of the twenty colonies covered by the Inspector General's reports. The taxes collected at the other thirty-seven ports amounted to only twenty-eight per cent of the total. The table below shows the collections for three average years.

TABLE 10. COLLECTIONS UNDER THE SUGAR ACT AT FIVE MAJOR PORTS
OF FOUR COLONIES, WITH PERCENTAGES OF THE
TOTAL TAX COLLECTED[35]

	1769 Amount	Per cent of Total	1770 Amount	Per cent of Total	1772 Amount	Per cent of Total
Boston and Salem	£ 9,975	24.9	£ 8,393	27.1	£14,476	33.9
New York	7,244	18.1	5,927	19.1	6,437	15.1
Philadelphia	7,054	17.6	7,511	24.2	7,651	17.9
Charleston	3,660	9.1	2,087	6.7	2,436	5.4
TOTALS	£27,933	69.9	£23,918	77.3	£31,000	72.5
Totals at all ports	£39,938	...	£30,910	...	£42,570	...

Massachusetts alone paid more than one-fourth of all Sugar Act taxes. In both New York and Massachusetts the imperial taxes under the Sugar Act alone by 1772 equaled or exceeded the total provincial collections for all other purposes in time of peace.[36] During the eleven years it was in operation the Sugar Act took from Massachusetts alone about one hundred thousand pounds. America was taxed—at least certain provinces were. The intensity of the opposition to additional taxes by the various colonies can be measured directly by the relative burdens imposed upon their trade by the Sugar Act.

The sums collected under the various sections of the Sugar Act were accounted for separately in the records of the colonial collectors. From time to time these sums were transmitted directly to England the same as other funds arising under general British tax measures. The total was subject to direct appropriation by Parliament. None of the receipts under the Sugar Act could be used by the ministry to pay salaries of colonial judges, governors, and other civil officers without appropriation for this purpose. In this respect the funds arising from the Sugar Act were in a class different from those from the Townshend Act. Thus the Sugar Act was to all intents and purposes a general taxation of the American colonies for the British treasury. The Treasury papers record the remission of the receipts from this act to the exchequer in London in great detail. It involved the principle of the direct taxation of the colonies for imperial purposes. Only the Revolution ended this practice.

REFERENCES

CHAPTER 7

1. 4 George III, c. 15, secs. 1-3.

2. Similar arguments were advanced in the colonial newspapers. The *Boston Evening Post*, January 2, 1764, says this act "will prevent Great Britain from exporting in woolens, linens, braziery, cutlery, beer, cheese, and other manufactures to these colonies, to the amount of many millions yearly. This must and will be the case every reasonable man will admit, as the grand resource the colonies had for their remittances is stopped, I mean the produce of the French, Dutch, and Spanish settlements in the West Indies." Many petitions from colonial legislatures contained similar arguments. See that of South Carolina in the *South Carolina Gazette*, February 6, 1765, and reprinted in the *Boston Gazette*, March 18, 1765.

3. The total importations of molasses were very large. Only estimates can be made prior to 1767, because records were kept in terms of containers instead of standard measures. After 1767 they were kept by the customs officers in gallons. The molasses regularly entered at the customhouses for the period 1768-72 follows.

	gallons		gallons		gallons
1768	2,862,552	1770	3,634,737	1772	4,878,804
1769	4,437,296	1771	3,793,465	Total	19,606,854

This makes an average annual importation for the five years of 3,921,371 gallons, only about three per cent of which was from the British islands. Boston is assumed to have been the center of the molasses smuggling trade. Import figures do not support this conclusion after 1767, as the average legal importations at that port for the five-year period were 1,129,006 gallons annually, or approximately one-third of the total imports. If there was much smuggling during this time, Boston used extremely large quantities of molasses. Compiled from *Customs* 16:1, Public Record Office, London.

4. In 1769 the total imports of brown sugar were 45,453 hundredweight foreign and 49,672 British. *Ibid.*

5. For the years 1768, 1769, 1770, 1772 total imports of coffee were 15,083 hundredweight, of which 7,592 were imported at Philadelphia, *Customs* 16:1.

6. In 1772 there was a total import of 76,788 pounds of pimento, of which 39,336 were imported at Philadelphia. *Ibid.*

7. The Inspector General's report for 1768 lists coffee imports of 2,781 hundredweight as imported subject to duty and only 56 hundredweight as carrying certificates that the duty had been paid in the West Indies. *Ibid.*

8. The total rum imports that year were 664,544 gallons, of which 617,793 came from British possessions. *American State Papers*, X, pp. 35-43.

9. The fullest account of this practice is in Lowell J. Ragatz, *The Fall of the Planter Class in the British Caribbean, 1763-1833* (New York, 1928), pp. 102-3. In some islands fully half of the sugar certified as British was of French origin. Some estates exported sugar without producing any at all. Molasses, rum, and sugar were naturalized in the same way.

10. *Boston Evening Post*, January 2, 1764.

11. French wines paid an import duty in England of £8 and other wines £4 a tun, 3 George III, c. 12, sec. 1. Channing says importation of French wines into England was prohibited at this time but gives no authority. *History of the United States*, III, 40. A small amount of French wine shows in the list of exports to the colonies in 1773. *Customs* 17:2.

12. So defined for revenue purposes by 5 Anne, c. 27.

13. For the first year the wine duties amounted to £5,772-14s-8¾d on Madeira wine; and only £536-4s-4d on wines from Great Britain. *Treasury* 1, bundle 430, f. 228 (Library of Congress, *Transcripts*).

14. *Customs* 16:1.

15. Imports of wine of all kinds at New York in 1763 were 1,126 pipes, 151 hogsheads, 7 tierces, 19 casks, and 777 quarter casks. For the years 1768-72 they totaled 1,227 tuns, or an average annual import for the five years of 245 tuns. In 1772 the imports were only 181 tuns, 157 gallons. The tun was equal to two pipes. *Ibid.*

16. The total number of tuns of wine imported by the continental colonies, including Quebec, Newfoundland, the Floridas, Bahama, and Bermuda, were:

	1768	1769	1770	1771	1772	Totals
Madeira	1,071	930	763	696	865	4,325
Port	509	867	803	480	833	3,492

Fractions of tuns reported each year are consolidated in the totals. Compiled from *Customs* 16:1.

17. *Customs* 17:2.

18. *Ibid.*

19. The total imports of Madeira wine for the five-year period at the chief ports in tuns were: Quebec, 36; Boston, 353; New York, 987; Philadelphia, 755; Virginia, 585; Charleston, 728. Compiled from *Customs* 16:1.

20. Compiled from *Customs* 16:1. Tables of tons of shipping entering and clearing from New York, Boston, Philadelphia, and Charleston for the years 1768-72, taken from *Customs* 16:1 are included in V. D. Harrington, *The New York Merchant on the Eve of the Revolution*, pp. 359-68.

21. 4 George III, c. 15, sec. 29.

22. 4 George III, c. 15, sec. 27.

23. 4 George III, c. 15, sec. 28.

24. *Ibid.*, sec. 28.

25. 4 George III, c. 15, secs. 23, 25, 28.

26. 4 George III, c. 15, sec. 30.

27. *Ibid.*, sec. 45.

28. *Ibid.*, sec. 46.

29. *Ibid.*, sec. 44.

30. *Ibid.*, sec. 27.

31. *History of the United States,* III, 90-91, fn. 2.

32. *Treasury* 1:461.

33. Compiled from *Customs* 16:1.

34. *British Colonial Policy, 1754-1765,* p. 283. Receipts under the act of 1764 are given as follows: 1765, £3,217; 1766, £21,990; 1767, £29,244. These are net amounts. Gross amounts for the act of 1764 are estimated as £4,600 per year more. This makes a total for the three years of £63,651. The totals for 1768-72 shown above are £164,874. The London accounts in *Treasury* 1:461 for 1773-74 for the Sugar Act alone are £66,605. This makes a total of £295,130 which includes no collections in the West Indies for 1768-72.

35. Compiled from *Customs* 16:1.

36. Thomas Pownall, *The Administration of the Colonies* (2d ed., London, 1765), pp. 98-100. The ordinary expenses of government for Massachusetts in time of peace are given as £12,937 sterling, and those of New York at not more than £4,000.

8

OTHER TAX MEASURES

ALL TAX legislation after 1764 was based upon, and used, the elaborate machinery created by the later sections of the Sugar Act. Like that act, the new laws applied to the entire colonial Empire in America, and not just to a part of it. The chief burden of taxation under them fell upon colonial commerce. They were, therefore, a part of the program to substitute a new plan of regulating colonial trade for revenue purposes and use the proceeds to change the constitutional relations of the colonies to the home country.

The new acts ran into intense colonial opposition, which was supported by the British merchants and manufacturers interested in the American trade—particularly that of the continental colonies. It is no part of this discussion to enter into the constitutional and political controversy that finally ended in open armed rebellion. It is pertinent, however, to point out that all of the condemnation of the new measures went on with the exactions and extortions possible under the Sugar Act as an ever-present fact. All discussion of the new measures was based upon how they operated, or might operate, as a burden in addition to that already imposed by the Sugar Act.

Consideration of the new measures will be limited to their relation to the trade and navigation system and their effect upon the old loyalties to the Empire based upon fair treatment of colonial trade.

THE STAMP ACT

Most of the discussion of the Stamp Act has assumed that it was a measure that affected only that portion of the old colonial Empire that ultimately became the United States. Such an impression is misleading.

The Stamp Act applied to all British colonies in America, including Newfoundland, the Canadian provinces, and the West Indies. There were no exceptions. The standard American accounts emphasize the tax on newspapers, almanacs, pamphlets, advertisements, instruments used in court actions, land grants, liquor licenses, and commissions of various kinds.[1] These clauses are important because they spread the opposition to taxation by Parliament to new and influential elements in the population. They were of secondary importance as probable revenue producers.

A major point made in the opposition was that the Stamp Act levied an internal tax. It is true that the act contained clauses that would have made possible the creation of a system of imperial internal revenue in the colonies supplemental to that provided in the Sugar Act and enforced by a new system of imperial courts. But the main burden of the tax would have fallen upon, and was intended to fall upon, trade and shipping.

Under the new law ships had to have stamps for every clearance; for every cocket or bill of lading; for every agreement covering compensation for transferring goods from one place to another; and for each of four bonds covering enumerated goods, non-enumerated goods, iron and lumber. On the average these stamps must have cost approximately two pounds sterling for every clearance. The variable factor was the number of separate shipments in a cargo. This depended upon the number of persons shipping goods, the number of merchants to whom they were consigned, and the nature of the goods exported. Obviously ships engaged in the coastwise trade would be the hardest hit because of their more numerous entrances and clearances from colonial ports. But no ships were immune, and those engaged in the direct trade to Great Britain or the West Indies faced a new and heavy tax burden.

That the real weight of the Stamp Act was expected to fall upon trade and shipping is shown: (1) by the long list of merchants' and ships' papers that had to pay a stamp tax; (2) by the use made of the customs officers and the navy in enforcing the act—resulting in the widespread hostility to these officers that broke out suddenly in so many places; (3) by the consignment of stamped paper to various centers to supply the expected demand for stamps. The last point needs elaboration.

The best proof of who is expected to pay a tax is the plans for its collection by those who are charged with its enforcement. We have such a report in the case of the Stamp Act in a sworn statement made by J. Lloyd in 1772.[2] This includes the names of all distributors, the value of the stamped paper consigned to each, and the returns received. Thus we know from whom the major tax payments were expected.

The largest consignments of stamped paper went to the colonies with a large ocean trade. Thus on the continent stamps were consigned as follows: New York, £12,934; Massachusetts, £12,413; Pennsylvania, £11,852; South Carolina, £10,818; and Virginia, £9,684: a total of £57,701, or 47.5 per cent of the value of all stamped paper consigned to the continental colonies.[3]

The consignments of stamps to the West Indies shows even more clearly that the large returns were expected from the stamps on merchants' and ships' papers. In this area the white population was small and the slave population large. There were few newspapers, books, pamphlets, or printed advertisements. There were only limited court actions and almost no new patents to land. In spite of these conditions, the largest single consignment of stamps made to any colony went to Jamaica—a total of £15,781. At that time there were about 17,949 whites on the island.[4] Other relevant consignments were Barbados, £11,855, with a white population of 16,139; St. Kitts, £7,820, with a white population of less than 4,000; Antigua with an even smaller white population was consigned £7,761, or more than was expected from either North Carolina or Maryland.[5]

In addition to the tax on their shipping, the Stamp Act subjected British merchants doing business in America to new and heavy expenses. Nearly all American business was done on a credit basis. Where there is credit there is paper evidence of the indebtedness. Every such paper had to carry a stamp. Total credits extended to Americans ran into several millions of pounds sterling. The greater proportion of these were advances to tobacco, rice, and indigo planters in the areas south of Pennsylvania.

Inevitably, with credits extended to thousands of individuals, there was a considerable amount of litigation. Consequently, a large proportion of the stamp duties on court proceedings would have fallen upon British merchants who had obligations due them from American producers. Thus the Stamp Act was basically anti-trade because it taxed and burdened British and colonial trade.

The penal clauses of the act reflect the practices already approved in the Sugar Act. Penalties were to be assigned, one-third to the governor, one-third to the informer, and one-third to the crown. One-half of all seizures at sea went to the crews of the vessels making them.[6] Offenses against the Stamp Act and all other revenue acts were made triable in the new courts of admiralty at the option of the informer or the prosecutor.[7] This section was retained when the main act was repealed.

The act was in force from November 1, 1765, to March 17, 1766—a period of four and one-half months. It operated without much opposition in a part of the West Indies and in the newly conquered provinces, Lloyd's return shows total cash receipts of £3,292—9s-11d, nearly two-thirds of which was from Jamaica alone. Clearly this and the £500 from Barbados came from stamps on ships' papers.[8]

The unanimity with which British merchants joined in the opposition the Stamp Act was in no small part due to the burden it placed upon their own business, as well as to the possible injury to their trade from American opposition. Even the West Indies sugar planters joined in the protests because this new act hit them and not merely their customers to the north.

The extent to which British trade would have been taxed under the Stamp Act can only be estimated. Total known clearances from the continental colonies, Bermuda and the Bahamas, averaged more than 6,000 per year from 1768 to 1771.[9] The additional clearings from the West Indies considerably exceeded 2,000 per year. Thus there was an annual clearance from colonial ports of 8,000 or more ships. If, as estimated, the costs of the stamps averaged two pounds per clearance, shipping alone would have paid one-sixth of the expected annual return from the act of £100,000. One-fourth of this, at lowest estimate, would have fallen upon ships owned in England. When the other charges upon evidences of indebtedness and papers used in courts are included, probably one-fourth of the total taxes levied by the Stamp Act would have fallen as a charge upon British merchants doing business with America.

In the discussion in Parliament which accompanied the repeal of the Stamp Act it was openly charged in the House of Commons, and not denied, that the American Stamp Act riots had been incited by British merchants. The only existing Stamp Act cartoons were published and widely circulated in England.[10]

A study of the spread of colonial opposition to the Stamp Act shows that it began in Virginia where the planters would have been burdened by stamp taxes on new land grants in the western part of the colony. This opposition was supported by the merchants in the eastern counties. It then appeared in violent form in the shipping centers of New England, New York, and Philadelphia and was carried to the southern ports by the crews of the ships from the north as they arrived for their annual cargoes of southern produce. Nearly all of the later loyalist elements in the mercantile population supported the opposition to the Stamp Act. Lloyd's official report of returns from the sale of stamps shows that the act was as effectually prevented from going into operation in Antigua, Grenada, and Bermuda as it was in Massachusetts.[11]

Although the American mercantile interests had been brilliantly successful in forcing a repeal of the Stamp Act and in securing some modifications of the Sugar Act, their victory carried with it the seeds of further trouble. The agitation in America and the strong tone of the resolutions adopted by some colonial legislatures, questioning the right of Parliament to extend its regulations within the colonies, caused alarm even among the friends of America in England.

Most of the merchants who supported the American cause were Whigs. The widespread constitutional discussion unleashed by the Stamp Act controversy caused some to question the extent of the American claims. Some believed that the American position included an asserted constitutional right to set aside the trade and navigation laws upon which the commercial prosperity and political supremacy of England was believed to rest.

As the suspicion spread that the Americans might be aiming to break away from the imperial trade system, the mutual confidence between the merchants doing business in America and their colonial customers was undermined. The same suspicion undermined the ability of the British merchants to plead the American cause in England. Pitt had to put through the Declaratory Act as a part of the price for the repeal of the Stamp Act. This act in turn sowed deeply the seeds of distrust of British policy toward America.

As the Sugar Act remained in force and continued to raise increasing amounts of revenue and, as the policy of the king and his friends to put through their program for reorganization of the colonial empire had not changed, a renewal of the taxation schemes was inevitable.

THE TOWNSHEND ACTS

The illness of Pitt in late 1766 opened the way for Charles Townshend, Chancellor of the Exchequer, to assume leadership of a new program affecting the colonies. This was a double-barreled scheme of reform and revenue. His ideas were embodied in four measures, three of which became law within a period of four days from June 29 to July 2, 1767. The last was not passed until after his death.

To raise additional revenue he had two laws passed. The first authorized a Board of Customs Commissioners for America to organize the customs service on the model of the British service and to supervise in detail such part of the American customs as might be assigned to them by royal commission. Efficient administration was expected to increase the revenue from all other sources.

The second act authorized a new list of import duties to be collected at American ports. The third provided for drawbacks on tea exported to the colonies, the fourth liberalized the procedures in the new imperial admiralty courts in the colonies, presumably to the advantage of the colonists.

Of these measures only the Tea Act can be classed as even remotely resembling the older trade acts. It was designed to encourage the use of tea in the colonies by repealing the inland, or excise, duty in England of one shilling per pound; allowed a complete drawback of all customs duties paid upon importation into England; and permitted the exportation of tea from England to the colonies in any quantity, so long as it was in the original packages in which it was imported into England. Thus after July 5, 1767, tea could be exported to the colonies free from all British duties. Such legislation was designed to encourage the legitimate trade in tea within the Empire.

The Revenue Act, on the other hand, was thoroughly anti-trade. It singled out a group of articles of British manufacture which had formerly been shipped to the colonies without restriction and imposed upon them new import duties collected at the American ports. The list included five grades of glass, red and white lead for use in paint, painters' colors, and sixty-seven grades of paper.

All of these articles were of English manufacture. The raw materials for all of them existed in unlimited quantities in some or all of the continental colonies and several glass works were already in operation.[12] The better papers were made from linen rags, of which there were enormous supplies in the colonies, and a few successful paper mills were already in operation.[13] Lead deposits were plentiful and the treatment of the raw material to change it into the forms used in paint was known. The oil in which the paint was ground was made from flaxseed, which was a major crop in some of the colonies and an important export to England. The colonists also had mills for making linseed oil.[14] The chief ingredients of painters' colors were also plentiful. An import tax upon British manufactures of these articles could operate only as a protective tariff to encourage the manufacture of American products to compete with those produced in England.

In addition to the American tariff upon articles manufactured in England, there was a new import duty of three pence a pound on tea collected at American ports.

Townshend expected the new duties would yield a total of about £40,000 per year. In this he was over-optimistic, as the highest yield in any one year was less than half that sum. As the new colonial duties came hard on the heels of a reduction of the land tax in England, the constitutional controversy over taxation was reopened in an acute form. Americans could point out that as taxes were reduced on English taxpayers, they were increased on the colonists.

The constitutional controversy was intensified because the new duties fell upon the trade and shipping of the same colonies that were already carrying the major burden of taxation under the Sugar Act.

The provisions that revenue from the act could be used for expanding the customs organization indefinitely and that net receipts over the cost of collection could be applied to the payment of the salaries of colonial governors and judges were especially offensive. Under this arrangement royal officials in the colonies were to be supported by parliamentary taxes, but expenditures were to be made without specific appropriation by either Parliament or by any colonial legislature. The American revenue thus became a fund that could be expended by the king for political purposes just as was the secret service fund in England.

The turmoil over the principle of taxation and the use of the revenue has effectively obscured all discussion of the amount of revenue produced by the act. Here again we have the three sources of information referred to in discussing the Sugar Act. The report of the Inspector General is the more serviceable, as it includes the total amount of each article subject to duty imported at each port each year. This shows that white glass was chiefly used by the northern, and green glass by the southern, colonies. Paint and painters' colors also went largely to the colonies north of Maryland. Tea went predominantly to the northern colonies.

The results for the three years the act was in full operation are shown in the table below. This omits paper, as the task of computing the tax on sixty-seven kinds of paper at forty-three different ports is more difficult than the results justify. The paper duty at best was a nuisance tax and the yield was small. Paper went mainly to the commercial and governmental centers. The total distribution of the tax was approximately the same as for other taxes. Thus in 1768 a total of 46,960 square yards of wallpaper was imported, of which 22,919 yards were landed at Boston.

TABLE 11. TAX COLLECTIONS UNDER THE TOWNSHEND REVENUE ACT AT FOUR PRINCIPAL PORTS, 1768-70, EXCLUSIVE OF PAPER. CONTINENTAL COLONIES ONLY[15]

	Boston and Salem	New York	Phila- delphia	Charles- ton	Total All Ports
White glass @ 4s-8d per cwt.	£ 684	£ 355	£ 355	£ 215	£ 2,345
Green glass @ 14d per cwt. ..	169	135	78	300	1,523
Lead and painters' colors @ 2s per cwt.	168	116	155	91	814
Tea @ 3d per lb.	5,524	4,644	3,236	637	16,460
TOTALS	£6,545	£5,250	£3,824	£1,243	£21,142
Percentage of Total	30.9	24.8	18.	5.8	

Colonial opposition took the form of nonimportation against the taxed articles. This reduced the importations of glass and painters' colors in 1769 to about one-half of the amounts imported in 1768. Still further reductions followed in 1770 so that the repeal of the duties, other than that on tea, did not reduce actual total receipts by more than £1,500. Total collections under the Revenue Act had dropped from £13,202 in 1768 in the continental colonies to £2,727 in 1770.[16]

The concentration of taxes upon the trade and shipping of a few ports opened the possibility that the entire collection machinery could be paralyzed by mob action against the customs officials, as had been done so successfully in the case of the Stamp Act. There is no evidence that Americans knew the relative amount of the collections at the various ports. Officials of the Treasury in England had that information, and the Ministry clearly knew what it was doing when it provided for Customs Commissioners with headquarters in Boston. The immediate concentration of armed forces to protect them was based upon the known tax returns from that port, rather than upon any overt acts by the people of Boston. From a revenue point of view Boston was one-third of the total problem.

The Townshend Acts were not designed solely to bedevil the thirteen colonies that finally revolted. The Revenue Act applied equally to every colony and plantation in America, including Canada and the West Indies. There were no exemptions.

When the bill was before Parliament it was intended to give the new Commissioners of Customs jurisdiction over the customs service of all American ports. Its authors were obviously ignorant of the geography of the Empire in America and did not realize that London was actually nearer to many American ports in terms of communication, than was any port on the continent. After the bill was passed, the London and other merchants interested in the trade to the sugar islands became aware of the great inconvenience the new measure would impose upon them if they had to take all their complaints to an administrative board located in Boston or any other port on the American continent. Their protests were so vigorous that the Treasury Board was forced to rule that the West Indies should be excluded from the jurisdiction of the new board.[17]

It was a fateful decision. For the first time in the history of the colonial Empire it was divided for administrative purposes. It was never again to be united. The new board, three thousand miles from London, was so far removed from the center of imperial administration that it was not amenable to changing public opinion. Its entire operation created hostility to the home government. *The actual separation of the continental colonies from the rest of the Empire dates from the creation of this independent administrative board.*

The Customs Commissioners by their commission were given jurisdiction only from Davis Strait on the north to Florida Strait on the south, but included Bermuda and the Bahamas. They had no jurisdiction over the sugar islands, but that area was subject to all the provisions of the other acts.

As the Inspector General had no jurisdiction over the customs

officers in the West Indies, we have no reports from the port officials in that area comparable to those from the continental ports.
There are no consolidated returns of the collections under the
various tax measures.

Beer estimates the gross collections under the Sugar Act for
1767 at £33,844 for all the colonies.[18] This is £6,185 more than
was collected gross from the continental colonies in 1768, which
would indicate that the receipts from the West Indies under the
Sugar Act were about one-fourth of those reported from the continental colonies.

There are no comparable data concerning the receipts from the
Townshend Revenue Act; but using the known exports of tea,
glass, paper, and painters' colors from England in 1773 as a measure of what should have been collected in the various colonies,
the collections in the West Indies were probably one-fifth of those
collected in the continental ports.

We are now in a position to consolidate the burden of all the
tax measures. The table below shows the situation in 1772 when

TABLE 12. TOTAL TAX COLLECTIONS UNDER ALL LAWS IN THE CONTI-
NENTAL COLONIES IN 1772, EXCLUSIVE OF PENALTIES AND FEES[19]

	Boston and Salem	New York	Phila-delphia	Charles-ton	Total All Ports
Navigation Acts	£ 1	£	£ 75	£ 355	£ 1,490
Sugar Act	14,476	6,437	7,651	2,332	42,570
Townshend Revenue Act	1,340	7	2	277	3,300
TOTALS	£15,817	£6,444	£7,728	£2,964	£47,360
Percentage of Total	33.4	13.5	16.3	6.2	

the gross collections were at their height. It still further emphasizes
the concentration of taxation upon the trade and shipping of the
four continental colonies where revolutionary sentiment developed most rapidly.

There have been many general statements that Townshend
raised a revenue by enforcing the trade and navigation acts. A
glance at the table above discloses how little of the revenue actually reported came from the Navigation Acts, cited by customs
officials as 25 Charles II and 4 George III. These provided for

colonial export duties on enumerated products shipped elsewhere within the colonial Empire than to England. The most common of these were indigo, rice, fustic, and tobacco. In no year from 1767 to 1774 did such duties exceed five per cent of the total collected and only in 1773 did they total £2,517 and were only £1,160 in 1768, the year of maximum collections under the Townshend Revenue Act.[20]

The total amounts taken from the Americans by the various revenue measures have been greatly underestimated. Channing is the only writer in the colonial field that attempts a specific statement. He estimates a gross collection of two hundred thousand pounds for the period 1768 to 1774.[21]

The table below has been compiled to cover the entire period

TABLE 13. TOTAL COLLECTIONS IN AMERICA UNDER THE DIFFERENT REVENUE LAWS, EXCLUSIVE OF SEIZURES AND COLLECTIONS IN THE WEST INDIES FROM 1768 TO 1774

	Sugar Act[22]	Stamp Act[23]	Townshend Revenue Act[24]	Total	Navigation Act[25]
1765	£14,091	£3,292	£	£ 17,383	£ 2,954
1766	26,696	....	.....	26,696	7,373
1767	33,844	....	197	34,041	3,905
1768	24,659	....	13,202	37,861	1,160
1769	39,938	....	5,561	45,499	1,294
1770	30,910	....	2,727	33,637	1,828
1771	27,086	....	4,675	31,761	1,446
1772	42,570	....	3,300	45,870	1,490
1773	39,531	....	2,572	42,103	2,517
1774	27,074	....	921	27,995	672
TOTALS	£306,399	£3,292	£33,155	£342,846	£24,639

of colonial taxation by Parliament. It does not tell the entire story because receipts from 1768 to 1774 are for the continental colonies only and do not include collections in the West Indies. It also omits receipts from seizures.

We have no separate account of the customs duties collected in the West Indies. The best estimate that can be made indicates collections in these islands under the Sugar Act and the Townshend Act at between one-fourth and one-fifth of the sums collected in the continental colonies. Using the lowest estimate for the years

1768-74, total collections are increased by £52,845 to a total of £395,691.

In addition to collections on imports there were the sums taken from the colonists by seizures for some alleged violation of some regulation. We have reports of such seizures from the continental colonies for the years 1768-74. Property seized by customs officers was sold and the net proceeds divided: one-third to the governor, one-third to the informer, and one-third to the treasury. Thus the sums reported represent not more than one-third of the value of the property taken from the colonists, and probably much less. Seizures were disposed of at forced sale and in many cases there was collusion, so that sums reported were considerably below actual values. Hancock's sloop *Liberty* which he valued at £1,000, was bid in by the Customs Commissioner for only £102-15-0½, or just over ten per cent of its actual value.

Seizures by the navy were divided: one-half to the crews making the capture and one-half to the treasury. As such seizures were sold under the same conditions as those made by customs officers, the amount received was always far below actual values of the property taken.

Actual values of the property seized could not have been less than five times the sums reported by customs officers and four times those reported by the navy. Applying these ratios we get the following results. Receipts from seizures by customs officers in the continental colonies from 1768 to 1774 totaled £6,080,[26] which represented not less than £30,400 of American property. Similar seizures reported by the navy amounted to £7,639,[27] representing colonial property worth not less than £30,556. Thus seizures alone must have cost the Americans not less than £60,956, which, added to the direct collections, gives a total of £456,647, as the direct takings of the customs officers exclusive of fees, direct plunder, and costs of defending suits in the admiralty courts.

All of these charges fell upon the shipping and trading part of the population. As has already been shown, the heaviest burden was borne by a few colonies. These were the leaders of the resistance movement.

FEES

In addition to the burden of direct taxation already discussed, there was a system of fees levied upon those who had to do business at the customhouses. This amounted to an additional tax. The sums so taken are not recorded in the receipts reported by the customs officers and the total incidence of this charge can only be estimated.

So long as officers of the customs were on salary they were paid out of the revenue collected. In 1765 all colonial customs officers were authorized by act of Parliament to take fees for their work in addition to whatever salary they were paid. Tables of fees were officially approved and, if any customs officer was on duty at a port where no table of fees had been approved, he was authorized to take the same fees as charged at the nearest port that had an authorized schedule.[28]

This law quickly led to the taking of fees at all ports. Quebec put in force the schedule of charges at the port of New York. In effect it increased existing taxes by the amount of the fees collected.

There were fees for entering and clearing; for entering a vessel out; for bonds required under the Sugar Act; for certificates for goods entitled to bounties in England and for goods imported subject to duty; for cockets covering all goods exported; for every entry of goods imported by each merchant in a single ship; for bills of health; for registering a ship or for certifying a lost register; for registering seamen; and for an endorsement on the register when a new master took charge of a ship.

The fees varied somewhat from port to port. An examination of those charged at Savannah and New York in 1771 indicates that the lowest possible total fees for entering and clearing a small vessel engaged in intercolonial trade was about £1 sterling at Savannah and $8.75 at New York. Fees for larger ships and those engaged in the European or West Indian trade totaled twice that amount. Vessels engaged in the purely local trade within a province were subject to somewhat smaller fees.[29]

An average charge of a pound and a half for every recorded entry of a vessel seems conservative. In 1771 there were 6,327 such entries recorded at the ports of continental colonies alone.[30] Fees on this trade must have approximated £10,000 per year. In addition, approximately fifty per cent more was collected on the shipping trade in the West Indies, a very large part of which fell upon merchants from the continental colonies.

Fees as a form of taxation became a major grievance of the colonies with no large ports. As fees became uniform it cost a shipper as much to enter and clear with a partial cargo as with a full one. This steadily increased the relative cost of doing business at the minor ports. Complaints poured into England from merchants whose trade was thus handicapped and from the colonies whose commerce was injured. These complaints bulk so large in the official records that they seem almost more important between 1770 and 1774 than objections to the revenue laws.

The most bitter complaints came from Jamaica, West Florida, Newfoundland, and Connecticut. Some of the colonies attempted to enact fee bills of their own to replace the obnoxious fee practices of the customs service. The governor of West Florida claimed that fees charged vessels plying between Mobile and Pensacola amounted to one-half what was received for freights. The most voluminous complaint came from Jamaica, where it was shown that ships were charged two fees, one at Kingston and the other at Savanna la Marr. The agent of Jamaica described such charges as "unheard of and exorbitant."[31]

Merchants and seamen especially resented these charges because they realized that they were being singled out for a business tax, every penny of which went into the personal pockets of the customs officers and none of it to the general revenue to pay colonial officers and promote the general defense. There was no way to evade the charges. Vessels could not enter a port without paying the fees and if any ship was encountered at sea without all the required papers it was subject to seizure. Every required certificate, bond, or paper was supplied only on payment of a prescribed fee.

Only the outbreak of hostilities ended the controversy. It was most acute in the years when the agitation over other forms of taxation had subsided. As it was a grievance of the shipping interests and not of the public generally, it is recorded chiefly in official records and not in the local newspapers and controversial pamphlets. The loyalty of a particular class was being alienated by continued injustice.

In estimating the total cost of the revenue system an item of about £150,000 must be added for the period 1765-75 to cover the fees collected by the customs officers. This charge, like the direct taxes, fell most heavily upon the trade at the ports of Boston, New York, Philadelphia, Charleston, and Savannah. These fees were not a part of the normal navigation system, but an additional burden imposed as a part of the revenue laws.

Gathering together the various items taken legally and openly by the customs officers, including revenue collections, seizures, and authorized fees, we have an estimated total of £606,647 as the known burden imposed upon American trade by the revenue measures. In addition there was an unknown and unmeasurable burden imposed by plain revenue racketeering which will be discussed in the next chapter.

REFERENCES

CHAPTER 8

1. G. E. Howard, *Preliminaries of the Revolution,* Chap. vii; Edward Channing, *History of the United States,* III, 46-64; Curtis P. Nettels, *Roots of American Civilization,* pp. 613-33, are excellent accounts from the strictly American point of view.

2. *A.O.3*:1086. Public Record Office, London.

3. *Ibid.*

4. Frank W. Pittman, *Development of the British West Indies,* p. 374.

5. The consignment to North Carolina was £7,446 and to Maryland, £7,428. *A.O.3*:1086.

6. Section LIX.

7. Section LVII.

8. Report of J. Lloyd, October 18, 1772. Total sales included: Quebec, £316-10-8; Montreal, £173-3-9; West Florida, £50; Georgia, £45; Jamaica, £2,097-2-0; Barbados, £500; St. Kitts, £8-13-6; a total of £3,292-9-11. *A.O.3*: 1086, Public Record Office, London.

9. *Customs* 16:1. This did not include the large number of smaller vessels doing a strictly local business that did not clear regularly, but could have been forced to secure stamps for such papers as they carried.

10. *British Antidote to Caledonian Poison,* 7th ed. (London, 1767).

11. There were no cash returns from any of these colonies. The stamp distributors' accounts were short in all of them, showing that stamps got out of their hands and could not be accounted for. The balances not accounted for were Antigua, £2,275; Grenada, £756; Bermuda, £786. For all America the unaccounted balances totaled £64,155-12-5½. *AO3*:1086.

12. Victor S. Clark, *Manufactures in the United States* (Washington, 1916), pp. 168-69; J. L. Bishop, *A History of American Manufactures* (Philadelphia, 1868), I, Chap. x.

13. Bishop, *op. cit.,* Chap. viii.

14. *Ibid.,* pp. 121, 143.

15. Compiled from *Customs* 16:1.

16. *Treasury* 1:461, Public Record Office, London.

17. Treasury Board to the Commissioners of Customs in England, August 7, 1767. *Treasury* 11:28, p. 144.

18. G. L. Beer, *British Colonial Policy, 1754-1765* (New York, 1907), pp. 282-84.

19. Compiled from *Customs* 16:1.

20. "Gross Receipts of American Customs," *Treasury* 1:461, Public Record Office, London.

21. *History of the United States,* III, 91.

22. Amounts for 1765-1767 are from figures quoted by G. L. Beer, *British Colonial Policy, 1754-1765,* p. 283; sums for 1768-72 are compiled from *Customs* 16:1; and those for 1773-74 are from *Treasury* 1:461.

23. From *A.O.3*:1086.

24. From *Treasury* 1:461.

25. Amounts from 1765-67 are from Beer, *op. cit.;* those from 1768-74 are from *A.O.3*:1086.

26. *Treasury* 1:461.

27. *Ibid.*

28. George III, c. 45, sec. 28.

29. Complete tables of fees charged at these and other ports are in the Treasury papers. Those at Savannah are listed in sterling. Those at New York are in dollars; presumably the Spanish milled dollar. At some ports they were in terms of local currency. *Treasury* 1:482, Public Record Office, London.

30. *Customs* 16:1.

31. Most of these complaints are recorded in *Treasury* 1:482, 486.

9

ERA OF CUSTOMS RACKETEERING

THE revenue provisions of the acts of 1764 and 1767 alone did not create enough friction to affect the loyalty of the great mass of Americans. To be sure there was widespread discussion of the constitutional issues involved. There was a renewal of nonimportation agreements, but there was no general opposition as there was in the case of the Stamp Act. In more than half the ports the new revenue act produced scarcely a ripple. Why the difference? The evidence indicates that it was the use made of the incidental provisions of these acts to attack fundamentally the liberty and property of Americans that in six short years transformed thousands of loyal British subjects into active revolutionists.

The major part of the damage was done between the years 1768 and 1772 by the tactless, arbitrary, and mercenary operation of these laws by a new race of customs officers and particularly by the conduct of the American Customs Commissioners at Boston.

NEW CONDITIONS CAUSE FRICTION

The same day that the Townshend Revenue Act was passed another act creating an American Board of Customs Commissioners with jurisdiction over all colonies north of the Florida Straits, including Bermuda and the Bahamas, received the approval of Parliament.[1] Within six months the personnel had been selected, the headquarters fixed at Boston and the Board had assumed its duties.

The selection of personnel was unfortunate. Robinson and Paxton had been customs officers at Rhode Island and Boston respectively. Hulton had wide experience in the British service but did not know America. Temple knew America well, as he had served as Inspector General of Customs and knew nearly every port and the local conditions, but his advice was ignored and he was removed from the Board. Burch went along with the majority. It was currently reported that Paxton had paid Townshend a high price for the American appointment.[2] If he did, that was not unusual, because it was a custom to treat salaried offices as annuities to be bought and sold like ranks in the army. Those who had the appointing power were not always above accepting a gratuity for making appointments.

The selection of Boston as headquarters for the Board was unfortunate for the future of the Empire. Boston had long been the cultural, intellectual, and commercial metropolis of America. Whatever happened there was quickly known wherever ships could sail or newspapers be circulated. Massachusetts, Connecticut, and Rhode Island were chartered provinces. The new program of colonial reorganization threatened them and their cherished liberties more than any other section. They were all actively interested in commerce. Their ships and seamen carried New England products and New England grievances to every port in America and Great Britain.

In addition Massachusetts had a governor and a lieutenant-governor closely connected politically with the party of King's Friends in England who were heading a movement to change fundamentally the existing form of American colonial government and set up a centralized type of control patterned more or less on the French and Spanish models. In no other colony was there a governor and subordinate officials actively interested in creating a local following of American King's Friends. Bernard and Hutchinson were the secret advisers of the ruling faction in England and their advice had more weight in shaping the new American legislation than that of other American officials.[3]

From the day they landed, the Customs Commissioners became a part of the Bernard-Hutchinson faction and devoted the vast powers entrusted to them to a promotion of basic changes in the century-old colonial-imperial system. They entered upon their new duties with the attitude of the staff of an army occupying an enemy country.[4] Some of them assumed the airs of royal pro-consuls sent out to bring law and order to a rebellious colonial world. Had it not been for the unfortunate personalities of Robinson, Paxton, and Hulton there might have been no Revolution. From 1768 to 1772 almost open warfare existed between the agents of the Commissioners and the trading fraternity of New England and some of the other major ports.

This warfare, however, was very uneven. In Boston the Commissioners insisted that their authority had to be backed by armed force. In other districts the duties were paid by American and British importers without friction and with no appeal at any time by the customs officers for assistance from the executive authority. New England and Charleston, South Carolina, were the areas of most intense warfare against American trade. North Carolina, Virginia, and Maryland were scarcely molested.[5] There were relatively few complaints from Pennsylvania, New Jersey, or New York. At the latter port, located at the very headquarters of the commanding general of all British troops in America, there is no instance recorded of the customs officers asking for military protection. Even in the middle of 1775, with British authority entirely gone and American troops camped near the customhouse, merchants entered and cleared their vessels at the customhouse and paid the duties.[6]

Reasons for this difference can only be suggested. The chances for personal profit from customs extortions were in direct proportion to the number of ships and amount of trade. Of the forty-four regular ports south of Canada the Commissioners reported in 1769 that most of the duties were collected at ten and that the other thirty-four were chiefly preventive and cost more than they yielded.[7] Hence there were twenty or more ports where there was not sufficient opportunity for plunder to attract a certain type of customs officer.

The governor of each province had a good deal of authority over the customs service and received one-third of the value of all seizures. His attitude was important. If he was not interested in adding to his personal income by extortions imposed upon shipping and insisted upon a program of fairness and just treatment, there was little opportunity for oppressive tactics in his province. If a colony was desirous of encouraging trade and building up its commerce, customs officers had to be reasonable. This was particularly true of West Florida, East Florida, Georgia, North Carolina, Nova Scotia, and Canada. In Pennsylvania and Maryland the proprietary interests went out of their way not to offend important groups because they might join in attacks upon the proprietary interests. In Virginia and Maryland the merchants were largely representative of the Scotch and other interests closely associated with the supporters of the ruling political faction in Great Britain. Attacking traders with such connections could have unpleasant repercussions at home. For some reason it was not done.[8]

The period of intensive warfare against American shipping coincided in time with the active policy of nonimportation as a means of securing the repeal of the revenue measures. It is possible that the whole oppressive program was a counter-measure to force an abandonment of nonimportation by putting pressure upon American merchants and their shipping.

Taxation Provisions Used for Racketeering

The clauses in the Sugar Act of 1764 and the Revenue Act of 1767 that became the basis of the legal plundering of American commerce were: (1) the bonding provisions—one for enumerated goods, one for non-enumerated goods, and one each for iron and lumber—which the law recited must be given *before* any goods were laden on board any vessel; (2) that any vessel that was decked or was of more than twenty tons burden found more than two leagues from shore had to have bonds and other clearance papers. The penalty in each of the above was the confiscation of ship, tackle, stores, and cargo. In addition was the provision that all vessels had to carry cockets listing in detail every cargo item on board. Penalty was forfeiture of the goods not included on the cockets. Another was the provision that a master had to go to the customhouse when arriving in a port district, report his vessel and its cargo, and receive a permit to enter and unload. Any breaking of bulk before proper entry laid a ship open to seizure. Landing or disposing of any article, regardless of conditions, was breaking bulk.

To these must be added the legal provision that the customs officer who informed of any breach of the above provisions was entitled to one-third of the value of all confiscations; the governor a third, and the revenue the other third. Seizures made at sea went one-half to the crew and one-half to the revenue. All trials were in the admiralty courts.

In addition to these provisions in the laws were certain practices that had the force of law. In the admiralty court goods or ships once seized were the property of the crown unless legally claimed by the owner.[9] To maintain a claim the owner had to prove the innocence of goods or ship. Thus there was no burden of proof upon the customs officers. The entire burden of proof was upon the claimant. Even if the seizure was made unjustly and the goods or ship awarded to the owner, it was the practice of the judge to certify on the record "probable cause" for the action of the customs officers. This certification restored the property to the owner but imposed upon him all or part of the costs, including the fees of the judge, and barred any future damage suits against the customs officers in the civil courts. Thus no matter how unfair a seizure might be the American claimant suffered serious financial loss. The dice were all loaded against him. Every suit he brought against the customs officers merely added to their revenues. It was these known practices that made admiralty courts so odious from one end of America to the other.

ROBBING THE LITTLE FELLOWS

In the controversy that developed over the enforcement of the revenue laws the greatest burden fell upon those who were financially weakest. They were not able to protect themselves by well-placed bribes or by contesting illegal seizures in the courts. In the main they had to endure such treatment as they received. It was cheaper to submit to illegal exactions than risk seizures and court costs.

Only a small part of what happened between 1768 and 1772 can be pieced together from the fragmentary reports that are in the papers of the Customs Commissioners and reported in the newspapers. From such accounts as are available it is clear the little fellows were the victims of purely technical provisions of the laws. In general they were engaged in the coasting trade or in operating small vessels in the West Indian trade with an occasional venture to Great Britain or the wine islands. The technical clauses used to entrap them are discussed below.

Ships engaged in the foreign trade were charged with breaking bulk before entry. In the past this had meant discharging a material part of their cargo at places not under the control of a customs officer. Massachusetts had a very long coastline, reaching past Cape Cod to Rhode Island on the south, including Nantucket, Martha's Vineyard, and other islands. On the north it included the entire coast of Maine and its indentations. There were only two regular customhouses—Boston and Salem. There were several other points where naval officers were maintained by the Port of Boston, such as Nantucket and Martha's Vineyard.

As there was very little direct trade between Rhode Island and England, goods bound for Newport or Providence had commonly been loaded on ships bound for Boston and transhipped at Nantucket. There was no ground to suspect fraud in the customary practice as everything was done under the eye of a customs officer and the papers showed the exact transaction. Without warning, ships following the regular practice were seized on arrival at Boston for breaking bulk before entry.[10]

Ships coming from the West Indies, and from the colonies to the southward, frequently stopped at Martha's Vineyard; sometimes wind-bound, sometimes because of storms, sometimes to make necessary repairs. If a vessel shifted cargo to make repairs, disposed of a few lemons that were in danger of spoiling, discharged a few bushels of grain to relieve local distress, or some members of the crew sold their little private ventures, the vessels were charged with breaking bulk before entry even when there was not the slightest reason to suspect fraud.[11]

The bonding clauses were a common source of abuse and loading *before* bonds were given was a common excuse for seizure.

This especially harassed the little wood and lumber boats plying along the coast of Massachusetts and Connecticut. They loaded regularly at points remote from any customhouse. As they were engaged wholly in purely local trade and could not possibly have violated any trade law, they had never before been required to enter, clear, give bonds, etc. They were now subject to seizure and otherwise annoyed.

The abuse of the bonding clauses was not confined to the continental colonies, but extended even to the West Indies. Turks Islands were an important source of salt for the fishing industry. Ships going there entered and cleared at New Providence. The customs agent at New Providence reported in 1771 that Lieutenant Dundas of the British armed schooner *St. Lawrence* was seizing vessels and sending them in for trial because they were loading salt without first giving bond for non-enumerated goods. This forced vessels to go to New Providence, 180 leagues from Turks Islands, give bond, then proceed to Turks Islands, which was dangerous navigation and took a month for the average sailing vessel. With the salt on board they then had to return over the same dangerous route to clear their vessels at New Providence. He called it a "cruel practice" on the part of the customs service. Americans called it war against British commerce for the personal profit of naval officers equipped with commissions as customs officers.[12]

The clause that was subject to the greatest abuse and produced the maximum inconvenience and friction among local merchants and shipowners was section twenty-nine of the Sugar Act. This required cockets covering all articles shipped from one colony to another. The Customs Commissioners insisted that this clause applied to all trade whether inter-colonial or within a province. Ships were seized at Charleston, South Carolina, at New York, at Boston, and at many other ports for carrying goods from one port to another within the same province without regularly entering and clearing. There was no charge of fraud in any case that has come to light.

At Boston the Commissioners applied to Attorney-General Sewell for an opinion on this and the bonding clauses. He ruled that they all applied to shipments from one colony to another and did not apply to shipments from one point in a colony to another point in the same colony.[13] In spite of this legal advice, they ordered a ship bound from Salem to Boston with a partial cargo of molasses seized because it did not carry a cocket listing all goods on board. The owner contested the suit and Judge Auchmuty of the Vice-Admiralty court at Boston returned the ship and cargo to its owner as there was no violation of law. He, however, entered a ruling of "probable cause" because the owner of the molasses did not have in his possession a certificate covering the importation at Salem. The costs of the suit were thus thrown on the owner.[14]

Not satisfied with a legal defeat at Charleston and the double defeat at Boston, the Commissioners appealed to the Treasury Board in London for an opinion from the Attorney-General in England. He ruled as did Sewall, Auchmuty, and Leigh that clause twenty-nine applied only to shipments from one colony to another.[15] Within a little more than three months this ruling of the Attorney-General of England was known in America and widely publicized in the newspapers.[16]

In spite of the adverse ruling of the highest law officer in the Empire the Customs Commissioners enforced their rule that local boats had to enter and clear, even if bound only to points a few miles distant within the harbor district. Even open sand-boats plying to and from Boston to Cape Ann were forced to comply with the new rules. Thus every coaster was forced to enter and clear and pay the fees, which amounted to about three dollars for a clearance.[17] As these vessels were not carrying articles subject to duty, no additional revenue was secured from this practice, only additional fees. Every penny of this increased financial burden went as extra compensation to the customs officers, because fees were their personal property. This practice was especially obnoxious because it merely burdened trade, had no relation whatever to enforcing the trade and navigation laws, and was known to be held illegal by the law officers of the crown.

Judge Auchmuty's ruling that the owner of the molasses in the case of the *Hope* should have had a certificate of legal importation was stretched into a formal requirement that all articles subject to an import duty must have with them certificates covering the time and place of their importation, the duties paid, the name of the original purchaser, etc. No article could be loaded on board any vessel for shipment to another point without such a certificate. Its absence might lay the owner of the boat open to seizure. The possession of such goods without covering certificates might give legal grounds for an attempted confiscation.

In the absence of a common circulating medium trade went on by a process of barter. Certain commodities became a common medium of exchange, like cigarettes by our armies of occupation. Anybody would accept such commodities in payment of goods or services because they could be passed on and even used to settle bills due in England. Molasses, wine, oil, and indigo were the articles most widely used for this purpose. All but oil were subject to import duties in the colonies.

It has been assumed that good salable wine was wanted only for beverage purposes. That was its ultimate use, but in the meantime it might be used to settle accounts in a number of places. As has already been indicated, wine from Madeira was imported mainly at a very few ports with a direct trade to southern Europe. Once arrived in America it began to circulate because of its commodity value in exchange. The local distribution was usually by means of the little coasters.

When certificates had to accompany every cask of wine or barrel of molasses there was trouble. As these articles changed hands they soon came into the possession of individuals who could produce no certificates and had no way of knowing who was the original purchaser. Consequently, such goods had to be disposed of on a black market, supplied with false certificates, transported overland, or labeled something else. Thus goods regularly imported and duties paid might be forced to take on the appearance of a petty smuggling trade. If there was trouble with the customs officers, it was usually some small trader or shipowner who took the rap.

The Customs Commissioners set up an elaborate coast guard service along the coast of the northern colonies, composed of naval vessels, and especially commissioned craft. Crews on board were commissioned as customs officers. Some were paid regular salaries, but most relied upon what they could make out of seizures, just like privateers in time of war. They acquired a reputation of rummaging vessels in most offensive ways and of seizing goods and ships on the most trivial and technical grounds. The most notorious of these, the *Gaspee* and the *Liberty*—John Hancock's former sloop—were attacked and destroyed by the outraged sailors and shipowners. There were several other similar but less well-known episodes.

Along with the new and offensive coast guard service, or Spanish *Guarda Costas*, as they were generally referred to in the public press, was a regular system of informers. These were "stool pigeons" employed by customs officers and especially by the Customs Commissioners. Some may have been paid small sums out of the very large "incidental expenses" of the Commissioners, but others were promised a share in what could be seized. They always were ostensibly engaged in work other than the customs service. Some served as sailors on board merchant vessels to report any little thing that could give ground for a seizure. Others worked about the ports and alehouses, picking up what gossip they could from the sailors. Others were honest but necessitous men who were promised a small share in the part of the seizures that belonged to the customs officers. They were hated more than regular employees and were roughly handled when discovered.[18] They too preyed mostly upon the small traders.

One of the most notorious cases happened at Philadelphia. Seizures by officers at that port had been small.[19] John Swift, the collector, planned to increase his income by employing informers. One of these reported he knew where there was some wine that was not covered by proper certificates and could be seized for illegal importation. The action of the informer became known, a mob formed and severely mishandled him. To save himself the informer confessed to the mob that he had only acted as he did because his family was in need and Swift had promised him a small share in the expected condemnation.

Swift was so alarmed by the public hostility aroused that he reported the entire incident in great detail to the Customs Commissioners, stated that he had offered the poor fellow a shilling a pipe—or less than one per cent—out of his share if they got a conviction and stated he thought he had a right to dispose of his third of such seizures as he saw fit. He was in such fear for his own personal safety that he had converted all the customs cash in his hands into good bills and had mailed them to the Commissioners at Boston.[20]

Thus the use of informers to increase the personal gains of the customs officers does not rest upon mere assertions in the patriot newspapers, but upon the signed statements of the customs officers themselves. Their admissions disclose a practice more reprehensible than that charged in the most partisan newspapers of the time.

INVASION OF SEAMEN'S RIGHTS

The provision that the master of a vessel must have in his possession cockets covering all articles on board, when construed literally, trespassed upon the rights of ordinary seamen. It was a custom-of-the-sea of long standing that various employees on board a vessel should, in addition to their regular wages, have the privilege of engaging in certain small ventures of their own. Whatever a sailor carried in his chest was his to dispose of as he saw fit. Sometimes by agreement other articles, such as an animal or a barrel or two of produce, were carried free as the property of the mate or other seaman to be disposed of when and where he chose. Prior to 1768 such petty ventures were not treated as a part of the cargo and were not subject to the rules of entry and payment of duties.[21]

Under the Customs Commissioners this ancient custom-of-the-sea was no longer respected. Search at sea became a regular practice. In such search articles on board were checked against the cockets and other clearance papers. Articles not covered were subject to confiscation. It had never been a custom for the master of a vessel to include the little ventures of his crew as a part of his regular cargo. In most cases he did not know what was in such petty speculations. He was not responsible for them in any way.

The searching parties from the new coast guard vessels ignored this old custom-of-the-sea. They were directly interested in what could be seized. Whatever they found on board not covered by the cockets they took. In too many cases they were rough and ruthless, broke open trunks, boxes, and seamen's chests and seized what they could.[22] To members of the crew any seizure was equivalent to confiscation, because they had neither the time or the money to contest the matter in court. So far as they were concerned, there was no law to protect them. A small loss to men of that group was serious, because it represented so large a part of their capital. Even in time of war they had not been exposed to much greater losses.

This invasion of the ancient rights of seamen created feelings of personal injustice and group animosities toward the customs officers that rapidly dissolved the cement of loyalty. A condition of open warfare between the new customs service and the seafaring population and their friends was soon in full operation. It was not a cold war either. In every major port—Boston, Salem, Providence, New London, New York, Philadelphia, Charleston, and even Bermuda[23]—the hostility of the seamen and mechanics toward the whole revenue system was far more pronounced than among the merchants or any other group of the population. Every known riot involving customs officers was dominated by seafaring men. There were few loyalists among the entire class of sailors and longshoremen. The volumes dealing with loyalists and their claims discloses an amazing absence of names from this group. To them the contest was much more than a discussion of abstract constitutional principles. They were supporters of the old mercantile system of the British Empire as it was before 1764, including the rights of seamen.

Entrapping Merchants by Sudden Changes in Practice

In the era of customs racketeering one of the common tricks was to overlook minor deviations from the letter of the law for a time and then suddenly insist upon compliance. By this device either rich seizures could be made or many small ones. Either one added materially to the personal fortunes of the customs officers. The records show cases of this kind from Charleston, South Carolina, the coast of Connecticut, from Massachusetts, and from Quebec. It is reasonable to assume that there were many other cases that did not get into the records.

There were two common grounds for seizure that were subject to this variation in practice—giving bonds before goods were placed on board and checking the cargo for exact compliance with the cockets.

It was the practice at most ports for ships to secure a permit to load, find such freight as they could, then go to the customhouse, report their cargoes, give bonds, secure certificates, and comply with all the rules of clearing regularly. There was no possible suspicion of evasion of any of the trade, navigation, or revenue laws in the regular practice. The law, however, specified that bonds should be given *before* any goods were placed on board. In many cases it was physically impossible to comply with the letter of the law. Hundreds of ships had to load at points remote from the residence of any customs officer and could not possibly comply with such regulations until they reached the nearest customhouse. It had been the usual practice for customs officers to coöperate with the trade in adjusting local practices to local conditions. A sudden change in practice could entrap a number of ships, lay them open to seizure, or force them to pay for being let off.

A similar situation existed in the case of wood and lumber boats and the innumerable small craft that operated along such coasts as Long Island Sound. Such craft had never been required to enter, give bonds, clear, carry cockets, etc. A sudden change in policy provided an opportunity for a rich harvest from minor exactions levied upon these craft under the threat of confiscation.[24]

In 1768 the grossness of this abuse resulted in complaints and appeals to the Treasury Board in London and a consequent reference to the Attorney-General of England for a formal opinion as to the legality of the practice. He condemned such abuses in no uncertain terms. He held that the customary practice at a port was a part of the law. If a specific administrative regulation was not enforced this amounted to public notice to the trading fraternity. They were legally entitled to govern themselves accordingly. If there was to be a change in such indulgences and the law enforced literally, public notice should be given a sufficient time ahead so that merchants could know of the change and plan to comply with it. Any other practice was too obviously an effort to entrap honest traders and subject them to vexatious charges for the personal profit of the customs officials.[25]

There is no evidence that this instruction was passed on by the Customs Commissioners in Boston to the local port officials. The evidence suggests that it was suppressed. Many months after this opinion was given, abuses of this kind happened at a port very recently visited by one of the regular customs inspectors from Boston. The inference is that he suggested to the local customs officer how he could increase his income by sudden seizures.

Most of the molasses was imported from the French sugar islands, where it was obtained by a process of barter. Many ships loaded at points remote from the customhouses. Apparently there was no attempt to gauge exports except by counting the containers. There was frequently careless loading. Masters of vessels knew only approximately the number of gallons on board. Clearance papers probably understated the amount on board, because if there was any shortage when a vessel reached port it might be charged with breaking bulk.

When the Customs Commissioners set up careful gauging of all liquid imports the actual number of gallons found on board did not always agree with the number stated to be on board by the cockets. What difference this made is not clear. The duty was paid on the number of gallons actually found on board. There was no concealment and little chance for fraud. The accounts show that such excess revealed by gauging every container was made an excuse for seizure of vessel and cargo.[26]

That racketeering was not confined to ports under the direct control of the Customs Commissioners is revealed by an impatient letter from Benjamin Wright at Savanna la Marr in the West Indies to his chief, Aaron Lopez, in Providence, June 2, 1770. "I never set down to write you since I have been in your employ so confused as I now am—the damned Custom-house officers put one almost mad with their extravagant demands." Things must have been pretty bad, because he had related in earlier letters how he had used money to secure favors from them.[27]

CARLETON TOLERATES NO CUSTOMS RACKETEERING IN CANADA

There have been many reasons advanced why Canada, a recently conquered province, should have remained loyal when the self-governing provinces revolted. One reason that has not been given is that Governor Guy Carleton was a statesman who had the courage to correct abuses before they became causes of serious popular discontent. Among other things he did not permit the customs officers in his province to practice the extortions that were too common in other colonies, although they attempted to do so.

His first clash with them was over fees. Salaries of customs officers at Quebec had been adjusted upward in 1765 on the ground that they did not have any regularly established fees. In the fall of 1769 Customs Inspector Wootin visited Quebec and told the officers they were legally entitled to take fees and, since none had been established for that port, they could charge the same fees as those at the nearest port with authorized fees. Boston was the nearest by air line and Halifax by water. They adopted the fees charged at Boston. All this without consulting Governor Carleton.

Complaints were quickly voiced by the merchants who were thus subjected to a new tax in the form of fees. Carleton immediately took up the matter with the Commissioners at Boston in language that haughty body was not accustomed to receiving. After protesting the new fees he added:

The officers of His Majesty's Customs are here upon so good terms with the People, as not even to require the least Assistance from Government, but to secure this, tis necessary they should not render themselves odius by any rapaciousness or oppressive demands. This would be Sacrificing the King's Interests, and in a very material Branch, to gratify the mercenary desires of a few of his lowest Servants, which I hope never to see here, nor in any other Province where I have the honor to command.

Inspector Wootin, he continued: "should have communicated his measures and produced his extraordinary Powers, if any such exist, to that Government the King has thought proper to establish here, and not to have smuggled them in, under a Cloak of Secrecy, which will equally cover things just and fraudulent."[28]

The contrast in the popular standing of his own customs officers with those at Boston, where the Customs Commissioners, themselves, claimed they could not perform their duties without a great show of armed strength, must have been painful.

Within a month he had an even more serious case of racketeering to deal with. The Collector, Mr. Ainslie, was away and the Deputy Collector, Thomas Mellish, was in charge. On November 10, 1769, he seized the sloop *Mary*, Richard Copelman, master, after it was fully loaded and the master had come to the customhouse to clear his vessel, because bond for non-enumerated goods had not been given *before* goods were placed on board.

A week later the case came to trial in the admiralty court at Quebec. Witness after witness testified that prior to this seizure it had been the regular custom at Quebec for ships to give bond for enumerated goods at the time of clearance and not before. Captain Copelman had a clean record as a fair trader and had never before had any trouble with customs officers. There was no evidence whatever of any fraud. His papers were all on deposit at the customhouse and he could not have escaped if he had tried. In the face of this evidence, the judge ruled that the ship and cargo should be returned to the owners as the intent of the law was to prevent fraud and not to oppress the innocent or fair trader. But, as bond had not been given before loading as required by law, he ruled there was probable cause for the seizure which put the costs of the suit and court fees on the owner of the ship.[29]

This was the first seizure of this kind in his province and Carleton determined it should be the last. He immediately transmitted a full account of the affair to the Commissioners with a blunt assertion that it clearly indicated malice or avarice on the part of the customs officer, that he would tolerate no such actions in his province, and demanded that the Board immediately require the Collector to return to his post or appoint a suitable successor. He told them:

This Matter has made a Noise in this place. . . . Such Behaviour might be attended here with the most pernicious Consequences to the King's Service and render the Officers of His Revenue as odius at Quebec as I understand they are in some of the other Provinces. . . .

The Revenue Laws were framed to prevent and Guard against Frauds, for which purpose great Powers are vested in the Officers . . . but it never was or could be the Intention of Legislature to arm them with such Powers to entrap honest Men, for the sake of enriching the executive Officers, which in this Affair appears too plainly the case.[30]

No patriot in Boston could have stated the American case more plainly. Carleton was entitled to one-third of the value of the *Mary* and her cargo. It was probably a very rich prize. He is the only governor in America that entered on the record a refusal to share in such plunder. His statement concerning the reputation the customs officers had acquired in other colonies is proof that even the staunchest Tories knew of the customs racketeering and despised it.

Mellish demanded that the case of the *Mary* be appealed to the authorities in London and complained that he had no support from authority—the same plea made by the Customs Commissioners when their attempted racketeering aroused popular resentment in Boston.[31]

Did the Board reprove Mellish for his attempt to confiscate the *Mary* and her cargo on such a technical charge? No, indeed! Instead they asked the home government to issue orders compelling Carleton to carry out the directions of the Board.[32] Carleton was too big a man to be pushed around that way. The record discloses no further instances of customs racketeering in Canada. The cement of empire was not permitted to be dissolved in that province.

HENRY LAURENS AND CUSTOMS RACKETEERS

The customs officers did not confine their exactions to sailors and owners of small vessels. They even attempted to plunder two of the wealthiest merchants in America. The first attempt was made upon the fortune of Henry Laurens of South Carolina.

Laurens was probably the richest merchant in the southern colonies, where he had built up a commercial business comparable to the great English houses engaged in colonial trade. He owned ships and plantations; imported and sold slaves; exported rice, indigo, naval stores, and miscellaneous colonial products; supplied credit to the planters of a large area; did a banking and general mercantile business; and was a general supplier to merchants in South Carolina, Georgia, and North Carolina.

His chief mercantile connections in England were with merchants who were classed as the political opponents of the King's Friends. He had other correspondents in Spain, Portugal, Madeira, and in every important port in the British Empire. Most of his ships engaged in overseas trade were owned in partnership, as was the custom of the time.

The extent and nature of his business made him a conservative in local politics. He took little part in the Stamp Act controversy and was opposed to sending delegates to the Stamp Act Congress. With his extensive commercial and credit relations he had to trade well within the law. Any seizure would have involved his partners in losses and have impaired his credit. With all his vast operations, he never had any trouble with the customs officers prior to 1767.[33]

In March, 1767, Daniel Moore arrived in Charleston as Collector. George Roupell was his deputy and Egerton Leigh was Attorney-General, Judge of the Vice-Admiralty Court, member of the Council, Surveyor General, and maintained a private law practice. All were interested in making all they could out of their jobs.

Moore quickly acquired a reputation for rapaciousness. His first act was greatly to increase the fees of the customhouse officers—that included his own. As Charleston was one of the busiest ports, this was no slight addition to his income. He was even charged with demanding fees for indigo certificates. His exactions soon aroused the resentment of the merchants, who had him prosecuted on the indigo certificates charge. He escaped with a small fine and assured the merchants that he could "sweat them at law with their own money."[34]

His first move was to seize the *Active*, one of the many small vessels engaged in the coastal trade from Wynyaw to Charleston, both ports in South Carolina. This was in part a move to make a profit from the confiscations and in part an effort to force all coasting vessels to enter and clear. If they did, the total fees would be greatly increased. The charge against the *Active* was that she had not entered, cleared, given bonds, carried cockets, etc. Judge Leigh ruled that vessels going from one point to another within the same province did not have to clear and give bonds. There was not the least evidence of fraud or intention to violate either the trade or revenue acts and the vessel was released.[35] Judge Leigh, however, certified there was "probable cause" for the seizure and assessed costs, including his own fees, of £150 against the owner of the vessel, which was probably worth only £80. It was now clear what he meant by "sweating the merchants at law with their own money."

Then followed in rapid succession three more seizures of vessels belonging to Laurens. The *Active* had been seized in May, 1767. That same month Laurens sent the *Wambaw,* a schooner of about fifty tons burden, with tools and provisions to his plantation in Georgia. The vessel was cleared from Charleston without any objection from the customs officers, who did not require even a bond for non-enumerated goods. The plantation was up the Altamaha River some fifty miles from the nearest customhouse.

On the return trip the *Wambaw* took on a load of shingles as ballast. This came under the head of wood and might require a lumber bond. Laurens had instructed the master to take no chances. As it was impossible to go to the customhouse at Sunbury, he went to Frederica, nine miles away over almost impassable roads, found two reliable merchants who were also magistrates and gave bond before them. With this proof and the load of shingles the *Wambaugh* returned to Charleston on July 17, 1767, where it was seized and libeled on orders of Moore for not having given a lumber bond at a customhouse. Prosecution was delayed a few days and the suggestion made that the customs officers would release the vessel for a liberal fee. Laurens was not doing that kind of business. When it came to trial the admiralty court condemned the *Wambaw* and her cargo and assessed the costs against Laurens, including a fee for Judge Leigh of £277. As there was no evidence of fraud, Laurens was permitted to buy his vessel back for £175. This was later complained of by Roupell, the deputy collector, because he said the schooner would have brought more at an appraised sale—and he claimed one-third as his share in the loot.[36]

In the meantime Laurens had sent another of his small

schooners, the *Broughton Island Packet,* loaded with tools and provisions to his Georgia plantation. This was regularly cleared at the customhouse and bond given for enumerated goods. There was no return cargo available at the plantation, so a number of logs and chunks were thrown in as ballast and the schooner returned to Charleston on July 30, 1767. On her arrival it, too, was seized because it could produce no lumber bond. The logs might have some use as firewood but had no commercial value. They were, however, "wood" and therefore might come within the letter of the law. The schooner was ordered to trial.

Moore claims he advised with Leigh as Attorney-General, paid him £50 for his opinion, and that he advised that the seizure be made. Sitting as trial judge in the admiralty suit, Leigh ruled that the charges against the *Broughton Island Packet* were frivolous, that there was neither evidence or charge that there was any intent whatever to violate any trade or navigation act or defraud the revenues. The charge was dismissed and the costs assessed, one-third to Roupell, who had brought the suit, and two-thirds to Laurens. The latter also had to pay the fees of Judge Leigh, which totaled £216-15. No "probable cause" for the seizure was entered on the record. This left Roupell open to a damage suit for false seizure. Laurens sued in the civil courts and was awarded damages of £1,400.[37] Ultimately this was paid out of the revenue.

These three seizures in a few months aroused intense hostility among the Charleston merchants. About this time Moore found it convenient to leave the province for his health, leaving Roupell in charge.[38] For some reason the latter decided to attempt an even bolder attack upon the business and fortune of Laurens. This time he picked on the *Ann,* a large ocean-going vessel in the direct trade to Europe.

The *Ann* arrived from Bristol on May 24, 1768, consigned to Laurens. She was entered regularly at the customhouse and began preparing for a return voyage. Captain Fortner, the master, thought he had given the usual bond in regard to enumerated goods before leaving England, but had no certificate to prove that he had done so. Laurens, taking no chances, prepared another bond covering enumerated goods and had that delivered at the customhouse by his messenger. Captain Fortner then proceeded to load with rice. Later he asked Laurens about a pipe of wine, but was advised not to load it as it would require additional bonds. A part of the cargo was deerskins, which were also enumerated under the Sugar Act. Laurens considered taking out an additional bond for nonenumerated goods, but decided they were covered by the earlier bond. About this time he left for Georgia to look after his business there, leaving his agents in charge.[39]

In his absence, Captain Fortner accepted a pipe of Madeira wine, some pink root, and some cattle horns, all non-enumerated goods.[40] When the ship was fully loaded, Laurens' clerk took Captain Fortner to the customhouse with the manifests of cargo, which were found to include the few non-enumerated articles. Everything else was in order.

Additional bonds covering non-enumerated goods were demanded. These were promptly prepared and tendered with a request to clear the vessel. The offer was refused and the *Ann* was ordered seized for loading non-enumerated goods prior to giving bond in violation of clause twenty-three of the Sugar Act.

The case of the *Ann* is no less important than that of the *Liberty*. Both were attacks upon the fortunes of future presidents of the Continental Congress. It was obvious that Laurens was being singled out for persecution and plunder by the customs officers. He had three ships seized in less than a year while other merchants, following identical practices, had not been molested. Laurens' credit was definitely endangered by the suit. He owned only one-fourth of the vessel. His creditors and correspondents owned the rest. The ship had been consigned to and loaded by him. If he could not handle ships without risk of seizures when consigned to him at his own home office and at one of the busiest ports in America, he was not a good risk. He had to win this fight.

The *Ann* was a rich prize. A decree against her would have involved confiscation of ship, tackle, furnishing, and all non-enumerated goods on board. This totaled not less than £1000 sterling. Laurens retained the best legal talent in Charleston. Pinckney and Rutledge—famous names in South Carolina—appeared as his defense attorneys. Not a single lawyer with any standing would accept the job as advocate for Roupell.[41]

When the case came to trial all the employees of the custom-house and many merchants were called as witnesses. Customhouse clerks admitted that it was common practice to accept bonds at the time vessels were cleared. One testified that proper bonds for the *Ann* had been tendered to him at the time of a regular request for a clearance and refused on orders of Roupell. Merchants testified that a Captain Maitland had cleared his ship the day before under identical conditions. Merchant after merchant testified under oath that they believed that the seizure was due to malice.[42]

Leigh was definitely on the spot. The series of seizures of ships belonging to Laurens and the vexatious nature of the suit against the *Ann* were resented in all Charleston circles. He decided that the *Ann* should be released to her owners and that Roupell and Laurens should each pay his part of the costs. This meant that Laurens was assessed two-thirds of the costs besides the fees due Judge Leigh. This meant that he was again out of pocket another £100 sterling besides what he paid his attorneys.

Roupell had offered to drop the suit against the *Ann* if Laurens would surrender the judgment in the case of the *Broughton Island Packet*.[43] That was too much like bribery for Laurens. Roupell attempted to appeal Judge Leigh's latest decision to London but was unable to supply the necessary bond. Instead he made out an elaborate report of the whole series of suits against Laurens and sent copies to the Treasury Board in London and to the Customs Commissioners at Boston. The latter forwarded their copies also to London with a request that the opinion of the Attorney-General be taken.[44] He ruled that where a customhouse had been permit-ting vessels to give bonds at the time of clearance there should be no change in that practice without the fullest notice to the mer-chants, that any other procedure was too obviously an effort to entrap honest traders.[45]

In the meantime Laurens had determined on a public exposure of the whole nefarious situation in the customhouse at Charleston. He first published a lengthy statement in the *South Carolina*

Gazette of July 11, 1768, while the case of the *Ann* was still pending. This exposure was so clear that public opinion compelled Leigh to dismiss the charges. It also was widely copied in other colonial newspapers and thus reached the public at the very time of the news of the attack upon Hancock. Furthermore Laurens followed up his newspaper attack by pamphlets in which the actual entries in the records of the court of Vice-Admiralty were reproduced.[46] This led Judge Leigh to publish a reply entitled *The Man Unmasked,* and Laurens replied by a second pamphlet, called *Appendix to the Extract of Proceedings.* Laurens circulated his pamphlets in America, the West Indies, and even in England.[47] The publicity thus given to the affair finally forced Judge Leigh in self-defense to arrange for a compromise of his ill-gotten fees. When the agreements on this score were finally signed, an anonymous article appeared in the *South Carolina Gazette,*[48] apparently from the pen of Laurens, as follows:

We consider that no part of the money so wrested from us, does, or could be expected to go into the treasury. On the contrary it is wholly swallowed up by a set of Revenue Officers, ever formidable to liberty, the numbers of whom was before much too great for safety of the constitution. With this kind of men dressed out in the spoils of your fellow subjects, O! Britons! and laced all over with the gold that should have been remitted to you, are our streets filled. Ask your minister, how many of them are Englishmen.

Other newspapers of America took notice of the affair, and the *Pennsylvania Journal*[49] published the following, almost as an editorial:

An anecdote just published by Mr. Laurens, of South Carolina, may serve to shew the danger that is likely to result in America from late revenue acts. . . . Our property is thereby not only taken from us without our consent, but when thus taken, is applied still further to oppress and ruin us. The swarms of searchers, tide waiters, spies, and other underlings, with which every port in America now abounds, and which were unknown before the Board of Commissioners was established among us, are not it seems, quite sufficient to ruin our trade, but infamous informers, like dogs of prey thirsting after the fortunes of worthy and wealthy men, are let loose and encouraged to seize and libel in the courts of admiralty the vessels of such as are advocates of the rights of America. If they can find any colour of pretense, the judge, who is dependent on the will of the Minister, and paid at his pleasure out of the American customs, is ready to pass sentence of condemnation; but if the vessel is acquitted, no loss or inconvenience is to accrue to the prosecutor. For if he is sued and damages against him recovered, the damages are paid out of the American revenue.

There follows a detailed account of Roupell's action in the case of the *Ann*. Thus Laurens came to be known as a prominent victim of the new regulations in much the same way as Hancock.

The newspapers of the period give many similar incidents where the victims were less well known, and hence attracted less attention individually. The mass of them was so great, however, that an undeniable impression was made upon public opinion in America.

The publicity which Laurens had given to the customs racketeering in Charleston forced the government in London to do something to correct the situation. Moore was removed, Roupell was ordered replaced, orders were issued forbidding one person to hold the offices of Attorney-General and Judge of the Vice-Admiralty court, Leigh was compelled to choose and decided to retain the position as Attorney-General. Then on September 7, 1768, an Order in Council created four new courts of Vice-Admiralty in America, one of which was at Charleston, gave the judges a fixed salary of £600 per year, payable out of the revenue, and forbad them to accept any fees or gratuities of any kind on pain of forfeiture of their offices.[50]

In 1772 Leigh was rewarded for his part in the Laurens affair by being made a baronet.[51] Honors of that kind were common political rewards. From June, 1768 on, Laurens became the recognized leader of the patriot party in South Carolina. Open mistreatment had done much to dissolve the cement of loyalty which he and his friends and associates had held for the British Empire under which they had prospered.

ATTEMPT ON JOHN HANCOCK'S FORTUNE

In the long list of plans to plunder American merchants, the attack upon John Hancock received greatest immediate attention and had the most important historical consequences. The seizure of the *Liberty*, the best-known incident in this attack, has usually been treated as an episode in local New England history or a piece of bad luck for a wine smuggler. It was neither. Instead, it was the most important in a whole series of events connected with the attempt to change fundamentally the constitution of the British colonial Empire.

Hancock was the wealthiest of the New England merchants and possibly the richest American merchant. In many respects his business resembled that of the great English merchants engaged in colonial trade. He did a large wholesale importing business, mainly from England; extended credit to many retailers; owned a good deal of real estate, mostly in Massachusetts; owned and operated a number of ships largely used as common carriers; and was a very large dealer in whale oil.[52]

His interest in wine was minor and none of his ships plied regularly to south Europe as did those from New York, Philadelphia, and Charleston. What wine he handled seems to have been for his own use, for some of his friends, and small amounts received to cover payments for exported New England products. There is no record that he ever imported a full cargo of wine. As has already been pointed out, Boston was quite unimportant as a colonial wine port.

Like Laurens, his chief correspondents in England were merchants who were political opponents of the "Kings Friends."[53] He had been very active in putting pressure upon the British merchants to secure a repeal of the Stamp Act. Locally he had acquired much prominence by his work in restoring law and order in Boston after the Stamp Act riots. His wealth, his independence, his large number of loyal employees and his capacity for political organization made him a person to be reckoned with.

He continued his opposition to the new revenue legislation and had no more respect for the Commissioner of Customs than he had for the stamp distributors. He was interested in military affairs and was captain of the Cadet Company, the only uniformed, regularly drilled and equipped military organization in Boston.

He went out of his way to show his contempt for the Commissioners of Customs and make them disliked in Boston. When they arrived in Boston Governor Bernard arranged a public reception and welcome for them, including a street procession and other welcoming exercises. Hancock and his Cadet Company were directed to supply a guard of honor for the governor. Hancock curtly refused to participate in any way. A few months later Bernard announced plans for his official public dinner at the time of the annual election and again notified Hancock to attend him with his company. The latter suspected that the occasion was planned to show special official approval for the Commissioners, which would put him in an embarrassing position. Consequently, he wrote the governor that he and his company would attend if the Commissioners were not invited; but, if they were to be present as guests of the governor, he and his company would not attend as usual. Bernard was angry at such disrespect for his official position, and as commander in chief, peremptorily ordered Hancock and his company to attend him at the public dinner. This order Hancock refused to obey, his men supported him and threatened to resign in a body. The affair was soon the talk of the town and the officials of the city formally voted to refuse the use of Faneuil Hall for the governor's banquet if the Commissioners were invited. Never before had a royal governor in America been so openly flouted and important royal officials so publicly insulted.[54]

The officials thus insulted began a very warm war. Within the customs organization were two distinct factions. One was headed by Temple and the old customs organization and had the general support of most of the merchants. The other was headed by Governor Bernard and his followers, backed by Commissioners Robinson, Paxton, and Hulton. These two groups had their supporters in England. Temple's support ran generally to the Customs Board in England and the Rockingham Whigs.[55] The Bernard faction had the support of the Hillsborough-Pownall-Halifax-Grafton-North combination of King's Friends. In general the Temple group of customs officials was not in ill repute with the American trading fraternity. The major hostility was directed against the Bernard-Hutchinson-Paxton-Robinson faction and their appointees. The racketeering and political persecution centered in this group and the attack upon Hancock originated in this faction.

Within the ruling faction there were crosscurrents of personal ambition to secure the most lucrative positions in the colonial service. These were the positions of collector at the large ports, the admiralty court appointments, and the more important offices in the colonial service. The suspension of Fisher as Collector at Salem on trumped-up charges and the attempted appointment of the Secretary of the Board in his place backfired in England, and Fisher had to be restored on direct orders from the Treasury Board in London.[56] The plot to undermine and displace Attorney-General Sewall leaked. Sewall had powerful friends in England. The ruling faction attempted to deny that they had any such plans against Sewall and fired Sam Venner, their Secretary, who had told Sewall some of the things that had been done against him. They then kicked their solicitor, David Lisle, upstairs by having him appointed collector at Piscataqua. He, too, had been indiscreet in giving Sewall information about the plot against him. The story of this intrigue is interlaced with that of the attack upon Hancock. It has never been written up, but would be revealing if it could be pieced together. Robert Auchmuty, Samuel Fitch, Thomas Irving, and Ben Hallowell all play major and minor roles in this political comedy of errors.[57]

The first move against Hancock was in connection with the *Lydia*, his favorite London packet. This vessel, laden with spring goods, arrived on Friday, April 8, 1768, and tied up at Hancock's Wharf. Two tidesmen, Owen Richards, the notorious informer, and a companion, came aboard. Some hours later Hancock visited his ship, found the two tidesmen, and inquired their business. They explained they were there by order of the Collector and Comptroller. Hancock made no objection, but gave strict orders that they must not be allowed below deck.

This order was observed until Saturday evening about seven o'clock, when they both went into the steerage and refused to leave. Hancock and a party came on board about eleven o'clock, found them in the steerage, demanded a sight of their orders, which were defective, and asked them if they had a writ of assistance. Richards said they had no such writ. Hancock again ordered them on deck and when they refused he had his men forcibly pick them up and deposit them on deck and close the companionway. Then he asked

Richards if they were trying to search the ship. They denied any such intention. To which Hancock answered that they could search the vessel if they chose, but could not tarry below deck.

All of this, in the form of sworn statements, was laid before the Commissioners. They at once referred the entire matter to Attorney-General Sewall with an instruction to file a criminal information against Hancock for interfering with customs officers in the discharge of their duty.[58]

Sewall looked up the law in his usual careful way and wrote a formal opinion that the case was without merit. In the first place the tidesmen had been sent on board to watch the unloading and under the law their place was on deck. They were given no authority to search. They could go below only on orders to search. Furthermore, Hancock had acted wholly within his rights in having them put back on deck. There was no violation of the criminal statute which described attacks by armed men. Hancock and his companions were unarmed and had not physically injured either Richards or his companion. He advised against any criminal prosecution, especially by information, as that method was novel in America and could do more harm than good.[59]

This opinion had the same effect on the majority of the Commissioners as the traditional red flag on a bull. The entire record was sent to the Treasury Board in England for an opinion from the Attorney-General. In addition they demanded specific authority to issue a mandatory order for Sewall to file the criminal information as requested.[60]

In this whole communication from the Board there is not the slightest charge that there had been any violation of the trade and navigation laws, or any attempt to import goods contrary to the revenue act. The entire argument for the prosecution of Hancock is stated on political grounds. There are few records of prosecutions in English history so brazenly personal and political as this official demand for the criminal prosecution of Hancock. A portion is given below.

We cannot omit mentioning to your Lordships that Mr. Hancock before named is one of the Leaders of disaffected in this Town, that early in the Winter he declared in the General Assembly that he would not suffer our officers to go even on board of any of his London Ships, and now he carries his Opposition to Government to an even higher pitch [here follows an account of the refusal of Hancock and his Company to attend the Governor's official dinner and Bernard's order for them to do so]. Mr. Hancock thereupon tore the seal off his Commission, and all the rest of the company, except nine declared they would not continue any longer in the service. This infatuated man now gives out in public that if we Commissioners are not recalled, he will get rid of us before Christmas.[61]

The specific law under which they demanded that Hancock be prosecuted, 14 Charles II, c. 11, provided penalties on conviction of a fine of £100 and imprisonment until released by order of the Exchequer. Indefinite imprisonment of Englishmen for daring to voice political opposition to highly unpopular legislation and refusing to be present when unpopular royal officials were fed at public expense was indeed a strange doctrine in America.

Foiled in this attempt to get Hancock, the Commissioners waited for the *Liberty,* which was known to have been at Madeira. There was much loose talk that she carried a good deal of wine which would be landed without paying duties in spite of the Customs Commissioners. It is probable that some of Hancock's admirers expected him to duplicate the recent exploit of Captain Malcolm on a more spectacular scale.

Hancock's advisers in England, however, had warned him that mob action and violent disregard of even patently unconstitutional legislation were unpopular and might make early repeal of the revenue laws impossible. Consequently he and his followers were carefully avoiding any actions that could be interpreted as openly defying the law. Their program was to convince the British public that the Americans supported law and order, and that the officers charged with the enforcement of the revenue laws were acting lawlessly.[62]

The *Liberty,* owned by Hancock and used by him as a common carrier, arrived in Boston from Madeira on May 9, 1768, and was entered at the customhouse the next day with a cargo of twenty-five casks of wine. The regular duties were paid.[63] For the next month the *Liberty* lay at Hancock's wharf apparently preparing for a voyage to London. A new cargo of 200 barrels of whale oil and 20 barrels of tar, both of American origin, had been placed on board. On June 10, one month after the *Liberty* had been regularly entered, late in the afternoon, Hutchinson says "about seven o'clock or near sunset,"[64] representatives of the Boston customhouse, acting under a direct written order from the Board of Customs Commissioners, searched the *Liberty*, found the new cargo on board, forcibly seized the vessel, and had her towed out into the harbor and anchored under the guns of the *Romney*, a British warship.[65]

On June 22, the following suit was filed:

Joseph Harrison, Esq. vs. Sloop Liberty
20 barrels of tar
200 barrels of oil[66]

Claimants were cited to appear on July 7, the case was continued to July 18, and finally on August 1, 1768, ship and cargo were ordered confiscated.[67]

Is not this seizure and confiscation proof that the *Liberty* was concerned with the illegal landing of wine the night of May 9, when she entered Boston Harbor?

Not at all. No reference of any kind to wine is made in the charge. It is a suit against the *Liberty* and a new cargo of tar and oil. A writ of assistance was used in making the search. Surely they were not searching the *Liberty* on June 10 for wine that allegedly had been unloaded illegally a month earlier. Even Lieutenant-Governor Hutchinson admits that the seizure was "for want of a permit," that means a formal permit to load, which the law provided should be given after bond had been filed.

This seizure and confiscation is clearly under clause nineteen of the Navigation Act of 1660 and clauses twenty-three and twenty-nine of the Sugar Act. The first required bond for enumerated goods, the second bond for non-enumerated goods, and the third a permit to load before any goods were placed on board. As has been pointed out, the universal practice at most ports in America was to load and then furnish the various bonds, certificates, and other papers necessary for a proper clearance.

The law, however, was specific. The 200 barrels of oil and the

20 barrels of tar found on board the *Liberty* were there in violation of a specific provision of the law. Doubtless every other ship in Boston Harbor that was preparing for a voyage could have been seized on a similar charge, but no other ship was disturbed. The Customs Commissioners were after Hancock and were determined to harass him as much as possible. The proceeds of all forfeitures were divided: one-third to the governor, one-third to the informer, and one-third to the crown.

If the *Liberty* had been seized immediately after May 10 there would have been only the value of an empty ship to divide. By waiting until June 10 they got the ship with new provisions, 200 barrels of oil, and 20 barrels of tar, which gave about twice as much to divide. In addition they had a case against the *Liberty* incapable of successful defense. The presence of the goods on board was proof of the violation of the letter of the law and insured condemnation.

A riot followed the seizure of the *Liberty* and started a chain of events closely linked with the Revolution. The spontaneous rising on June 10 was not of men interested in protecting a wealthy wine smuggler, nor was it the work of a carefully organized and drilled mob. Hancock's employees and the others about the wharf knew why the *Liberty* and her cargo were being taken. It was the first instance in Boston of a seizure on such technical grounds and the only seizure known to have been made at that port on such a charge. The crowd also knew how the proceeds of seizures were divided.

The riot was undesired by the Boston leaders and was unfortunate. It was, however, such a plain case of public plunder—not for any violations of the law affecting either the revenue or the course of trade, but obviously for the personal profit of the governor and the customs officers—that the crowd reacted as would Western cowboys when rustlers came boldly in daylight to steal their employer's herds.

Thus the *Liberty* seizure and confiscation supply no evidence that Hancock was a smuggler, but are the plainest evidence that he had valuable property taken by Governor Bernard and the customs officers and appropriated to their own personal use for following the regular commercial practice. The admiralty record shows that

Bernard received his third on November 9, 1768. We do not know just how the customs officials divided their third.

The *Liberty* case has been confused by the discovery of an alleged information signed by Thomas Kirk, one of the tidesmen placed on board the *Liberty* when she docked April 9, 1768. Both he and his companion swore the next morning that none of the *Liberty's* cargo had been disturbed during the night.

One month later, on June 9, Kirk signed an information which is very different from his regular report. This information recites that while he was on board the *Liberty,* a Captain Marshall with several men, none of whom he knew, came on board about nine o'clock. A proposition was made concerning the unloading of some wine. When Kirk refused the proposition he was forced below deck and confined for about three hours. During that time he heard noises like heavy walking and sounds like the ship's tackle being used to hoist out goods. He was then released and threatened with dire consequences if he revealed what happened.[68]

When questioned, his companion denied any knowledge of such occurrences, but admitted he might have been asleep. Kirk asserted his companion was drunk and had gone home to bed.[69] Captain Marshall had died during the month and could not be called for questioning.[70]

Kirk states nothing of his own knowledge. He only heard noises. He mentions no noticeable changes on deck the next morning, nor does he mention any ascertainable disturbance of the ship's cargo. No member of the regular crew or any other employee of Hancock is mentioned. Are we to believe that Hancock permitted all of his employees to leave a newly arrived ship with valuable cargo on board and turn it over with unlocked doors and hatches to the tender mercies of tidesmen, particularly recently appointed supernumeraries? So far as the Kirk statement shows, he simply invaded the *Liberty* without reporting his presence to anyone, without seeing or being seen by the owner of the vessel or any of his employees.

Surely some of the crew or other of Hancock's men were on board all night. After his experience with the *Lydia* a few weeks earlier Hancock cannot be presumed to have trusted tidesmen aboard any ship without several dependable men to watch their actions. Especially would he be expected to be suspicious of the actions of tidesmen who were not regular employees. With all the talk that was circulating in Boston and the known personal hostility of the Commissioners, it must be presumed that Hancock kept the *Liberty* and all his other ships carefully guarded by his own trusty employees.

The Treasury papers in London contain many reports by customs offices of difficulties and opposition encountered by them. None of them are so lacking in specific facts and details as this sworn statement of Kirk's. On the contrary they invariably name persons, actions, incidents, describe individuals, and otherwise give evidence that could be used in court.

This information is an amazing document. The signer is a self-confessed perjurer. If his statement on May 10 was true this one must be false. If this is true his earlier sworn statement is false. In either case he is a self-confessed liar. There are no possible witnesses indicated. He rules out his companion—says he was home drunk. Both were apparently sober when placed on board and were sober when they reported the next morning. Captain Marshall, the accused, was dead and could not be called to testify. Kirk recognized none of Marshall's alleged companions. He does not even identify them by size, build, dress, actions, language, or in any other way.

In addition Kirk was himself personally interested in the outcome of his testimony, which would bar him as a witness in any fair court. Legally he was entitled to one-third of all sums that could be secured as a result of his evidence. His proportion alone might run from ten to more than a hundred times his annual earnings as a tidesman, depending upon whether one considers the value of the *Liberty* and her oil or the far larger sums attempted to be extorted from Hancock by the later suits.

The customs racketeers at Boston were not satisfied by what they realized from the seizure of the *Liberty* and its load of oil. They had not broken Hancock's political influence in Boston. He was stronger than ever and was now urging nonimportation agreements on a continental scale. A personal suit against him might yield much more spoils to divide and, by impairing his fortune, end his political leadership. There were differences of opinion as to the wisdom of starting further prosecution. Sewall was reluctant to begin a suit as novel as this would have to be.

Ben Hallowell, the Comptroller at Boston, had been the moving spirit in the actual seizure of the *Liberty* and in securing the Kirk information. Immediately after the riot he was supplied with a most liberal expense account out of the money in the hands of the Commissioners and rushed off to England to make a personal report to their political superiors.[71] He also carried important confidential communications from Bernard and Hutchinson. He consulted the right people, found active support in the Hillsborough faction, put on an interesting show by his testimony before the House of Lords, got the Commissioners' side of the now warm war before the public, and was evidently advised to break Hancock if possible.

Soon after reports from Hallowell reached Boston indicating political conditions in England favored the plotters, things began to move. There was a deal in regard to possible promotions. The soldiers had landed and Boston Harbor was crowded with naval war craft. It seemed that public opinion could be defied.

The records of the Commissioners reveal a most suggestive list of expenditures. On October 27, 1768, John Hincks was given £100 "for carrying on sundry prosecutions subject to the Board's orders." The next day Robert Hallowell, deputy collector and a close relative of Ben Hallowell, was paid £60 for a pipe of wine for a Captain Coiner. Why he needed so much wine on that day or why he was entitled to any at public expense is not stated. It is the only present of that kind shown on the records as a gift to anyone. The same day the clerk paid Attorney-General Sewall and Samuel Fitch "20 half Johannes each" or a total of £72 sterling as retainers' fees "for sundry causes depending for the Crown."[72] The only known causes were the pending suits against Hancock. The retainer fees are excessively high, as previous payments were about ten per cent of the sums in this case.

The next day, October 29, 1768, Sewall filed the long-delayed suit in Judge Auchmuty's court not only against Hancock, but also against five other merchants, each personally for £9000, or a total of £54,000, for allegedly aiding in unloading 100 pipes of wine valued at £30 each on the night of May 9, 1768, when the *Liberty* entered Boston.[73] That is an enormous penalty for an alleged evasion of £700 in wine duties.

The Sugar Act had a provision that any person in any way connected with or abetting the unloading, transporting, receiving, storing, or concealing uncustomed goods could be sued for triple the value of the goods allegedly landed. The Board determined to base its new suit upon these provisions, using the alleged Kirk information as partial evidence. Much more would be needed, but money and official pressure might supply it.

This is the most unusual suit in the entire history of British revenue laws in America and possibly had no parallel in England. The alleged events happened entirely upon land within the limits of the Province of Massachusetts Bay. It was a dragnet attempt to uncover evidence of a conspiracy to violate the revenue laws. Criminal conspiracy should have been tried in the regular courts of the province under the rules of the civil and criminal law with a jury to pass upon the evidence. Instead the case was brought in the Vice-Admiralty court at Boston, without a jury, and under rules of evidence and procedure highly unusual, if not openly illegal. It was an action against persons for what amounted to criminal acts, not against property, as was the suit against the *Liberty*. The marshal of the Admiralty Court arrested Hancock's person and placed him under excessive bail. This made the action essentially criminal and should have been begun by an indictment instead of an "Information," as was pointed out by Sewall in the case of the *Lydia*.[74]

In addition witnesses were examined by interrogatories, that is, a list of questions was made out in writing by the Advocate-General and the witness required to answer them in writing. Witnesses were not put on the stand and compelled to give their testimony in open court in front of the accused, where their entire appearance, demeanor, and manner of answering became a part of their testimony. In no case was the attorney for the accused permitted to cross-question them in open court. Amendments to the Federal

Constitution, VI, VII, and VIII, are obviously the result of the denial of such rights and the publicity given to the methods used in this most spectacular persecution in the pre-Revolutionary period.

Information concerning this second suit against Hancock and others was carefully kept from the Board's superiors in London. In none of the mass of reports and letters still preserved in the Treasury Papers in London is there any mention or report of the matter. Even Secretary of State Hillsborough apparently received his first information concerning these new suits from a letter from General Gage, who was in Boston at the time the suits were filed and stated in his letter of November 3, 1768, that "some Prosecutions were commenced in the Court of Admiralty against two of the most popular Leaders."[75] This at once aroused Hillsborough's curiosity and on December 24, following, he asked Gage for full information concerning the "Grounds" for the new prosecutions.[76] Gage's reply of March 5, 1769, and the accounts of the trial in the newspapers appear to have been the only actual information supplied officially to the home government.

The Commissioners took personal charge of the prosecution and the securing of evidence. Hancock's office was entered and his desk rifled.[77] His most confidential employees and his nearest relatives were secretly examined in the judges' chambers and subjected to third-degree methods.[78] One tidewaiter was dismissed and then offered his job back and a liberal reward if he would give the testimony desired.[79] The case was spun out for nearly five months, apparently to give time to examine every sailor that had ever worked on Hancock's vessels, or who might have been in Boston about the time the *Liberty* docked.

Warrants for summoning witnesses were handed to the Commissioners in blank to be filled in secretly, thus concealing the names of prospective witnesses, not only from Hancock's attorneys, but from the Advocate of the Board as well.[80] Money in large amounts was supplied by the Board to be used in securing evidence and tampering with witnesses.[81]

The testimony of one witness was so contrary to the truth that he was indicted for perjury by the local grand jury, but, before he could be brought to trial, the Board gave him a job on one of its revenue boats outside of the province and thus removed him from the jurisdiction of the Massachusetts court.[82]

The ordinary principles of the civil law, as well as the common law, were ignored in the taking of testimony. New witnesses and new evidence were introduced after Hancock's defense witnesses had testified. Other witnesses were called into the judge's chambers, examined secretly, and subjected to typical third-degree methods to extort information from them. It was not a trial in ordinary court but persecution under conditions of Star Chamber procedure.[83]

This is the only case in colonial history in which happenings in the court were reported from day to day and supplied in a news service to papers widely published in most of the colonies and even in England.[84] The persecution of Hancock thus became known from one end of the Empire to the other. The case stank with an odor that reached as far as London.

The wide publicity given to this extraordinary trial left permanent impressions on men's minds. The reference in the Declaration of Independence to depriving persons of trial by jury clearly refers to this trial because it was known from one end of America to the other, and there was no similar case that received material publicity, even locally. It is also probable that the constitutional provisions for indictment by a grand jury, trial by jury, forced self-incrimination, confronting witnesses face to face, excessive bail, depriving persons of property without due process of law, and excessive fines found in the earliest state constitutions and embodied in the fifth, sixth, seventh, and eighth amendments to the Federal Constitution are there because of the procedures of this trial.[85]

Hancock was prosecuted in what amounted to a criminal action without an indictment by a local grand jury. He was compelled to give evidence against himself through the seizure of his papers, and the forced testimony of his most confidential employees and his nearest relatives. As the court procedures were not in accordance with usual legal processes, an attempt was made to deprive him of valuable property without due process of law. He was denied trial by jury and was not permitted to have witnesses against himself examined in open court in his presence. He was required to furnish bail of £3,000, which was manifestly excessive, as he had large physical properties within the jurisdiction of the court and there was no possible reason to suspect he would attempt to flee the province. The proposed fine of £9,000—three times the alleged value of the cargo—was excessive even if the alleged offense had been committed. Especially is this true where one-third of the proposed fine—£3,000—was to go into the personal pocket of the governor who was a direct party to the suit, and an equal amount was for the personal profit of those who concocted the evidence against him. These were the very injustices that the constitutional provisions referred to were designed to outlaw for the future.

As the prosecution was not only against Hancock but also against five other residents of Boston, each for £9,000 sterling, Governor Bernard was seeking as his third of the plunder a total of £18,000 sterling—a sum larger than his regular total salary as governor for ten years. Another £18,000 sterling was sought for distribution among a small number of fifty to one hundred pounds-a-year customs officers—a sum probably greater than their combined total salaries for twenty years. Such efforts to use official position for personal plunder are "racketeering," even according to the standards of the modern city underworld.

The extraordinary efforts of the Board, the unusual expenditures, the arbitrary procedure in the court seemed to indicate probable conviction regardless of the facts. But time was running against the conspirators. By March, 1769, it was obvious that Governor Bernard would be recalled. The Commissioners began to be blamed in England for stirring up much of the trouble in Boston and in other colonies. The Ministry was gravely embarrassed by the troubles growing out of sending troops to Boston. The Treasury Board bluntly informed the Customs Commissioners in Boston to mend their ways and try to win the respect and confidence of honest merchants.[86] They also became very inquisitive about how the Commissioners were expending the revenue funds in Boston. The men most interested in plundering Hancock were either out or on their way out. It was a bad case at best. Somebody decided it should be dropped.

Finally, March 25, 1769, Robert Auchmuty's permanent commission as judge of the Vice-Admiralty Court in Boston was read in open court, thus insuring him a permanent salary of £600 a year out of the colonial revenue—a very large income for officials at that time. On the same day Attorney-General Jonathan Sewall, who had just received a similar appointment for Halifax, entered a motion formally withdrawing the suit and so wording his withdrawal that it could not be reopened.

Such is the evidence. Hancock had established a reputation throughout the Empire for stubbornly standing up for his rights. No other American had been singled out for so much personal abuse and for such personal persecution as he had been. He stood his ground, kept his head, engaged in no controversies in the press, and insisted upon his legal rights. It was this reputation that made him President of the Second Continental Congress for three years and first signer of the Declaration of Independence. The American people were placing their future in the hands of a tested patriot who had proved his worth by his sacrifices in the common cause, not a smuggler who used the popular agitation to make personal profits for himself.

A near attempt was made at Philadelphia to duplicate the tactics used in the effort to convict Hancock. Late in 1770 the Treasury in London sent an information to the Collector at Philadelphia to seize the *Speedwell* on her arrival, as she had on board some foreign tea. Careful search of the *Speedwell* by the Philadelphia customs officers failed to reveal any evidence of the alleged tea. There was a possibility that there had been tea on board, but that it had been disposed of before entry. This could only be determined by questioning the officers and every seaman on board under oath. Such a procedure would force them to give evidence that might tend to incriminate themselves.

The Collector was afraid to resort to such practices without legal advice and applied to the Attorney-General of the province, Andrew Allen, for his opinion. The latter wrote: "I am very clear in opinion that the Court of Admiralty cannot with propriety oblige any persons to answer interrogatories which may have a tendency to criminate themselves, or subject them to a penalty, it being contrary to any principle of Reason and the Laws of England."[87] Unlike the Hancock episode no publicity was given to this opinion and it has lain buried all these years. It is important, however, as indicating how American lawyers of all shades of politics were thinking.

The Commissioners were dissatisfied and informed Swift very bluntly that he should have prosecuted in spite of the absence of evidence and the adverse ruling of the Attorney-General. They insisted that the Admiralty Court had legal power to question all persons, compel them to testify, and could send commissioners into any county of the province to question those not found in Philadelphia where the court met. That power to set up an inquisition was not actually attempted, but the claim that it could be was probably known in Philadelphia, as Swift had both good sense and friends. The episode should be considered as an effort to continue the use of the extra-legal methods employed in the attack upon Hancock. It helps account for the universal American dislike for the Commissioners and the arbitrary power they represented.

The reasons for singling out Laurens and Hancock for the vexatious attacks just described has never been adequately explained. Neither had ever before been charged with violation of either the trade or the revenue acts. Both had outstanding reputations as fair traders. The retained private papers of each reveal no evidence of any connection with a clandestine trade as do those of Aaron Lopez of Rhode Island, who was not molested.

Other merchants, such as those doing business at Philadelphia, New York, and the hundreds of Glasgow merchants doing business in Maryland and Virginia, were not interfered with. Why were South Carolina and Massachusetts and their most prominent merchants picked out for worse treatment than others?

Politics and business have a mutual affinity for each other. The reign of George III was no exception. The attacks upon Hancock and Laurens came the same year and at a time when the cabinet was pushing its prosecution of John Wilkes. The latter was very popular in America, especially in South Carolina. Many in all the colonies associated the cause of Wilkes with that of their own struggle for the rights of Englishmen. The supporters of Wilkes in England were also those who most actively supported the American protests against taxation. The leading correspondent in London of both Hancock and Laurens was George Haley, who had married a sister of John Wilkes. If Hancock and Laurens could be broken financially, Haley and certain other rich Whig merchants who were actively opposing the program of the King's Friends could be seriously embarrassed. The business they lost would go to merchants with other political affiliations and their politically friendly American correspondents.

One does not expect political connections of this kind to be written out in permanent records. One has to infer such relations from other events. The political nature of the attack upon Hancock is clear. It is not so evident in the case of Laurens. The rewards given the chief actors in these unusual prosecutions are a good index to political relations. Leigh and Bernard were the active leaders in these attacks. Both were signally rewarded by the crown for their services—rewards that were not given to any other colonial officers of the same period. Both were created baronets—Bernard in 1769 and Leigh in 1772. No possible grounds are known for such awards but their activity in these prosecutions. Such honors, so awarded, suggest most strongly that the attacks upon Laurens and Hancock were political and directed from England—the object being to destroy political opposition in America.

The crown rewarded Leigh and Bernard. Americans, in turn, apparently recognized that the men thus attacked were considered as most dangerous by the crown and hence most valuable to the American cause. Hancock was made President of the Second Continental Congress and carried that body through Independence and the defeat and capture of Burgoyne. Laurens was his immediate successor and completed the alliance with France, thus insuring the success of the American cause. Hancock was again chosen President of that body to inaugurate the negotiations for peace after Yorktown—the only American to serve twice as President of Congress.

While the attacks described above were the most spectacular instances of customs racketeering, they are only a small part of the story. Hundreds of lesser Americans suffered as well. The clauses in the acts of 1764 and 1767 regulating the internal commerce of the colonies were made to yield a revenue for customs officers only. Just how much they were able to take from those whom they were privileged to plunder can never be determined, as it was exacted in the form of fees and bribes extorted under threat of prosecutions for noncompliance with some technical provision of the law.[88]

American hostility to this program was not directed against the navigation system nor was it the reaction of smugglers who found their illicit trade suddenly interfered with. The fair trader suffered even more than the unfair.[89] Over and over again complaints were made in the colonial newspapers that no seizures had been made of any goods that could have injured the trade and manufacture of England. It is almost impossible to find records of seizures of articles of foreign manufacture. The Customs Commissioners were not trying to keep trade within the Empire. They were solely interested in imposing a burden upon it. Even in their apologetic report of the burdens their new regulations were imposing upon the coasting trade, where small ships were admittedly being forced to give three separate bonds thirty or forty times a year merely for trading from one local port to another, they discuss regulations wholly in terms of revenue.[90]

The assumption that appears in many discussions of this period of American history that the Townshend revenue system was an effort to enforce the trade and navigation laws is without support by contemporary evidence. An examination of the thousands of pages of records left by the Customs Commissioners has not revealed a single instance in their seven-year administration of American customs where they expressed the remotest interest in promoting the trade of the Empire. Every regulation, every report to the home authorities, every reported seizure, every report of current colonial trade practices, and every suggestion for changes was made in terms of how these might affect the revenue. Every prosecution that has come to light was for some alleged violation of a revenue clause or some technicality upon which a seizure could be based.

The contemporary literature exhibits the strange spectacle of the Americans defending the century-old commercial system and complaining bitterly of the new policies that had the sole effect of hampering and injuring that trade. Hillsborough's correspondence and the published portions of the correspondence of George III also fail to reveal the remotest interest at this time in promoting the trade of the Empire. Instead, such comments as are found deal with how to tax the trade of the colonial Empire. Had these men gone out deliberately to wage war upon British colonial commerce they could not have done more harm than they did.

Efforts to Secure Writs of Assistance

Prior to the enactment of the Revenue Act of 1767 the only colonies that had supplied customs officers with writs of assistance were Massachusetts and New Hampshire. These had been issued on the request of Paxton largely as a measure for enforcing trading with the enemy acts. They never had been a part of the Navigation and Trade Acts, which had operated successfully for a century without them.

The Revenue Act of 1767 authorized their issue by the highest court in each province, but did not provide any form for such writs. Customs officers secured copies of the forms issued by the Exchequer Court in England. These were entirely novel to the judges and lawyers in America who had been trained in the common law courts. On instructions from the Customs Commissioners customs officers in each colony year after year were required to apply through the attorneys-general to the courts to issue this particular form of general search warrant. These repeated applications made writs of assistance an issue before the supreme court of every colony other than those of Massachusetts and New Hampshire from 1767 to the Revolution. In Connecticut, Rhode Island, New York, New Jersey, Delaware, Pennsylvania, Maryland, Virginia, and North Carolina the courts rejected these applications year after year.[91]

The question of issuing writs of assistance was directly related to customs racketeering and was especially connected with the new practice of the customs officers demanding that certificates of importation accompany all dutiable goods. Wherever such goods could be found—and after 1770 this meant tea, wine, molasses, coffee, and rum—a charge of illegal importation could be filed unless the person in whose hands such goods were found could produce a detailed certificate of importation. With the system of spies, snoopers, and stool pigeons honest traders were in grave danger. Tea, wine, molasses, and rum were articles of wide consumption. Every retailer carried them. They passed from hand to hand like money. Certificates could not keep up with them as they passed into retail and consumption channels.

Possession without certificate and proof of importation was a presumption of illegal importation. Proof was on the owner of the goods, not on the customs officers. General power to search and seize opened such unlimited possibilities of plunder and blackmail that most of the judges in America, even though they were the staunchest Tories, refused to issue such writs in the form demanded, even when subjected to the heaviest political pressure.[92]

Thus outside of Massachusetts and New Hampshire the question of writs of assistance was made a part of the whole issue of taxation by Parliament, self-government, and English legal rights. There were enough abuses in the use of such writs in the colonies where they were issued to cause them to be associated in the minds of Americans with the worst phase of plundering by customs officers.

ATTEMPT TO CONTROL INTER-COLONIAL TRANSPORTATION BY LAND

It has already been pointed out that there were clauses in the revenue acts that could be used to set up legal controls over shipment of goods by land from one colony to another. Land transportation was developing rapidly in the decade preceding the Revolution. Most of the good wagon roads were from the older settlements near the seaboard into the back country. But some ran from one colony to another. Roads of this kind which first became important were those from Boston to Rhode Island and

across the narrow neck from the Delaware River to the settlements on the east side of the upper Chesapeake Bay region of the
Maryland east shore. This last-named section became the testing
ground for the program to control goods carried by land from one
colony to another.

Robert Stratford Byrne, apparently a Scotchman directly from
Britain, got himself appointed Surveyor of Customs at Sassafras
and Bohemia, two large inlets on the eastern shore of Chesapeake
Bay, near the north end. He says he had been assured an income
of £500 a year, although the salary was much less. The balance
was expected to come from fees, seizures, and gratuities of various
kinds. There were practically no entries or clearances and consequently no fees.[93] Apparently he needed money and began to
hunt for goods that could be seized. The Commissioners of Customs in 1774 had sent instructions to all of their customs officers
"to exert themselves" to prevent the revenue system from col-
lapsing. So early in March, 1775, Byrne went out and exerted himself.

There was a well-developed main road from Duck Creek on the
Delaware River across Delaware to Georgetown on the Big Sassafras Inlet in Maryland and on to the other settlements on the east
side of Chesapeake Bay. Over this road went many heavy wagons
loaded with goods for Maryland stores. On March 2, 1775, Byrne
went out along this road and finally met two wagons heavily laden
with freight headed west. He stopped them in the name of the
law and demanded where they were from, where they were going
and what they carried. The answer was "from Duck Creek" and
the goods were mainly the property of Messrs. Lorain, Bolton, and
Anderson, to whose store in Chester Town they were going. Duck
Creek was in Delaware; Chester Town was in Maryland. Their
loads consisted of rum, sugar, coffee, piece goods, and other articles
of common trade. Here was direct evidence of goods carried from
one colony to another and, as some were subject to customs duties
on importation, they came under the technical provisions of the
revenue acts requiring certificates, cockets, bonds, etc.

Byrne demanded that the teamsters show him their cockets.
Asking a teamster on an American road in the woods, miles from

the sea and in a relatively uninhabited country, for a cocket for goods he was hauling and had been hauling along that same road for years, was an unheard act of impudence. A naval customs officer in uniform on such a road was as much of a novelty as would have been an elephant. The teamsters had no cockets, had never heard of them, and in language "such as the Gentiles use and lesser breeds without the law" are likely to use on such occasions they told Byrne they had no such documents and that they did not use them in their business. He then explained that under the law he would be required to seize their wagons, teams, and the goods carried by them. It was a good haul. His third would help to bring his income up to the £500 promised.

The teamsters drove on and Byrne trudged along beside the wagons for six or eight miles. Then the teamsters insisted they must stop to "bait" their horses. They had selected a spot near a mill owned by Oliver Gallop where there were several persons assembled. Byrne did not like the looks of things and insisted they should push on as the road ahead was lonely and he was alone. The teamsters informed him in highly professional American teamster language that they were hauling the goods and would do as they pleased.

While the wagons were halted and the teams were being fed an event happened that was almost as significant as the destruction of the tea at Boston. Country people going to and from the mill quickly assembled about the wagons, talked to the teamsters and began examining the goods on the wagons. There was a cask in one wagon that apparently contained gunpowder. A desire to possess this was loudly expressed in a tone that made Byrne even more nervous. He roughly ordered the country people to keep away from the wagons, as they were "the King's property."

That was the signal the crowd was apparently waiting for. They at once rushed him, pinned him to the ground, rifled his pockets, confiscated a new purse he carried in one of his pockets, took his money, gave him an uneven coat of tar so applied as to spoil every garment, kicked his shins, made him drink with them, rode him around on some rails (he called it a raft), made him beg for his life, and exacted repeated promises from him that he would never again commit another act of this kind. He was assured that if he were ever again caught in that part of Maryland his life would pay the penalty. The treatment and the talk were very persuasive. He claims that his entertainment there in the woods lasted about three hours. In the meantime the teamsters hitched up their horses and drove away with their loads.[94]

Byrne finally escaped from the mob and fled into the woods, where he concealed himself for two days. Then he made his way as secretly as possible to Annapolis, where he laid his case before Governor Eden and his council. At that council meeting was Daniel Dulany. The council after hearing Byrne and listening to his affidavit as to what had happened to him solemnly referred the case to the Attorney-General to investigate.[95]

Byrne at once wrote letters to the Commissioners of Customs describing his harrowing experience and enclosing a copy of his sworn statement. Byrne explained that he had been so roughly handled and that the arguments of the crowd had been so convincing that he dared not go back to his post without an armed guard to protect him. He begged the Commissioners to give him a different assignment and a leave of absence for two years so he could return to England for his health.[96] The Board paid him a liberal compensation for his alleged losses and complimented him for his action. He never returned to his post.

Thus ended the one attempt to put customs officers on inland roads from one colony to another with power to compel freight wagons to enter, clear, give bonds, carry cockets, and pay duties. America would indeed have had a centralized government had the Customs Commissioners succeeded in this effort. The rural people of Maryland stopped that attempt as effectively as Bostonians in a similar frame of mind stopped the argument over tea. There were no later attempts of this kind, as the cold war had already become a shooting war.

The End of an Era

The era of customs racketeering largely came to an end by the middle of 1770. Customs officers preferred the rich harvest of fees to the risk of being chased out of the colony by unwise seizures.[97] The publication of the letters of Bernard and the Commissioners disclosing they had asked for military protection had eliminated Bernard and gravely undermined what remaining prestige the Commissioners had. In January, 1770, they were indicted by the local grand jury for slandering Boston and the province of Massachusetts.[98]

Political changes in England, in turn, retired some of the most inveterate enemies of America. The end of the Wilkes agitation gave tempers a chance to cool. The "Boston Massacre" forced the withdrawal of troops from Boston and the end to customs officers calling for military force to support their arbitrary actions. The experience of the Commissioners in fleeing for their lives, having their employees indicted for murder for firing on the people of Boston the night of March 5, 1770, and the universal unpopularity of their conduct seem to have had a moderating influence on their later conduct.[99]

In addition they had a long vacation away from Boston. For more than eight months the Board did not meet. It was a sort of sit-down strike on their part to force the home government to place military force again at their disposal. It failed. The Treasury Board in London ordered them to resume work.[100] Parliament, yielding to the clamor from both England and America, repealed all the new taxes, except that on tea, on the ground that they were anti-trade and an injury to British commerce. The former political patrons of the Board were discredited. Temple had returned to England, where he could tell the truth about the unwise policies of the Commissioners. The political teeth of the Board had been effectually drawn and they were pretty thoroughly tamed. Before they could again become troublesome, the Hutchinson letters were made public, thus destroying the influence of their last important supporter in America.

But the damage had been done. From one end of America to the other the old devotion to the commercial colonial empire had been undermined. Only in the Virginia-Maryland-northern-North Carolina area did the merchants as a class remain loyal.[101] The reason seems obvious: In this area there had been no serious interference with trade, no irritating seizures, and no racketeering.[102]

Otherwise, from one end of America to the other the regulations designed to raise a revenue were opposed by the commercial-shipping classes.

The culminating episode was simple. Prior to the decision in 1772 to give the East India Company a practically legal monopoly of tea exports to America, tea had gone out with nearly every shipment of goods. Rigid enforcement of nonimportation would have involved opening every container as it arrived. The new plan placed all the trump cards in the hands of the radicals. For the first time they could duplicate the tactics used so successfully against the stamps. In this case, however, direct action was necessary at only four points—Boston, New York, Philadelphia, and Charleston—all points of extreme friction from 1767 to 1770. One riot did the job. Threats either sent the tea back or kept it from entering into commerce at the other three.

REFERENCES

CHAPTER 9

1. These are 7 George III, c. 46 and 7 George III, c. 41, respectively. Both are dated June 29, 1767. Pickering, *Statutes at Large*, XXVII, 509-12; 447-49.

2. Alderman Trecothic was said to have a copy of a will by which Paxton had given Townshend the reversion of an estate valued at £50,000. ("Journal of the Times" for December 27, 1768. First printed in *New York Journal*, January 19, 1769.)

3. This is revealed in their letters that were widely published in the colonial newspapers. The model Bernard held up was a relationship such as that between England and Ireland. He recommended specific changes in the charter of Massachusetts so as to reduce popular control of the government. E. Channing and A. C. Coolidge, *The Barrington—Bernard Correspondence* (Cambridge, 1912). Barrington was Secretary at War during the entire period, 1765-78, and very influential among the King's Friends. He and Bernard were cousins.

4. Their letters to the Treasury Board, February 12 and March 28, 1768, describe conditions as one of extreme opposition and state that force would be required to enforce the revenue laws. They merely echo what Bernard had been writing, *Treasury* 1:465.

5. Not a case of popular clamour against illegal seizures in these provinces has been found in the newspapers of the period. The papers of the Customs Commissioners contain no references to such troubles. C. C. Crittenden, *Commerce of North Carolina* (New Haven, 1936), reports only three seizures from 1767 to 1774, pp. 43-44. C. A. Barker, *Background of the Revolution in Maryland* (New Haven, 1940) found only four seizures in Maryland for the same years, p. 198.

6. Letter of Collector of New York to Customs Commissioners, July 8, 1775. *Treasury* 1:513.

7. Letter to the Treasury in London, November 14, 1769. *Treasury* 1:471.

8. I. S. Harrell, *Loyalism in Virginia* (Durham, N. C., 1926) pp. 33, 48, 62-65.

9. L. A. Harper, *English Navigation Laws*, pp. 110-16.

10. The fullest account of arbitrary practices was gathered and printed in a day-to-day account from September 29, 1768, to August 1, 1769, in "A Journal of the Times." In this form it was widely printed in colonial, and

some English, newspapers. The entire series has been reprinted by the author under the title *Boston Under Military Rule, 1768-1769.* Illustrations of the above are on pp. 36, 102-3.

11. *Ibid.,* pp. 68, 77, 79-80.

12. Letter from Mr. Symmer, agent at New Providence, *Treasury* 1:482.

13. Opinion dated February 1, 1768. *Treasury* 1:468.

14. Opinion dated May 1, 1768, in the case of the schooner *Hope. Treasury* 1:465.

15. Opinion of Attorney-General DeGrey, dated London, September 8, 1768. *Treasury* 1:465.

16. This was reported in the "Journal of the Times" for January 12, 1769, and repeated on February 4. In this form it was very widely published in colonial newspapers.

17. The accounts on this point are so full and so frequent all during 1769 that there can be no doubt of the practice. *Boston Under Military Rule, 1768-1769* (Boston, 1936), pp. 59-60, 84, 103.

18. At Providence, Rhode Island, May 18, 1769, James Saville, a tidesman, was seized while on duty, gagged; had his clothes cut from his body; was covered with turpentine and feathers from head to foot; was beaten; had dirt thrown on him; was carried about in a wheelbarrow; and was generally manhandled for an hour and a half. These facts are reported in a proclamation of the customhouse signed by Richard Reeve and offering a reward of £50 for the apprehension of the guilty persons (*New Providence Gazette,* June 10, 1769).

John Rowe records the tarring and feathering of an informer in Boston on October 28, 1769 (*Diary and Letters,* p. 194). The *Boston Gazette,* August 15, 1768, *Supplement,* records the near drowning of a subordinate employee of the customs, who was "making Virginia Fence on the brink of Charleston Ferry" and fell into the river. At Newburyport, Joshua Vickery, a supposed informer, was put in the stocks; carried through town with a rope about his neck; pelted with eggs, gravel, and stones; handcuffed, and kept in a dark warehouse over Sunday (*Essex Gazette,* September 27, 1768). At Salem a customhouse waiter by the name of Row was taken to the common, tarred and feathered; seated in a cart with a placard front and back; and in that condition conducted down the main street through the jeers of the populace. He was warned to get out of town and promised worse treatment if he ever returned (*Essex Gazette,* September 13, 1769).

At New Haven, Connecticut, an alleged informer was put "on an eminence," where he promised never to inform against anyone else. He was then given a coat of tar, two pillows of feathers were emptied over him, a pair of horns was fixed on his head, and he then was permitted to get out of town (*Boston Gazette,* September 18, 1769).

In Rhode Island two tidewaiters, after they had gone on board a ship, were stripped, rubbed with oil of tar and feathers, and then transferred to the hold of an empty vessel in the harbor (*Boston Gazette,* July 6, 1772). Many more illustrations could be given but these show the temper of the times. The reports to the Customs Commissioners contain many reports from places outside of New England.

19. They are officially reported as £64-6-11 in 1768; and £72-16-11 in 1769. *Treasury* 1:461.

20. Letter of John Swift, the Collector, to the Commissioners, October 13, 1769. *Treasury* 1:471.

21. Here is a typical contract with a captain, "Pay Master £7-10 to £8 a month, Pennsylvania currency—present of 5 or 6 gallons of spirits per voyage —privilege of carrying 18 barrels of flour freight free or same bulk in other goods." Stocker and Wharton to Christopher Champlain, Philadelphia, June 18, 1773. *Commerce of Rhode Island* (Massachusetts Historical Society, Series Seven, IX, pp. 440-41).

22. The *New London Gazette* for September 22, 1769, gives in great detail an account of the arbitrary and unwarranted seizures by Captain Reid of the *Liberty* (Hancock's former vessel). When remonstrated with by local merchants because of the breaking of casks and the rummaging of trunks and other private property, Reid answered "every man on board had a share in the prizes, the same as of an enemy, and therefore they had a right to make all the discovery they could."

23. W. B. Kerr, *Bermuda in the American Revolution* (Princeton, 1936) pp. 3-25.

24. The local newspapers had numerous complaints of this practice. See *New London Gazette* for September 22, 1769; *Boston Under Military Rule*, pp. 48, 103; *Pennsylvania Journal*, February 9, 1774.

25. Opinion of Attorney-General DeGrey in the case of the *Ann*, March 9, 1769. *Treasury* 1:472.

26. Several cases of this kind were reported at Boston, *Boston Under Military Rule*, pp. 45, 80, 113. Benjamin Wright at Savanna la Marr on June 17, 1769, wrote Aaron Lopez at Providence that there might be more molasses on board one of his ships than invoices show and to watch the unloading to avoid a seizure. *Commerce of Rhode Island* (Massachusetts Historical Society, Series Seven, IX) pp. 279-80.

27. *Ibid.*, p. 331. See also his letter of March 9, 1768.

28. Carleton to the Commissioners of Customs, October 25, 1769. *Treasury* 1:474.

29. Decree of Vice-Admiralty Court at Quebec, November 17, 1769. *Treasury* 1:474.

30. Letter of Carleton to the Customs Commissioners, November 22, 1769. *Ibid.*

31. Letters of Mellish to the Customs Commissioners, November 23 and December 2, 1769. *Ibid.*

32. Secretary Richard Reeve to the Treasury Board, August 14, 1770. *Treasury* 1:476.

33. Leila Sellers, *Charleston Business on the Eve of the Revolution* (Chapel Hill, 1934), pp. 49-50; David D. Wallace, *Life of Henry Laurens* (New York, 1915), pp. 44-76.

34. Sellers, *op. cit.*, pp. 192-93.

35. *Ibid.*, pp. 193-94.

36. Letter of Roupell to the Customs Commissioners, July 11, 1768, *Treas-*

260 NAVIGATION ACTS AND AMERICAN REVOLUTION

ury 1:465; D. D. Wallace, *Life of Henry Laurens,* pp. 137-39; Sellers, *Charleston Business on the Eve of the Revolution,* pp. 194-95.

37. This was in lawful money which was worth about one-seventh as much as sterling.

38. The Customs Commissioners later reported that he had been driven from Charleston by the merchants.

39. This ship was owned only one-fourth by Laurens: William Fisher, of Philadelphia, and two British houses were also interested in her, each for a fourth. Sellers, *op. cit.,* p. 198, states that Cowles and Co. of Bristol had a half interest in the vessel.

40. The official inventory ordered by the court. *Treasury* 1:465. The secondary accounts state there was also some rum, but this is not listed in the invoice. The difference is that a rum bond would have been required if there had been rum on board.

41. Letter of Roupell to Customs Commissioners, August 6, 1768. *Treasury* 1:463; letter of Customs Commissioners to Treasury Board, August 25, 1768, transmitting full details of events at Charleston. *Treasury* 1:465.

42. Transcript of record in the case of the *Ann* supplied by Roupell. *Ibid.*

43. Sellers, *op. cit.,* p. 199.

44. These are in *Treasury* 1:463, 465.

45. Opinion dated March 9, 1769, signed by DeGrey. *Treasury* 1:472.

46. *Extracts from the Proceedings of the Court of Vice Admiralty in Charleston, South Carolina* (Charleston, 1769). See also D. D. Wallace, *Life of Henry Laurens* (New York, 1915), pp. 140-47.

47. According to Wallace, Laurens, before publishing his pamphlets, sent the manuscript to Philadelphia and to influential persons in England. In this way it came to the notice of the ministry, who forced Leigh to give up some of his ill-gotten gains. *Ibid.,* p. 145.

48. July 27, 1769.

49. October 19, 1769. This was reproduced by Rind's *Virginia Gazette,* on November 16 following.

50. *Treasury* 1:465.

51. Sellers, *op. cit.,* p. 201.

52. There is no good biography of Hancock. The best treatise on his commercial activities is W. T. Baxter, *The House of Hancock* (Cambridge, Massachusetts, 1945), Chap. xii-xv.

53. *Ibid.*

54. Memorial of the Customs Commissioners to the Treasury Board in London, May 12, 1768. *Treasury* 1:465.

55. *Bowdoin-Temple Letters,* Massachusetts Historical Society *Collections* Sixth Series (Boston, 1897) IX, 29, 54-55, 70-74, 76-77, 283. Joseph Harrison, Collector at Boston, when he visited London in 1766, was a guest at Rockingham's home, where he served as an assistant to Burke, who at that time was secretary to Rockingham. *Ibid.,* 72-73.

56. Treasury Board to Commissioners of Customs, December 26, 1768. *Treasury* 1:465.

57. The official records of many details of this intrigue are in *Treasury* 1:465, 471. John Adams was involved in some way. He claims in his "Diary"

that Sewall asked him to accept the position of Advocate-General for the court of Vice-Admiralty at Boston, a position held by Sewall at that time. C. F. Adams, *The Works of John Adams* (10 volumes, Boston, 1850-56) II, 210, 212. The records of the Customs Commissioners show he was employed by them in one case about this time. There is a summary of part of this struggle for preferment in O. M. Dickerson, "John Hancock Notorious Smuggler or Near Victim of British Customs Racketeers," *Mississippi Valley Historical Review* (March, 1943), XXXII, 532-34.

58. Memorial of Customs Commissioners to Treasury Board in London, May 12, 1768. *Treasury* 1:465.

59. This very important opinion of Sewall's is printed in *William and Mary Quarterly* (October, 1947) Third Series IV, 499-504.

60. May 12, 1768. *Treasury* 1:465.

61. *Ibid.*

62. A. E. Brown, *John Hancock, His Book* (Boston, 1898).

63. Report of Customs Commissioners to Treasury Board in London, June 15, 1768. *Treasury* 1:465.

64. Thomas Hutchinson, *History of the Colony and Province of Massachusetts Bay* (L. S. Mayo, editor) (3 vols., Cambridge, Mass., 1936), III, 137.

65. The sworn statements of what happened are in *Treasury* 1:465. G. G. Wolkins has printed all of these in an excellent article "The Seizure of John Hancock's Sloop Liberty," Massachusetts Historical Society, *Proceedings, XV* (Boston, 1921-33) pp. 251 ff.

66. Vice-Admiralty Court Records, Office Clerk of the Supreme Judicial Court, Boston, Massachusetts.

67. *Ibid.*

68. Wolkins, *op. cit.*, prints a copy of Kirk's statement, which seems to be an accurate transcript, taken from *Treasury* 1:465.

69. Letter of Customs Commissioners, June 15, 1768. *Treasury* 1:465.

70. A. E. Brown, *op. cit.*, p. 156.

71. He was allowed compensation for travel to and from England and paid an allowance of a guinea a day from July 7, 1768 to May 19, 1769, while in England. That would be equal to fifty dollars a day at the present time. He also got himself in line to replace Temple as a member of the Board of Customs Commissioners. On September 27, 1770, the record shows he received £393-1-0. He also drew his regular salary. *Treasury* 1:471.

72. Record of expenditures by the Commissioners. *Treasury* 1:461.

73. The amount of the suit is given as £9000 in the "Journal of the Times" for November 5, 1768. *Boston Under Military Rule*, pp. 16, 31. General Gage, who was in Boston at the time, says he heard the matter discussed and says, "The People prosecuted are Messrs. Hancock and Malcolm: accused of declaring publicly that they would land their Goods and would not pay the Duties. That they did accordingly land their Goods without paying the Duties by Law Established in defiance of the Officers of the Customs. They were arrested during my Residence in Boston. Hancock, one of the most Oppulent Men in this Country, I think for the sum of £13,000 and both after some time gave Bail. The Reason given why those Persons were not arrested before was that the Prosecutors were afraid and darst not attempt it—till they were

protected by the presence of the Troops; for Mr. Hancock and Malcolm were reported to have been Leaders or Abettors of the Mob. I confine myself to the general Heads of Accusation which I recollect to have heard; Some particular Circumstances relative to the Conduct of these persons were mentioned at the time, of which I have not sufficient Recollection to relate to your Lordship." Gage to Hillsborough, New York, March 5, 1769. Clarence E. Carter, ed., *Correspondence of General Thomas Gage* (2 vols. New Haven, Conn., 1931-33), I, 220. A full copy of the charges against Hancock is in Josiah Quincy, *Massachusetts Reports* (Boston, 1865), I, 459. This gives the sum sued for as £9000.

74. "This morning Mr. Arodi Thayer, Marshal of the Court of Admiralty for three provinces, with a hanger at his side, came to the house of John Hancock, Esq.; to serve him with a precept for £9000 sterling and having arrested his person, demanded bail for £3000 sterling. Mr. Hancock offered him divers estates to the value thereof, which were absolutely refused; he then made him an offer of £3000 in money, and afterwards of £9000, which were also refused; Mr. Thayer alledging that such were his directions. Mr. Hancock however having heard of the orders—prudently determined to give bail, as did five other gentlemen arrested for the same sum, and on the same account from like prudent motives." ("Journal of the Times," November 3, 1768, *Boston Under Military Rule*, p. 18.) There is a copy of Auchmuty's order for the arrest of Hancock in Quincy, *Reports*, I, 458. The marshal obviously did what he was ordered to do.

The others arrested at the same time as shown by the Admiralty Court Record in the office of the Clerk of the Supreme Judicial Court of Massachusetts were Daniel Malcolm, John Matchet, William Bower, and Lewis Gray. Nathaniel Barnard was the sixth person, but the Admiralty Record shows no service was secured in his case.

75. *Correspondence of General Thomas Gage* (C. E. Carter, ed.), I, 206.

76. *Ibid.*, 220.

77. *Boston Chronicle*, June 13, 1768.

78. "Journal of the Times," January 2, February 11, 1769. *Boston Under Military Rule*, pp. 43, 64.

79. "Journal of the Times," February 18, 1769. *Ibid.*, p. 66. Most of the statements in this widely circulated contemporary account are supported by the brief entries in the Record of the Vice-Admiralty and by the account of John Adams, who was attorney for Hancock and knew specifically what was done. *Works of John Adams*, II (Diary), p. 216. There is also full supporting evidence in Quincy, *Massachusetts Reports*, I, 459. Taken from notes made by Adams.

80. "Journal of the Times," January 5, 1769, *Boston Under Military Rule*, p. 45.

81. It is impossible to determine accurately the full amounts expended by the Commissioners in this prosecution, because the latter attempted to conceal many items under other labels. An examination of their expenditure accounts for 1768-69, transmitted to the Treasury Board in England, reveals the following that included probable expenditures in this case:

One William Rogers on May 4, 1769, was paid ten shillings "for giving

Information." While this sum seems small it was the pay of a regular tide-waiter for more than a week. Sewall and Samuel Fitch each were paid £72 sterling in two separate payments on October 27, 1768, and February 7, 1769, as "retainers fees in sundry causes depending for the Crown." These are exceptionally large fees, as all previous payments were for about five per cent of these sums.

Between July 8, 1768, and January 19, 1769, a period of less than eight months, and the period when maximum efforts were being made to secure evidence against Hancock, a total of £470 was paid to Green and Russell for "printing." John Mein received large sums for "Stationery." His paper, the *Boston Chronicle,* for months in 1769 conducted a smear campaign against Hancock. Among the Treasury Papers is a letter from Mein describing his services at this time and requesting a pension. Obviously it was granted because his name is in Lord North's list of pensioners after 1770 (*Correspondence of King George The Third,* V, 468).

A "Mr. Irving from Scotland," probably Thomas Irving, was given large sums for general spy and information work in Boston and a surprising increase in salary. Secretary Venner states that he, personally, could have had almost any financial remuneration he might have asked and the Board would have dropped the charges against him if he would have engaged in similar work. Memorial of Samuel Venner to the Duke of Grafton, May 1, 1769, *Treasury* 1:471.

The pretext of "refitting" the confiscated *Liberty* as a revenue boat was made to cover what looks like large items for some other purpose. Between December 19, 1768, and June 2, 1769, Robert Hallowell was paid £650 for this purpose. It took an additional £281 to "refit" the *Liberty* on August 21, 1769. The vessel had a probable value of £1000 before it was seized.

Excessive amounts are charged for "Barge and boats" and other services for the Commissioners while they were at Castle William during the summer of 1768, one payment in 1769, to Bergressen and New, alone, for "Barges and boat" amounted to £249. *Treasury* 1:461.

The above are only the most conspicuous items in the list of certified expenditures. The fact that so many items are for round sums in pounds indicates that they were not regular payments on properly itemized accounts.

82. Joseph Muzzele or Maysel. Items in "A Journal of the Times" for March 27 and April 22, 1769. *Boston Under Military Rule,* pp. 84, 92. There are intimations that this may have been the real informer.

83. *Ibid.,* pp. 46, 67, 68.

84. The full course of the trial can be followed in "A Journal of the Times" a day to day account prepared in Boston, first published in the *New York Journal,* thence widely copied into colonial and English newspapers. This publication started on September 28, 1768, and continued to August 1, 1769. It is the only service of this kind during the Revolutionary period. It has been gathered together and printed under the title *Boston Under Military Rule,* 1768-69, already referred to. See also Quincy, *Reports* I, 463 ff., for additional items.

85. The Virginia constitution of 1776 provided for trial by jury, examination of witness face to face, and prohibited excessive bail, Ben P. Poore,

Charters and Constitutions (2 vols., Washington, 1878), II. The North Carolina constitution of 1776 guaranteed indictment by grand jury, trial by jury, and prohibited excessive bail. *(Ibid.)* The Connecticut constitution of 1776 contained a general provision that the procedure must be according to the law of the land. *(Ibid.,* I, 258.) The Maryland constitution of 1776 required indictment by a grand jury, examination of witnesses face to face, and insured trial by jury. *(Ibid.,* 317.) The Pennsylvania constitution, 1776, included trial by jury, right to confront witness face to face, and prohibited forced self-incrimination. *(Ibid.,* II, 1541.) Vermont adopted a constitution in 1777, with a clause almost identical with the provisions in the Pennsylvania constitution. *(Ibid.,* II, 1860.) The Georgia constitution of 1777 prohibited excessive bail and excessive fines. *(Ibid.,* I, 383.) The Massachusetts constitution of 1780 required trial by jury, examination of witnesses face to face, by implication an indictment by grand jury, and prohibited forced self-incrimination.

The movement to add a bill of rights to the new federal constitution was started by Hancock's own proposals in the Massachusetts state ratifying convention. The sixth of these resolutions specifically required indictment by grand jury. *Documentary History of the Constitution of the United States* (3 vols., Washington, 1894-1900), II, 95. It is significant that the New York state convention expanded Hancock's proposals into almost the specific form of the present fifth, sixth, seventh, and eighth amendments. *Ibid.,* 191-92. The people of New York were fully aware of the dangers involved in the extraordinary prosecution of Hancock because the first full accounts of that trial were published in the *New York Journal.* Leading men in that state could hardly avoid thinking of that particular case when they proposed specific guarantees against any such future injustices. There was no other similar case that they could have had in mind.

86. Letter of Treasury Board in London to Commissioners of Customs. December 26, 1768. *Treasury* 1:465.

87. Report to the Commissioners of Customs by John Swift, Collector at Philadelphia. *Treasury* 1:482.

88. "The wretches employed to carry the grievous laws into execution—I mean the pilfering and most grievous part of them—are justly complained of everywhere—*here* from the Deputy Collector downwards to a man. They are strongly described by the character of those miscreants who were driven out of the Temple by Jesus with a scourge of small cords." Henry Laurens to James Grant of Florida, January 22, 1769. David D. Wallace, *Life of Henry Laurens* (New York, 1915), p. 147.

89. On January 12, 1769, a Portsmouth, New Hampshire, vessel was detained because a barrel of wine was found on board (*Boston Evening Post,* February 27, 1769). September 30, 1769, John Rowe records: "This day the Customs House officers made a large seizure from Capt. John Horner who I take to be a very honest Good man and for which I am very sorry should happen at this time." (*Letters and Diary,* p. 193.) The *Essex Gazette* for November 19, 1771, gives an account of the seizure of goods belonging to "a Gentleman of Fortune of one of the First Families and employed in one of the most important Offices in this Town." The *New London Gazette* for

September 22, 1769, gives in great detail an account of the arbitary and unwarranted seizures by Captain Reid of the *Liberty* (Hancock's former vessel which had been taken over by the revenue service). When remonstrated with by local merchants because of the breaking of casks and the rummaging of trunks and other private property, Reid answered that "every man on board had a share in the prizes, the same as of an enemy, and therefore they had a right to make all the discovery they could." Numerous other illustrations can be found in the newspapers for 1768-69. Most of these are from South Carolina and New England, but the same unpopular practices existed in other ports. The *Pennsylvania Journal*, February 9, 1774, has an article signed "Mercator," in which the author complains of the extortions "the Merchants have long experienced."

90. Letter to the Treasury Board in London, January 16, 1769, *Treasury* 1:471.

91. The originals of the reports by customs officers are in their reports to the Customs Commissioners, *Treasury* 1:491, 492, 493, 501. The only summary of the entire attempt is in R. B. Morris, ed., *The Era of the American Revolution* (New York, 1939), chapter 2, "Writs of Assistance as a Cause of the Revolution."

92. *Ibid.*

93. Recorded testimony of Byrne before the Governor and Council of Maryland, March 16, 1775.

94. Copies of Byrne's elaborate affidavit, and his letters to the Commissioners of Customs dated March 10 and March 17, 1775, elaborating on the treatment he had received are in *Treasury* 1:513.

95. Minutes of Maryland Council, March 17, 1775.

96. Letters of March 10 and March 17, 1775, *Treasury* 1:513.

97. There are many instances where customs officers, after an arbitrary seizure, actually had to flee. An example is William Shepherd, Surveyor and Searcher at Philadelphia, as recorded in great detail in his letter to the Commissioners of April 24, 1769. *Treasury* 1:471.

98. Letter of Secretary Reeve to the Treasury in London, January 4, 1770, enclosing a copy of the indictment. *Treasury* 1:476. Manwaring, a very unpopular tidesman, had his defense expenses on this indictment for murder, totaling £88-14-0, sterling, paid by the Board and was given leave to go to England for six months, obviously to prevent a conviction. Letter of Board to the Treasury in London, June 10, 1771. *Treasury* 1:482.

99. The clearest statement of this is in a letter from Commissioners Burch and Hulton to the Duke of Grafton, written from Piscataqua, New Hampshire, where they had taken refuge, dated April 3, 1770. The letter is obviously written to excite pity. *Treasury* 1:476.

100. *Treasury* 1:478.

101. Isaac S. Harrell, *Loyalism in Virginia* (Durham, N. C., 1926), pp. 62-63.

102. The fullest information on this point is in the long, detailed report of Inspector John Williams of conditions at the ports in this area July 14-25, 1770. According to his report there was less supervision by customs officers and less restraint on trade at these ports than in any other area in America. *Treasury* 1:476.

ENGLISH OPINION

FROM THE controversial pamphlets, the newspapers, the published letters to Americans, and from the records of the debates in Parliament, it is possible to get a pretty definite idea of the trends of English opinion on the Navigation Acts.

In considering English opinion it must be borne in mind that the British Empire constituted the greatest commercial unit of the eighteenth century. The unification had been brought about by the trade and navigation systems carefully worked out over more than a century of legislation and commercial development. English and colonial industries were adjusted to this system; people living in 1765 had not known from direct experience any other. Capital had been invested in colonial enterprises; in shipping, and in commercial and manufacturing business in the home country under the tacit assumption that this was a permanent part of the established order. Money had been borrowed and loaned, and laborers had established their homes in the belief that this system would never be disturbed. Wars had been fought and won to retain the commercial advantages thus painfully built up. The permanency of the system was less questioned than is the capitalistic structure of western European nations today. It was as much a part of British commercial practice and thinking as the tariff system of the United States is a part of the financial and commercial life of this country.

Practically every session of Parliament from 1764 to the outbreak of the Revolution saw minor adjustments in the elaborate system of regulations, rebates, export and import bounties, debentures, preferential tariffs, and shipping regulations intended to promote the interests of various politically conscious commercial groups. Many of these adjustments were distinctly favorable to the colonies.

THE THEORETICAL FREE TRADERS

The only serious critics of the system as a whole were a few theoretical free traders who formed the first school of modern economists. Sir Matthew Decker's essay on the *Causes of the Decline of the Foreign Trade* was going through its second edition in 1750. While this accepts the navigation system as beneficial in practice, it condemns it in theory.

Although this act is beneficial to us under our present diseases in trade, but would be needless were they perfectly remedied, yet it is even now not without its inconveniences; for a law that confines, in any degree, our imports or exports to particular ships or men, gives a monopoly to those for whose benefit the restraint is formed, which in this case is either the navigation of the countries whose growths we import, or else our own. And this monopoly is very prejudicial to our manufactures; for 'tis enacting that several necessities and materials of manufacture shall not be imported by the cheapest navigation, but by a dearer one, and of course that they shall pay dear freights, which must raise their price; and if the manufacturer buys his materials dear, he must sell his manufacture in proportion.[1]

This argument, like so many others against the established commercial system, was entirely theoretic. It assumed that the restrictions on navigation and trade made commodities and freight high, without going to the trouble to investigate specifically whether they were actually relatively high or low.

Discussing the Navigation Act in particular, he says:

Now as this act makes our navigation dear, it for that reason deprives us of the fishing-trade, the great nursery of seamen, which cannot be carried on but by a cheap navigation to vie with the *Dutch* and *French*, in which we make no progress worth speaking of: Therefore, in this case, this act has deprived us of seamen, instead of increasing them; and the acquisition of foreign seamen, in any degree being prevented by this act, gives a monopoly to our own sailors, by which means, in war-time, or any spurt of trade, they exact near double the wages that foreign seamen are content with; which oppresses our merchants, brings our goods dear to all markets, giving foreign manufacturers a great advantage against our own, and our sailors lying hid in order to get greater wages by their monopoly in the merchant's service, is one, amongst other reasons, for the difficulties we find in manning the king's ships.[2]

In less than ten years the very system he condemned produced ships and seamen to give England complete mastery of the seas of the world.

Decker, however, stood practically alone in his free trade theories. Businessmen and politicians were wedded to the plan that had worked for a century and made Britain the leading commercial nation of the age. Until the outbreak of the Revolution there was only an occasional pamphlet or article in the current periodicals that questioned the desirability of the navigation system, and these are either anonymous or under pen names. Among the pamphlets that were brought forth by the Stamp Act controversy, one urged the complete removal of all restrictions upon the colonial trade. It claimed that England would be better off and could sell more goods to the Americans if the latter were permitted to sell all of their goods wherever they could find the best market.[3]

In 1773 a writer under the name of "Rationalis" contributed articles to the *London Chronicle*, in which he held that the soil and climate of America were so similar to those of England that trade was unnatural and forced, and hence unprofitable. So long as there were extensive government bills to be paid in the colonies, merchants could receive their pay in bills on London or in cash; but, when the government payments ceased, the Americans had no means of remittance. This trade was not, in his opinion, beneficial to the colonies, "for although our goods are sold as cheap as in London . . . their inability to pay . . . is such, that they are continually prosecuted . . . and their houses and lands taken from them and often for . . . the luxuries of both Europe and Asia, which their inability to pay for should dictate to them to do without."[4]

Adam Smith's attack upon the commercial system came too late to affect the course of the major controversy, but it has influenced historical interpretation of the causes of the Revolution. He is the best-known of the economic writers of this period who advocated free trade policies on theoretical grounds. His position is frequently misrepresented, as his arguments are spread over a large part of Books IV and V of his *Wealth of Nations,* which first appeared in 1776. In the first place, he admits that restraints of trade are proper when the object is to build up an industry that is essential for national defense. He accepts the shipping sections of the Navigation Acts as proper measures for building up a body of English seamen and a supply of necessary shipping.[5] On the other hand he condemns the commodity clauses of these acts on the ground that they are not favorable to foreign trade.[6] However, he expresses the opinion that industry has become so adjusted to the protective features of the commercial system that complete free trade in England can never be hoped for.[7]

In his discussion of the colonial applications of the commercial system, Smith displays a considerable mastery of the legal phases, but reflects no familiarity with American opinion on the system. In discussing the features that laid restraints upon American industry he says:

> To prohibit a great people, however, from making all that they can of every part of their own produce, or from employing their stock and industry in the way that they judge most advantageous to themselves, is a manifest violation of the most sacred rights of mankind. Unjust, however, as such prohibitions may be, they have not hitherto been very hurtful to the colonies. Land is still so cheap, and, consequently, labour is so dear among them, that they can import from the mother country almost all the most refined or more advanced manufactures cheaper than they could make them for themselves. . . . In their present state of improvement, these prohibitions, perhaps without cramping their industry, or restraining it from any employment to which it would have gone of its own accord, are only impertinent badges of slavery imposed upon them, without any sufficient reason, by the groundless jealousy of the merchants and manufacturers of the mother country. In a more advanced state they might be really oppressive and insupportable.[8]

It should be noted that while Smith refers to the Navigation Acts as "badges of slavery," he nowhere intimates that Americans held this view of the commercial system; and at the same time he admits that, up to the time he writes, the restraints upon manufactures had done no practical injury to the colonies. The acts were "badges of slavery" only because they violated his own creedal preconceptions of sound economic theory.

After making this statement he proceeds to show that the commercial system had been instigated by the merchants, to the injury of the colonies and the mother country,[9] although he admits that it had resulted in the colonial trade becoming very large and very profitable.[10] This had resulted in the prosperity of the merchant class, but he believed that other classes had suffered from the special advantages given to this favored group.[11]

The theory that the colonies existed and had been built up and protected solely to provide a market for British products and profits for British merchants does not come from any contemporary American writer, but emanates from British sources. It is found in Smith's final condemnation of the mercantile system, written while the Revolutionary War was in progress. In this respect this part of his argument must be classed with other anti-war literature of the time. It embodies a theory of the origin of the war which, when pushed a little further, gradually acquired an extensive vogue in England because it tended to fix the blame for what had happened upon a system and a class instead of upon individuals and specific measures.[12] Besides, this theory agreed with the new theology of economics that was slowly becoming the vogue.

Smith sums up his argument:

But in the system of laws which has been established for the management of our American and West Indian colonies, the interest of the home-consumer has been sacrificed to that of the producer with a more extravagant profusion than in all our other commercial regulations. A great empire has been established for the sole purpose of raising up a nation of customers who should be obliged to buy from the shops of our different producers, all the goods with which these could supply them. For the sake of that little enhancement of price which this monopoly might afford our producers, the home-consumers have been burdened with the whole expense of maintaining and defending the empire. For this purpose, and this purpose only, in the last two wars, more than two hundred millions have been spent, and a new debt of more than one hundred and seventy millions has been contracted over and above all that had been expended for the same purpose in former wars. The interest of this debt alone is not only greater than the whole extraordinary profit, which, it ever could be pretended, was made by the monopoly of the colony trade, but than the whole value of the trade, or than the whole value of the goods, which at an average have been annually exported to the colonies.

It cannot be very difficult to determine who have been the connivers of this whole mercantile system; not the consumers, we may believe, whose interest has been entirely neglected; but the producers, whose interests has been so carefully attended to; and among this latter class our merchants and manufacturers have been by far the principal architects. In the mercantile regulations, which have been taken notice of in this chapter, the interests of the manufacturers has been most peculiarly attended to; and the interest, not so much of the consumers as that of some other sets of producers, has been sacrificed to it.[13]

This condemnation of the commercial system was not because it was disliked by colonials, nor because it was unfair to them or the object of their protests, but because Smith considered it had been unprofitable for the average English consumer and especially profitable to a limited class of English merchants and producers. It is especially illuminating that, at the very time Smith was writing this arraignment of the navigation-commercial system, the representatives of the revolting American colonies were voting their support of that same system.

The permanent position of leadership accorded the *Wealth of Nations* among devotees of the new economic science soon established it as a guiding English authority, and in the course of half a century led English writers to account for the revolt in America as the inevitable fruit of a program that was theoretically unsound and unfair to the colonies. It was an easy step to transfer the evils that Smith pictured as borne by the British consumer to assumed evils borne by the colonists. In the course of time George Bancroft, who was also a free trader, borrowed this English view and embodied it in his American writings, from which it has been uncritically accepted by others and has thus descended to the present time in a form quite different from that in which it was originally stated.

Reaction to American Constitutional Protests

The complicated commercial system rested upon legislation by Parliament, applicable not only to England but to every part of the far-flung Empire; and it was upon a public conscious of these laws and their advantages that the controversies raised by the revenue phases of the Sugar Act and the Stamp Act fell.

The constitutional issues raised by America precipitated a violent controversy in England, with its flood of articles in newspapers and magazines and its scores of pamphlets. Practically all of these recognized that the issues were those of the constitutional organization of an empire that was rapidly coming of age. The American objection to taxation met with active support and bitter opposition; but the American challenge of the constitutional power of Parliament to legislate for areas outside England created issues that were to endure to the end of the struggle. The Americans had in no case assailed the commercial system in theory, nor had they questioned the power of Parliament to regulate commerce. Their sole objection was to perverting such regulations into a taxation and grafting system which was dangerous to American political liberties, oppressive to its trade, and injurious to the total trade of the Empire.

Some of the ministerial party responsible for the legislative policies of 1764-65, however, professed to see in the American challenge of Parliament's constitutional powers an attack upon the parliamentary commercial regulations which were publicly believed to be the foundation of British prosperity.[14] Some may have been honest in fearing that a surrender to the American contention would endanger the entire commercial system; others certainly advanced such an argument for merely partisan purposes, knowing that it was false.

The bulk of American support in England came from the commercial, manufacturing, and shipping population living in the large cities and seaport towns. In politics these were Whigs of the Pitt faction. Many of them were directly interested in colonial trade, had investments overseas, and were personally concerned with colonial prosperity.

These were the very men whom Smith accused of profiting unduly through the operations of the trade and navigation system. It was upon this group that Americans relied to secure the repeal of regulations that proved burdensome in practice. The Grenville-Bedford faction saw an opportunity to divide the opposition and undermine the English support of the American faction by using the imaginary danger to the commercial system as a sort of political red herring to drag across the constitutional controversy.

With the enactment of the Stamp Act, taxation of the colonies became a political issue in England. With no direct voice in legislation, the Americans looked largely to those who were in opposition to the ministry in power to plead their cause and free them from burdensome legislation. Truth telling is not the only method of carrying on political discussions; and the ministry and its friends did not hesitate to becloud the issue by a misrepresentation of the motives of the Americans and appeals to the prejudices and fears of the British.

The period from 1763 to 1783 was not one of idealism in British public life. Corruption was open and unashamed. Motives other than those of direct personal gain were not much in evidence, and the easiest explanation for the action of others was to suggest some personal gain that might be desired. On the other hand, the driving forces back of the American Revolution were based upon ideals of ancient English liberties and turned largely upon abstract conceptions of political liberty and constitutional rights. A great many Englishmen understood this and based their discussions upon the constitutional issues involved.

Ministerial Charges Against American Motives

Grenville and his followers, however, were determined to see the issue differently, and they knew the argument that would produce the greatest suspicion of American motives. They charged that a repeal of the Stamp Act would mean the surrender of the Navigation Acts as well. A few samples of the stock arguments are given at this point. They began to appear in the newspapers early in 1766 and were never quite suspended until the Revolution was too far advanced to be adjusted.

The act of trade, that great Palladium of our English navigation, made in order to increase our naval power, our manufactures, and our commerce, and particularly with a view that England should reap the just and natural benefits of commerce with her daughter colonies . . . hath been trampled on by the North Americans, in the most bare-faced . . . manner for these last 60 or 70 years.

Then the author goes on to recite the evasions of the Molasses Act of 1733, by which he estimates the revenue loss amounted to £1,700,000. Besides, he claims a vast smuggling trade has been built up, that New England rum was run into the Isle of Man, Jersey, Guernsey, western Scotland, and southern England; that ships went regularly from one port in North America to Hamburg and Holland and returned with all kinds of European goods; that Dutch ships were permitted a direct trade with New York and Philadelphia; that the collector of Boston had an income of £3,000 a year by conniving at illegal trade; that merchants worth £50,000 to £100,000 refused to pay taxes; that at the same time, and as a result of this, England was burdened with a debt of £140,000,000 and annual taxes of £10,000,000.[15]

Another article a week later asserted:

The only shadow of an argument, that can be brought to support the repeal of the Stamp Act, is that our trade with that country will suffer, if we enforce the tax with spirit and rigour. I grant it will—but what then? It will suffer only for a time; and this necessary severity will support and secure it for the future. Whereas if the tax is repealed, it will give a blow to our trade, that will be felt for ages—it will open a channel to the Americans for a free commerce with all the world: The manufactures of this country will be rejected, in proportion as other nations underwork, and undersell us: In short America will be no longer British, but German, French, Spanish, Russian—and what not?[16]

The most shameless of the newspaper writers in the Bedford faction was "Anti Sejanus."[17] In March, 1766, he contributed the following: After the Americans "have got a little deeper into our debt they will set aside the Act of Navigation; and if we think of enforcing it, the same arguments that have lately been used, will come again upon the anvil, and it will be beat into our ears by those who have their properties in the colonies. 'For God's sake gentlemen, consider—if you enforce this act you will make them desperate. You will not only lose your trade to America, but will wipe off all that vast debt they owe you.' "[18]

Charles Lloyd, Grenville's chief assistant in the financial legislation of 1764-65, and one of the most active political pamphleteers, wrote in 1767: "It was plain, that although the Stamp Act was the pretext, the restrictions upon their trade, which are so necessary, and their desire *to be* independent of England, were among the real causes of many of the American tumults; that impatience of all government which some of the colonists expressed, that opposition both to the former and latter customhouse and commercial laws, which some even of their assemblies avowed, required to be immediately and effectually controlled."[19]

The ministry, he states, "were informed very minutely of a total dissolution of every part of government, and that although the Stamp Act was the pretext, yet the causes and the objects of their resentment were also the restrictions on their trade, and their subjection to Great Britain: these were really felt, while the Stamp Act, which was formed to execute itself, which affected scarcely any but those of whose ability the very payment was a proof, which was confessed by the Americans to be the most eligible of all the taxes which could be imposed . . . was only the occasion for these insurrections."[20]

Whately, who was at one time private secretary to Grenville, was more restrained. He did not charge the Americans with aiming at an evasion of the navigation system, but did insist that the modification of trade regulations in favor of the colonists amply justified a tax upon them. He also met the American contention that they were already taxed indirectly through the operation of the trade laws, by insisting that such laws were essential to commerce and were never intended to be a substitute for direct taxation.[21]

Another writer who took an attitude similar to that of Lloyd wrote: "It is not the Stamp Act which has aroused these riots and tumults in the colonies; no—this is only a pretence or subterfuge. Bolt the matter to the bran, and you will find that the real grievance, the true and ultimate object of complaint is the Act of Navigation; and it is to rid themselves of this burden, that they are now in a state of revolt and rebellion."[22] He goes on to state that if the Americans should secure the repeal of the Stamp Act they would then attack the Navigation Act. He ridiculed the idea that the resolutions of the assemblies were truly representative of opinion in America.

Aside from the obviously inspired articles in the *London Chronicle* and the few pamphlets and articles that emanated directly from the Grenville-Bedford faction, there were very few writers who charged the Americans with bad faith toward, or with being discontented with, the operation of the commercial system.

Sir Josiah Tucker, the economist, is one of the exceptions. In his widely circulated *Letter from a Merchant in London to his Nephew in America* he says:

What is the cause of such an amazing outcry as you raise at present? Not the Stamp Duty itself; all the World are agreed on that head; and none can be so ignorant, or so stupid, as not to see, that this a mere sham and pretence. What then are your real grievances . . . ? Why some of you are exasperated over the revival of certain restrictions laid upon their trade: I say a revival; for the same restrictions have been the standing rule of government from the beginning; though not enforced at all times with equal strictness. . . . But alas! an *American* . . . will ever complain and smuggle, and smuggle and complain, 'till all restraints are removed, . . . anything short of this, is still a grievance, a badge of slavery, an usurpation on the natural rights and liberties of a free people, and I know not how many bad things besides.[23]

CHARGES THAT AMERICANS WERE SMUGGLERS

Closely akin to the charges that the Americans were trying to overthrow the navigation system were attacks upon them as smugglers and evaders of the customs regulations. These were invariably presented as organized efforts to break through the navigation system, and not as efforts to evade tax regulations that were held unconstitutional by the Americans. A number of examples of charges of this kind by the Tories in America have been given. Similar material was prepared for consumption in England.

Josiah Tucker,[24] John Mein, John Dalrymple, and William Allen are the most conspicuous in this form of partisan abuse.

Mein was particularly interested in presenting an unfavorable picture of Boston, where he had resided for years and which he had to leave as a result of his paid opposition to the non-importation agreements following the Townshend Acts. A short extract will show the nature of his attacks.

We shall now give an example of Bostonian *Piety*. Boston Smugglers are far above lurking on the coast, and running their goods clandestinely. Under the cherishing wings of the Faction, they boldly lurk along-side the wharfs, walk deliberately to the Custom-House, *take* the *necessary oaths* with the utmost composure, and unload their cargoes; if any officers of the Revenue attempt to interfere, the whole Board of Commissioners, Collectors, Comptrollers, and Inspectors are knocked down or driven out of the town.[25]

Dalrymple insisted that smuggling had gone beyond all bounds in America.[26] Allen was intensely anti-American and asserted that Americans were concerned in extensive smuggling in England in connivance with the Dutch, and that one house in ten in London was supplied with tea from this source.[27] If this statement was true, there was more tea smuggling going on in England on the eve of the Revolution than there was in America.

The charge that the real opposition of the Americans was to the Navigation Acts, and the assertion that they were forcibly defying trade laws, had just enough plausibility about it to alarm a considerable section of British public opinion which opposed the taxation measures, but staunchly supported the general commercial regulations and the legislative authority of Parliament.

Although these arguments were put forward publicly by only a few persons, and many knew them to be unfair and even slanderous so far as the Americans were concerned, they made headway and had to be considered in all future legislation. The Declaratory Act, in the form in which it finally passed Parliament, was phrased largely to satisfy those Englishmen who looked upon the American denial of the constitutional authority of Parliament to levy taxes upon them as threatening the permanence of the navigation and trade acts.

ATTITUDE OF THE MERCANTILE INTERESTS

Public opinion unquestionably demanded that the commercial system should not be disturbed. Pitt's much misconstrued statement about Americans having no right to manufacture even "a nail for a horse shoe" was based upon this. He had to meet the two arguments (1) that British manufacturers would be ruined if they were to be heavily taxed for many years to come, while Americans entirely escaped taxation and at the same time developed competing manufactures as they saw fit; and (2) that such a policy could only have the effect of driving manufacturing industries out of England to America. He had to promise protection to British industry: hence his statement that, so long as America remained exempt from taxation and all revenue had to be raised upon the British taxpayer, the Americans must refrain from all direct competition with the British producer who paid the taxes.[28]

Many friends of America agreed with this position. That staunch defender of the colonies, Alderman Trecothic of London, voiced a similar opinion in the debates over the ministerial policy of sending troops to Boston. He said, "I would not have a paper of pins admitted into America, that was not made in this country. We should monopolize the trade of America. . . . We should content ourselves with that exclusive trade."[29]

Pitt accepted in theory the American point of view in regard to the Navigation Acts and was one of their most honored spokesmen; yet in discussing the proposed coercive legislation of 1774-75 he said:

As an *Englishman,* I recognize to the Americans their supreme unalterable right to property. As an *American,* I would equally recognize to England, her supreme right of regulating commerce and navigation. This distinction is involved in the abstract of things; property is private, individual, absolute; the touch of another annihiliates it. Trade is an extended and complicated consideration; it reaches as far as ships can sail, or winds can blow. . . . To regulate the numberless movements of its several parts, and combine them into one harmonious effect, for the good of the whole requires the superintending wisdom and energy of the supreme power of the empire.

On this grand practical distinction, then, let us rest; taxation is theirs, commercial regulation is ours.[30]

This was a point of view that received generous support in England and universal favor in the colonies.

The Americans depended upon their influence with British merchants to secure the repeal of burdensome legislation. Along with the repeal of the Stamp Act, the Boston merchants had asked for relief in regard to iron by way of a permission to ship bar iron directly to Europe. In declining to assist in securing such a change, the London merchants advised Hancock that restriction "is considered as beneficial to the iron manufacturies of these Kingdoms; to which, from good policy, reason and justice, a preference is due; and we beg leave to recommend your avoiding hereafter any applications which may be construed into the most distant means of interfering with the manufacturers of the mother country, either by furnishing her rivals with raw materials, or by the public encouragement of similar manufactures among yourselves, no small strength having arisen to your opponents, during the late struggles from each of those topics.

"In a word, the system of Great Britain is to promote a mutual interest by supplying the colonies with her manufactures by encouraging them to raise, and receiving from them all raw materials, and by granting the largest extension to every branch of their trade not interfering with her own."[31] Such a warning is significant, since it came from a body of Englishmen who sympathized with the Americans and who had just contributed their entire influence to help bring about a repeal of the obnoxious Stamp Act.

IMPORTANCE OF AMERICA TO ENGLAND

It is difficult to overestimate the economic importance of the American colonies to the British Empire on the eve of the Revolution. From a trading point of view the American market was almost as valuable as that of the continent of Europe. More than one-fifth of all British ships entering British home ports in 1774 were from the colonies. More than forty per cent of exports of British-made goods went to the colonies.[32] Forty-seven of the rising industrial towns were largely involved in producing goods for the rapidly expanding American market.[33]

As America demanded goods especially adapted to local conditions, entire districts were engaged solely in supplying that market. Thousands of sailors, dock workers, warehouse men, teamsters, and skilled artisans of all kinds were dependent solely upon the American trade for a livelihood.

There was a steady migration of labor to the colonies on the continent. Thousands more hoped to migrate. Millions of pounds of British capital had become invested in the colonies, particularly those south of Pennsylvania. The interest on this debt alone probably exceeded the total cost of the British army stationed in America.[34]

Nearly every class in England and Scotland was interested in some way in the trade with the American colonies. Even the English landed gentry who supplied the majorities to keep ministries in power were directly concerned. When orders from America for British manufactures ceased, thousands of laborers and skilled workers in manufacturing districts were thrown on the poor rates and thus increased the already heavy land taxes which the landed gentry had to pay.

In 1766 the merchants, the manufacturers, and the landed gentry united to force a repeal of the Stamp Act.

From 1767 to 1775 the imperialist group that surrounded the king sought to create divisions in this combination. The landed gentry was attracted by the promise of a revenue from America.[35] Some of the merchants could not accept the constitutional arguments so universally promulgated by the colonial assemblies.[36] Others accepted as true the steady stream of assertions from the court party that the Americans were seeking to escape from the trade and navigation system and that a program of force was necessary to preserve the old economic order. As late as 1775 the public was informed that the steady stream of naval vessels being dispatched to America was to enforce the Navigation Acts.[37]

The colonial program of boycotts and nonimportation seriously injured many friendly merchants who had become over-extended in trade. This was particularly true in 1773.[38]

The heavily advertised colonial program of home manufactures frightened some merchants who would lose some of their former trade if such schemes succeeded. It particularly alarmed the manufacturers whose chief markets were thus threatened with permanent loss. To all these groups and their employees the ministerial program of using force sounded plausible when it was pictured as a part of a definite program of preserving the trade of the colonies for the benefit of British merchants, shipowners, sailors, and manufacturers.[39]

Compromise Made Impossible by Partisan Charges

After the destruction of the tea at Boston and the ministry had raised the direct issue of coercion, effectual compromise was blocked by the spectre of American opposition to the trade and navigation laws. Burke in his speech in opposition to the acts against Boston and Massachusetts said: "I know, Sir, that great and not unsuccessful pains have been taken to inflame our minds by an outcry in this house and out of it, that in America the act of navigation neither is or never was obeyed. But if you take the colonies through, I affirm, that its authority never was disputed; that it was no where disputed for any length of time; and that on the whole it was well observed."[40] Here is a direct assertion that the ministerial party was using assumed American opposition to the Navigation Acts to frighten the British public into supporting their unwise measures, and that their propaganda along this line had been very successful.

Wedderburn brazenly pushed the charge against the Americans home by asserting: "They consider all the acts that restrain their trade as illegal and they want to treat with you upon an independent footing; but if you give up this tax [that on tea] it is not here that you must stop, you will be required to give up much more, nay to give up all."[41]

As the differences with the ministry gradually drifted into more and more dangerous channels, leading Americans became aware of the false position in which they had been placed by this British suspicion of their attitude toward the Navigation Acts and the deliberate misrepresentation that had taken place concerning their intentions. It has already been pointed out how Pitt was literally forced by public opinion to word the Declaratory Act as he did to save in legal form the constitutional rights of Parliament to regulate colonial commerce. The efforts at final compromise were in part wrecked by this background of fear and suspicion concerning the commercial system.

Numerous friends of America sought to make clear that such suspicions and charges were unfounded, and that the Americans were satisfied with the main features of the trade regulations. But the charge once made would not down. As the controversy over taxation and constitutional relations came to a head, this fear for the security of the commercial system stood in the way of compromise. One writer to the *London Chronicle* in 1775 even opposed the use of petitions to Parliament to adjust the disputes and permit trade to be resumed. His argument was:

Would not the Americans be encouraged to insist on a repeal of the Act of Navigation, the principal source of the wealth, power and glory of England? And would they not renew their congress, and make further combinations to injure the merchants and commerce of Great Britain, until they had obtained an unlimited trade to all other parts of the world; and did they not declare such sentiments publicly on the repeal of the Stamp Act, and on many other occasions, and are not these sentiments plainly implied in many of their late pamphlets, and even in resolves of some of their assemblies?[42]

The leading Americans realized the dangers involved in this poisoning of public opinion on this point, and the sections of the resolutions and other public papers of the Continental Congress which refer to trade relations were written primarily for the British reading public. Attention has already been called to the paper which was prepared by Franklin for publication at the head of Washington's army, but which was finally first printed in England. A similar sentiment appears in the *Address to the Inhabitants of Great Britain*.

It has been said that we refuse to submit to the restrictions on our commerce. From whence is this inference drawn? Not from our words, we having repeatedly declared the contrary, and we again profess our submission to the several acts of trade and navigation passed before the year 1763, trusting nevertheless in the equity and justice of Parliament, that such of them as upon cool and impartial consideration, shall appear to have imposed unnecessary or grievous restrictions, will, at some happier period, be repealed or altered. And we cheerfully consent to the operation of such acts of the British Parliament as shall be restrained to the regulation of our external commerce for the purpose of securing the commercial advantages of the whole empire to the Mother-country, and the commercial benefits of its respective members, excluding every idea of taxation internal or external, for raising a revenue on the subjects of America without their consent.[43]

This sounds conclusive enough, but it was at once seized upon by a writer in the *London Chronicle* and made to appear insincere.

These regulations are now all to be taken away, while the arts of evading the laws, against which they were made, are still to remain. . . . Previous to these Gentlemen's cheerful consent to the operation of acts of trade, the board of Customs is stated as a grievance, and the poor revenue officer is to be left alone in every part naked and defenseless, to be tarred and feathered, if he presume but to look in the face of an illicit trader.

And then . . . after we have made all these concessions, and removed every thing . . . which can . . . check . . . their smuggling, then, they tell us, that they will cheerfully consent to the operation of such acts . . . of parliament, as they shall find to come within their description of acts of trade . . . after having taken away all authority of parliament to command the observance of these laws and . . . all the efficacy of the courts of admiralty, which should punish the breach of them, they may . . . cheerfully leave them to their operation. Stript of all means of enforcement . . . they well know that they will have no operation at all.[44]

It is clear from the foregoing that there was a small but influential faction in England that persisted in charging the Americans with attempting to escape from the commercial system which bound the entire Empire. This charge sounded plausible to a good many people in England. And, as the profits of so many people depended upon the special advantages they enjoyed under the trade and navigation system, their fears that these privileges might be lost led many to believe the partisan charge against the Americans. No amount of denial on the part of the revolutionary leaders was sufficient to counteract completely the effect of this accusation, and war broke with the calumny still reiterated in England.

TESTIMONY OF CONTEMPORARY ENGLISH HISTORIES

The contemporary history usually reflects the prevailing prejudices and opinions that have been impressed upon the public mind by popular agitation.

In addition to Burke's elaborate speech on conciliation and the extensive accounts in the *Annual Register,* there are three histories of the Revolution published by Englishmen for the British reading public in the years immediately following the war.

Burke's speech, delivered in the House of Commons in 1775 before the beginning of hostilities, deserves special attention. It is historical in character. Burke had served for years as paid agent for one or more of the colonies; as member of Parliament from Bristol he represented one of the most important constituencies of merchants engaged chiefly in American trade; he had prepared the material for the *Annual Register* during the crucial years preceding 1775; he was extremely popular in America; and he had the personal confidence of the active revolutionary leaders. If any Englishman knew what the American grievances were and what was the main object of their resistance, certainly Burke must have known.

Furthermore, the question of American aims came up directly in the debate and Burke took time to deal with it. One of the ministerial supporters had openly hurled the partisan charge that the Americans were really aiming at the Navigation Acts. Burke expressed surprise that moderate men like Mr. Rire could fail to see the unfairness and absurdity of such charges. He closes this part of his argument with the following statement concerning the trade laws. Part of this was to meet an argument of Lord North that the laws were no real restraint on America, and that the trade of England with the colonies was due to mutual commercial advantages and not to the restraints of law.[45]

But I cannot agree with the noble Lord, nor with the pamphlet from whence he seems to have borrowed these ideas concerning the inutility of the trade laws. For without idolizing them, I am sure they are still, in many ways, of great use to us; and in former times they have been of the greatest. They do confine, and they do greatly narrow the market of the Americans. But my perfect conviction of this does not help me in the least to discern how the revenue laws form any security whatsoever to the commercial regulations; or that these commercial regulations are the true ground of the quarrel, or that the giving away, in any one instance of authority, is to lose all that may remain unconceded.

One fact is clear and indisputable. The public and avowed origin of this quarrel was on taxation. This quarrel has indeed brought on new disputes on new questions; but certainly the least bitter and the fewest of all, on the trade laws. To judge which of the two be the real radical cause of the quarrel we have to see whether the commercial dispute did, in order of time, precede the dispute over taxation. There is not a shadow of evidence for it.

Then he went on to say that such assumptions as to the motives and aims of the Americans were only "suspicions, conjectures, divinations in defiance of fact and experience."[46]

There were three full-dress histories of the Revolution published in England in the years immediately following the war.

The first, published in London in 1786, was obviously taken almost fully from the *Annual Register* and appears without any author's name under the titles: *History of the War in America,* etc.; *History of the Origin, Rise and Progress of the War in America,* etc.; *An Imperial History of the War in America,* etc. Edmund Burke is generally credited with the authorship of the material. Under the second title this history was reprinted in Boston. Nearly all the later writers made extensive use of this account, which was especially true in the case of Gordon.[47]

This history does not include American objections to the Navigation Acts as one of the active causes of friction with the home country. The omission is significant, because the author was unquestionably in a position to know what the American complaints were and what was the British understanding of these grievances. As it was written primarily for sale to a British reading public, it is still more strange that this point was not treated, if any great number of people living at the time believed there was any material truth in it.

The second independent British account of the war was by John

Andrews in 1785-86.[48] He used four volumes to tell his story. It is the most detailed account prepared by any Englishman with the possible exception of Trevelyan. He does not treat the Navigation Acts as a cause of the separation.

Finally, we have a history of the Revolution by Charles Stedman in two volumes that appeared in 1794. Stedman was a member of Cornwallis' staff and consequently came closely in touch with British officers, loyaltists, and Americans. Had there been any considerable discussion of the Navigation Acts or of the commercial system, he certainly would have encountered it. Being an Englishman, he could not well have been ignorant of the current partisan charge by the King's supporters that the Americans were trying to break away from the commercial system and that the constitutional argument was only a subterfuge. One would expect to find some substantiation of this charge had Stedman found evidence to support it. His history does not even refer to the Navigation Acts. Obviously he never discovered that they were a source of irritation in the colonies. As his services took him into both the middle and the southern colonies his opportunities for learning the facts were unusual. No other British writer had similar access to sources of public opinion in both England and America.

Thus the contemporary histories, written during or soon after the close of the Revolution, reveal less evidence that the British believed Americans were trying to escape from the Navigation Acts than is found in the controversial pamphlets and newspaper articles. Apparently the assertions along this line exerted enough influence to keep the governmental party in power while the policy of coercion was attempted, but produced no substantial following in the nation as a whole. The fact that trade returned so promptly to its old channels after independence tended to discredit the earlier partisan claims. The contemporary historians clearly did not consider them worthy of serious notice.

REFERENCES

CHAPTER 10

1. Matthew Decker, *An Essay on the Causes of the Decline of the Foreign Trade, Consequently of the Lands of Britain and of the Means to Restore Both* (London, 1750), p. 51.

2. *Ibid.*, pp. 52-53.

3. *The Tried Interest of Great Britain with Respect to the American Colonies Stated and Impartially Considered,* by a Merchant of London (London, 1766).

4. *London Chronicle,* October 19, 1773, p. 380.

5. *Wealth of Nations* (Bohn edition, 1896), I, 463.

6. *Ibid.,* p. 464.

7. *Ibid.,* p. 472.

8. *Ibid.,* II, 91.

9. *Ibid.,* p. 93.

10. *Ibid.,* p. 111.

11. *Ibid.,* p. 126.

12. It was not easy for any British minister to admit his errors publicly, even when he knew he was pursuing an ill-advised course. Lord North found it practically impossible to admit his error and repeal the entire series of acts passed after 1763, although even Lord Germaine considered this the wise policy in 1778 (*Correspondence of George III,* London, 1928, IV, 27, 35). It was much simpler to ascribe the entire trouble with America to a wrong economic policy pursued over a series of years. This removed the blame from specific individuals, absolved Grenville, Bute, North, Townshend, and George III, and thus made easier the healing of the bitter political controversies of the period.

13. *Wealth of Nations,* I, 178.

14. This position was taken by Lord Littleton: "It is said they will not submit to the Stamp Act as it lays an internal tax; if this be admitted, the same reasoning extends to all acts of parliament. The Americans will find themselves crampt by the Act of Navigation, and oppose that too." (February 24, 1766. Hansard, *Debates,* XVI, 167.) Grenville spoke in a similar vein (*ibid.,* 102). Burke, in a speech against the Repressive Acts in 1774, asserted that Rockingham found the "office-holders raised a violent outcry against any

alteration in the Stamp Act, insisting that such action would threaten the whole legal commercial system." *Ibid.*, XVII, 1245.

15. *London Chronicle,* January 14, 1766. The article is unsigned, but the information is such as only those close to the ministry could have had.

16. *Ibid.*, January 23, 1766, p. 77.

17. Unsigned article, *London Chronicle,* January 23, 1766, so identifies him. He was Rev. James Scott. *Dictionary Nat. Biog.,* LI, 37.

18. *Ibid.*, March 11, 1766, p. 236.

19. Charles Lloyd, *The Conduct of the Late Administration Examined,* etc. (London, 1767), p. 60.

20. *Ibid.*, pp. 83-84.

21. Thomas Whately, *Considerations on the Trade and Finances of this Kingdom and on the Measures of Administration with Respect to those Great National Objects since the Conclusion of Peace* (3rd ed., London, 1769), pp. 144-56. He lists the following acts as favorable to the colonies: whale fishery encouraged by removing the duty on colonial whale products; restraints upon exportation of rice relaxed in favor of Georgia and South Carolina; bounties on colonial hemp and flax; bounties on colonial timber; American bar iron permitted to be shipped to any British port; rice permitted to be reëxported through England without advancing the customs duties; heavy duties upon foreign indigo, coffee, sugar, and molasses; customhouse fees fixed by law.

22. *A Plain and Seasonable Address to the Free Holders of Great Britain on the Present Posture of Affairs in America* (London, 1766), pp. 8-9.

23. Josiah Tucker, *Letter of a Merchant in London to his Nephew in North America Relative to the Present Posture of Affairs in the Colonies* (London, 1766); also in *Four Tracts with Two Sermons on Political and Commercial Subjects* (Gloucester, 1774), Tract III, pp. 132-34; and R. L. Schuyler, *Josiah Tucker, A Selection from his Economic and Political Writings* (New York, 1931), pp. 321-22.

24. "General Gage, you say, declares in one of his letters that 'they have in *Boston* been able by successful Chicane, wholly to evade many Parts of one of our Capital penal Constitutions,' most probably this penal Statute was one of the Laws for the Regulation of their Trade, and for confining it to the Mother Country; which System of Laws you well know (tho' you will not own it) has ever been their Aim either to undermine, or overturn." *A Letter to Edmund Burke, Esq.* (London, 1775), p. 35.

25. John Mein, *Sagattarius's Letters and Political Speculations, Extracted from the Public Ledger* (Boston, 1775), p. 2.

26. John Dalrymple, *The Address of the People of Great Britain to the Inhabitants of America* (London, 1775), p. 35.

27. William Allen, *The American Crisis: A Letter Addressed by Permission to Earl Tower—on the Present Alarming Disturbances in the Colonies* (London, 1774). Although Allen is usually referred to as an American Tory, he is here classed as English, as he was in England at this time and did all of his publishing there.

28. "The Proper Question Respecting the Expediency of the American Taxation, Discussed," *London Chronicle,* February 20, 1766.

29. Cavendish, *Debates,* December 5, 1768, I, 85.

30. Quoted by Dickinson, *Writings,* I, viii-ix.

31. "London Merchants to John Hancock," June 3, 1766, *Boston Gazette,* September 8, 1766.

32. In 1772 imports from all Europe totaled £6,460,166 and those from America £5,489,080. All Europe received £5,162,718 of British-made goods, while £4,384,141 went to the colonies. In 1774 there was a total of 6,414 ships from all ports of the world entered at British ports. Of these 1,347 were from the American colonies. *Customs* 17:1, 2, 3.

33. Dora Mae Clark, *British Opinion and the American Revolution* (New Haven, 1930), p. 22.

34. *Ibid.,* chap. 2.

35. *Ibid.,* p. 132.

36. *Ibid.,* pp. 64-65.

37. *Ibid.,* p. 227.

38. *Ibid.,* pp. 28-30, 69.

39. *Ibid.,* 227.

40. Hansard, *Parliamentary Debates,* XVII, 1,237.

41. *Ibid.,* 1,269.

42. *London Chronicle,* January 31, 1775, p. 97.

43. Pamphlet edition, p. 6.

44. Unsigned article, "To the North American Merchants," *London Chronicle,* January 7, 1775.

45. This obviously was not an uncommon opinion of leading Englishmen of the ministerial party. It was elaborately stated by Tucker in 1774. See Schuyler, *Josiah Tucker* (New York, 1931), p. 36.

46. Hezekiah Niles, *Principles and Acts of the Revolution,* pp. 233-36.

47. William Gordon, *History of the Rise, Progress and Establishment of the Independence of the United States of America* (London, 1778).

48. John Andrews, *History of the War with America, France, Spain, and Holland,* 1775-83 (London, 1785-86).

II

WERE THE NAVIGATION ACTS A CAUSE
OF THE REVOLUTION?

As a result of the foregoing survey and analysis of the Navigation Acts as an issue in American and British politics, it seems possible to arrive at some definite conclusions. To save space these will be stated somewhat dogmatically, in the belief that ample proof has been supplied in the preceding chapters.

General statements in regard to the Navigation Acts are in need of extensive revision. As enacted in the seventeenth century and continued for more than a hundred years before the outbreak of the Revolution, they were not, by 1763, the cause of serious irritation in America, nor were they made the basis of complaints on any considerable scale by the American leaders of the Revolution. The clause confining the carrying trade between the colonies and Great Britain to English ships and English seamen was as popular on this side of the water as on the other. It was specifically ratified by Virginia and Massachusetts and was never made the basis of a formal complaint during the entire century preceding the Revolution.

The clauses of the successive acts creating a list of enumerated products met with less opposition and more general support in America than has been supposed. The idea that enumeration was generally burdensome to the locality producing the commodity in question is not supported by the facts. Practically all of the enumerated products were grown in the West Indies or in the southern colonies. These were not the colonies that led in the revolt, with the exception of Virginia and South Carolina. In each case they had other grievances, and neither colony complained of the enumeration of tobacco, rice, and indigo as a grievance on the eve of the Revolution.

The enumeration clauses were apparently nowhere a cause of complaint, serious irritation, or widespread agitation, either for change in the laws or for separation from the mother country.

On the other hand, there is positive proof that enumeration was a real economic advantage to the regions where such articles were produced. Enumeration gave them an assured market for all that could be produced. Prices fluctuated, but even a low price at times was better than no price. Production of such articles acquired a stability that invited the investment of vast amounts of capital in labor, slaves, plantations, tools, shipping, warehouses, factors' establishments, and consumable supplies. Much of this capital was British and most of the debts due British creditors after the Revolution were in the areas where enumerated products were grown and by planters engaged in their production. Some of the active leaders of the Revolution in the southern states wrote off large fortunes in debts due to British creditors by the repudiation of these debts.

In addition enumeration made possible the creation of centralized markets in Britain with all of the mercantile facilities to distribute the enumerated products to a world-wide market. Communication was assured in time of war as well as peace as a result of the great financial investments in Britain and America, thus guaranteeing the arrival in the colonies of fleets of ships to carry home the enumerated products at the right time and to bring in the necessary supplies for the production of the next crop.

These were real advantages not shared by the regions not producing such products. Separation from the home country, which ended enumeration, left all of the important enumerated products in a declining condition. They became sick industries. Rice and indigo never recovered their former world markets. It was more than half a century before American tobacco interests could create for themselves the world-wide markets and credit machinery they had enjoyed before the Revolution.

The clauses limiting American imports to British products or to such European and Asiatic products as came from England encountered some opposition and some evasion. This was limited, however, in time and in products, and in no case was the opposition coördinated and concerted. As time went on, objection to this limitation upon the course of trade diminished, and was practically nonexistent at the time of the Revolution.

The main reason for the steady acceptance of the routing of foreign commodities through Great Britain was the elaborate system of export bounties, export debentures, drawbacks, credits extended by British merchants, and other facilities that made England the most advantageous market in the world in which the Americans could supply themselves with goods. Such advantages continued to increase up to the outbreak of the Revolution and were a part of the whole complicated series of trade acts. These advantages obviously were not objectionable to the Americans.

Another phase of the trade acts was the definite encouragement of various local colonial industries by means of preferential tariffs in England, strongly favoring the colonial product; drawbacks of British duties for such portion of the product as had to find a market in foreign countries; and direct parliamentary bounties on colonial products, totaling millions of dollars and becoming more numerous in the years immediately preceding the Revolution. There are no American complaints on record against this practice. They strongly resemble the modern federal assistance to farmers in the United States.

The navigation and trade acts as a whole and considered as a part of a developed commercial policy had not resulted in widespread poverty or distress in any of the colonies. On the contrary all of the evidence shows that the continental colonies were generally prosperous, rapidly increasing in population, with every physical evidence of wealth more abundant than in England, and their wealth and prosperity boasted of by their own people and envied by their relatives in Britain. A constant stream of immigration from England, Scotland, and Ireland gave proof that colonial prosperity was well known in the home country. Finally, the rapidity with which the heavy colonial debts contracted during the French and Indian War were sunk demonstrated their fundamental prosperity as superior to that of Britain herself.

The limitations placed upon colonial manufactures were complained of by only a few Americans in New England and the middle colonies.

In general the objections to such limitations were confined to three articles—hats, woolen goods, and steel. The limitation on the first was in fact a limitation on the inter-colonial shipment of hats and in no case checked their actual manufacture. The prohibition against shipment from one colony to another applied as well to hats made in England as to those of local manufacture, and ultimately led to protests from English hat interests themselves. Much the same conditions applied to the regulation against wool and wool shipments. There never was a prosecution against American production of either woolen goods or steel.

Obviously manufacturing was too much in the household stage, the production of goods so largely for purely neighborhood consumption and those interested in the making of articles for export too limited in numbers and in geographic distribution to make paper restrictions a cause of the Revolution. No cases of actual enforcement occurred that are reported officially or in the newspapers of the period, which certainly aired every important cause of complaint.

Even Lord North admitted in the debates in Parliament in 1770 over the repeal of the main taxation program, that it was clearly not to the interest of Americans to engage in general manufacturing either for their own use or for export at this time.[1]

On the other hand the attempts of the Americans to develop manufactures of their own to take the place of the regular supplies from Great Britain, especially during the periods of aggressive nonimportation in 1765, 1767-70, and 1773-75, created real alarm in England. British merchants, manufacturers, laborers, and shipowners feared that their vast business interests involved in the

American trade were in danger. These fears led some of them to advocate and induced others to support the restrictive measures of Grenville, Townshend, and North that were ostensibly designed to preserve the old and profitable colonial markets. In this sense manufacturing in America became an important cause of the Revolution, not because Americans were oppressed and irritated by the trade acts limiting their manufacture, but because of the panicky reaction of men in England who were already engaged in manufacturing for general export and who feared the spectre of American competition which might permanently destroy their American market.

Evasion of the Navigation Acts was far less than has been assumed by many writers. There was probably no extensive evasion of the basic acts; and systematic smuggling in violation of the trade acts after the middle of the eighteenth century was limited mainly to two articles—tea and molasses. The repeal of the inland duties on tea in England, followed by the granting of drawbacks of the customs duties upon exportation to the colonies, removed most of the profits in the smuggling of tea and greatly diminished the practice. Lowering of the tax of six pence a gallon on foreign molasses to three pence and finally to a penny terminated any general illegal importation of molasses after 1766, and complaints on that section of the trade acts practically disappeared as a special issue. After 1766 there was no discrimination between British and foreign molasses, consequently that article was no longer under the trade laws.

The assumption that all shipowners and seamen violated the trade and navigation acts is without real foundation or tangible evidence. The smuggling charge was made against the Americans by some of the partisan Tories and was vehemently denied by leading revolutionary leaders.

The areas where illegal trading was, by common report, supposed to be most extensive were places where the Revolution received only lukewarm support or where the Tory population was very large, such as New York, Philadelphia, and Newport. Lawbreakers have never been famous for their patriotic following of lofty ideals. Even here the charges do not apply to the bringing in of foreign articles but to customed articles, largely British.

It is highly probable that as many, or even more, professional smugglers remained Tory as espoused the cause of the Revolution. Official evidence indicates that there may have been extensive smuggling from England in Virginia and Maryland where the great majority of the merchants were Tories. This is based upon the voluminous reports of Inspector General John Williams in 1769. He, however, was reporting in terms of the apparent evasion of the tax upon the importation of British manufactures without paying the duties. He indicates no suspicion that there was any general evasion of the trade acts by the importation of goods of foreign manufacture. There are many other reports by customs officers of presumed smuggling at other ports, but in every case they are referring to evasion of the revenue laws and not to violations of the trade and navigation acts.

There was organized opposition to the Sugar Act and the Townshend Revenue Act, especially in New England and the middle colonies. This was not due to the opposition of the Americans to the trade laws and had no possible relation to their attitude toward the old navigation and commercial system. This is shown by the letters, resolutions, and memorials of the Americans themselves.

Their opposition to the measures enacted after 1763 was not because they were trade regulations, *but because they were not laws of that kind.* They recognized these later acts as revenue laws, and hence a violation of the fundamental constitutional relationship that had been developing through the past century, under which all powers of taxation in the colonies belonged to their local assemblies. To the Americans the new program endangered their dearly-won powers of self-government and threatened them with the loss of political liberty. Such laws also burdened British commerce instead of regulating it. This is not a mere assertion of American writers. The fullest statement of this attitude of Americans everywhere is in the formal unpublished reports made by the Customs Commissioners to the highest officials in England.

Failure to understand this fundamental issue as seen by the revolutionary leaders and by those who were attempting to enforce the revenue laws has led to a confusion of the resistance to the acts passed in the reign of George III with opposition to the general trade and navigation acts. The wholesale attempts to avoid paying the new duties have been falsely assumed to be a part of the general opposition to and evasion of the Navigation Acts.

The ministerial faction in England and some of their partisan adherents in America seized upon American opposition to the revenue measures to charge that the real objection of the Americans was to the trade and navigation acts. This charge was vehemently denied by leading Americans and their friends in England. At the time the accusation was made, it was generally recognized as unfair and put forward for partisan purposes.[2]

There was an almost universal acceptance of the desirability of the trade regulations in both England and America as one of the essential foundations of British commercial and industrial prosperity. Besides, the American trade had been developed so long and so much capital was invested in it, so many British subjects made their living out of it, so many localities were so largely dependent upon the continuation of the old commercial relations, and so many millions of pounds had been loaned to American merchants and planters, that a charge that Americans were seeking to break down the complicated legal regulatory system upon which that trade was founded created real alarm. This fear gave the ministerial faction enough popular support for their ill-advised measures to enable them to stay in office and attempt to carry them out. Laws bitterly denounced in America as unconstitutional taxation measures and destructive of British commerce were defended in England as acts designed to restrain the Americans within the commercial system, and thus preserve the commercial relations upon which British prosperity had been built and a vast war debt contracted.

In this way the Navigation Acts became a cause of the Revolution, but not in the sense commonly presented. They were not the source of serious complaint by the Americans, but were used in England to justify and continue the measures after 1764 that were the object of American opposition and ultimately the cause of revolt. Such charges of American intentions stood in the way of effectual compromise as the issues approached the verge of civil war. The fear that concessions such as would satisfy the Americans would be only a prelude to a complete abrogation of the commercial system enabled the ministry to attempt to carry through its policy of asserting the authority of Parliament, by coercion if necessary.

The American leaders recognized this danger and tried in every way possible to convince the British public that they were not seeking to escape from the navigation system. This is shown in the resolutions of the Continental Congress, and in Franklin's specific offer to have the Navigation Acts reënacted by the colonial assemblies and even guaranteed for one hundred years, if the British would abandon their claims to parliamentary taxation.

Contemporary American and British historians understood the nature of the controversy so thoroughly that they did not include the Navigation Acts as one of the causes of the Revolution.

An examination of the contemporary literature on the eve of the Revolution leads to the conclusion that the trade and navigation system had built up in the course of a hundred years a self-sufficient commercial and political Empire that was the wonder of the world. The colonial sources of supply of raw materials, shipbuilding facilities, and loyal seamen made the British Empire potentially the most powerful nation in the world.

In the Seven Years War this loyal potential enabled Britain to sweep the seas clean of French and Spanish naval and commercial shipping, seize the French colonial empire with its added potential, and some of the richest prizes of the Spanish colonial empire. In 1763 the British Empire was in much the same relative world position as was the United States in 1945.

This vast commercial and colonial Empire was disintegrated and dissolved in ten years by a policy that undertook to substitute trade taxation for trade protection and encouragement. The cement of fair and relatively equal treatment in matters of commerce was dissolved by what happened in a few years of customs racketeering. This included the exploitation of American commerce by a new race of customs officers who sought to operate the customs service for their own personal profits. The bonding provisions of the new revenue laws were used to give legal color to the seizure of vessels on the most technical grounds. Excessive fees were exacted. New and unheard of burdens were imposed upon the coasting trade. Strictly local trade within individual provinces was forced to enter, clear, give bonds, carry cockets, etc., in spite of the rulings of the highest legal advisers of the crown. Informers, spies, stoolpigeons, and swarms of other officers, all supported out of the proceeds of the American revenue, or from fees and seizures for borderline causes, were created. The ancient rights of seamen to engage in little ventures of their own were made the basis of new prosecutions against their employers and seizure of their own little stocks of capital.

The new Board of Customs Commissioners devoted its energies to waging war upon ships, seamen, merchants, and commerce in the interest of revenue; multiplying officers and employees for this purpose; inaugurating a new and rapacious coast guard service manned by unprincipled individuals interested chiefly in personal plunder. This new coast guard service behaved like pirates and was soon at open war with the formerly loyal American seamen. The officers of the navy were made customs officers and assigned to the same task of plundering American commerce for their own personal gain under the name of enforcing the new revenue regulations. The Union Jack on a British vessel had formerly stood for the protection of British commerce. Now its appearance aroused feelings like that of the old Jolly Roger.

From the beginning the Customs Commissioners were obsessed with the idea that the Americans were rebellious and the Commissioners needed military and naval power to enforce their decisions. Englishmen do not yield readily to coercion, and especially resent the threat of force. Formerly loyal, the Americans planned open and passive resistance to measures they considered illegal exercises of authority by placemen of a "wicked ministry."

The efforts of the Commissioners to use the revenue laws as a cloak to set up in America a centralized authority over domestic and foreign commerce through the extended use of admiralty courts; multiplication of writs of assistance: power to compel attorneys-general, colonial supreme courts, and even governors to do their bidding; and directed prosecution of suits for enormous sums against wealthy merchants who dared organize political opposition to their exactions, created in three short years a hostility toward customs officers from Quebec to the Caribbean hitherto unknown in British colonial relations.

None of the new exactions and demands for the exercise of arbitrary authority had any relation to the trade and navigation laws. They were thoroughly anti-trade. Americans said so in season and out of season. The majority of British merchants and manufacturers interested in the colonial trade agreed with the Americans and agitated for a repeal of the anti-trade legislation. Finally in 1770 even the King's Friends conceded that taxation of British manufactures going to colonial markets was contrary to sound trade principles and moved for the repeal of all the new taxes except that on tea.

This was retained because it was a real source of revenue for support of the numerous placemen which the King's Friends in England needed to keep themselves in office. It was the only fund out of which colonial officials could be paid. While the concessions were a great relief to the Americans, they were inadequate. The customs service was still administered for revenue and not for trade purposes. Three years of gross mistreatment at the hands of a plundering revenue service had created in important places a deep sense of resentment. The old sentiment of loyalty was gone.

A century of wisely administered trade and navigation laws had developed the greatest and most loyal colonial Empire in the world. Abandonment of that policy destroyed that Empire in less than ten years. The former cement of favored trade relations that bound colonies and home country together had been dissolved. The new policy of taxation and exploitation of America in the interests of a political faction in England was a distintegrating force that destroyed loyalty. The degree of damage was different in different areas, depending upon the way the revenue acts were administered. In some areas they were so administered as to produce very little hostility. In general these were the areas where there was little concentration of the import trade from England or from the West Indies. The heavy taxation, the excessive fees, and the seizures were concentrated in a few trading colonies. These were the centers of the revolutionary movement. The areas where the old trade and navigation laws operated relatively undisturbed by the new taxation program remained loyal.

REFERENCES
CHAPTER 11

1. Hansard, *Debates*, XVI, 855.
2. The partisan assertion that the Americans were trying to escape from the regular century-old commercial relations with Britain is found in the printed articles prepared by employed partisan writers, and in the King's speech from the throne in 1770. *Journal of the House of Lords*, XXXII, 394

BIBLIOGRAPHY

NOTE

Statements that the Navigation Acts were an active cause of the Revolution go back historically to George Bancroft, who began publishing his *History of the United States* in 1834. The volumes dealing with the pre-Revolutionary period were completed during the intensely nationalistic period of the "Roaring Forties" and at a time when both England and the United States were experimenting with free trade. Bancroft rewrote the causes of the Revolution in terms of current free trade theories.

No other American historian has had so great an opportunity to impress his historical concepts permanently upon a nation as did Bancroft. His was the first full-dress history of the nation. He had no competitors. He was very much in the public eye. Money and documents flowed to him. His history was almost a national enterprise.

Bancroft profoundly influenced later discussion of the Navigation Acts. He described them in condemnatory language: he pictured them as selfish and oppressive from the start; he confused the expression "English ships" with ships owned in England and described the entire carrying trade as a monopoly of residents of England; the few legal restrictions upon manufacturing certain goods for export from the colonies were cited as prohibiting all manufactures in America even for home consumption; he confused revenue legislation with the Navigation Acts; he assumed that temporary colonial objections to the acts of 1660 to 1690 continued with increasing tempo until the Revolution, and repeatedly insisted that the Navigation Acts were the primary cause of the Revolution. He cites as his sources of information Adam Smith, *Wealth of Nations;* Chalmers, *Introduction to the History of the Revolt of the American Colonies;* Montesquieu; and Burke.[1]

Bancroft dominated the field of American history for about fifty years. During that time free schools were established in all the states with American history as one of the regular subjects. Chairs of history were appearing at leading universities. American history was becoming a popular subject of study.

Prior to Bancroft the history books for schools did not include the Navigation Acts as a cause of the Revolution. After 1850 such texts regularly included it and soon every pupil in America had to learn that the Navigation Act of 1660 was the "first cause of the Revolution."[2]

A generation after Bancroft published his volumes on the causes of the Revolution, Mellen Chamberlain prepared the chapter on the causes of the Revolution for what was long the most scholarly and scientific history written by Americans.[3] While he did not accept all of Bancroft's statements he was manifestly influenced by them. He used some source material. He discovered that the commercial regulations did not all work badly and that Americans did not, in fact, condemn them. To reconcile this conflict between the Bancroft thesis and the obvious facts, he offered the explanation that the Navigation Acts were evaded.[4] He gave no evidence to support this assertion. That unsupported statement has been widely copied into later writings. He also created a new myth concerning Writs of Assistance—that they were wanted to enforce the Navigation Acts, when they were solely concerned with the revenue laws.

In his critical essay, however, Chamberlain recognized the slender factual data upon which his discussion was based and even questioned the entire validity of the theory that the Navigation Acts were a real cause of the Revolution.[5]

The Bancroft-Chamberlain explanation was accepted and perpetuated by two prominent historical figures of the twentieth century, George E. Howard, author of *Preliminaries of the Revolution* and Claude H. Van Tyne in his *Causes of the War of Independence.* Thus for nearly a century the leading general histories of the Revolution presented the Navigation Acts as a chief cause of the Revolution. School and college texts conformed to the general pattern. It became a part of American thought on the subject and affects much of the literature since 1860. The presence of this theory is an historical concept that has to be faced by all students of the pre-Revolutionary period.

General histories and special studies have been adequately cited in the footnotes. It does not seem necessary to repeat the titles here. Consequently, the formal bibliography is limited to official records and contemporary materials.

The following is a list of what was examined. As many items did not mention the Navigation Acts or the commercial system directly they are not cited in the footnotes, hence the list is far more than a compilation of works cited.

British and American Official Papers

The details of British regulations of commerce have to be dug out of the entire mass of parliamentary legislation from 1660 to 1775. Use has been made of both the Pickering and Ruffhead editions of the *Statutes at Large.* Cobbett's *Parliamentary History of England* was the chief reliance for details of discussions of controversial measures.

For the United States the Ford edition of the *Journals of the Continental Congress;* Peter Force, American Archives (9 vols., Washington, 1837-53); and the *American State Papers* proved most valuable. Statistics of American trade after 1783 are mainly from the latter source.

Manuscript Records

Aside from the sources of contemporary opinion in regard to the trade and navigation system the most important source of information for this study has been the Treasury papers preserved in the Public Record Office in London. These give details of the actual operation of the various laws, both in Great Britain and the colonies. The following have been examined in detail.

A.O. 3, vol. 1086. Detailed accounts of the Stamp Act and its yield.

Customs 3. Ledgers of imports and exports, Great Britain, general, vols. 63-75.

Customs 4. Ledgers of imports and exports after 1790, Great Britain, general, vols. 1-4.

Customs 14. Ledgers of imports and exports, Scotland, vols. 1-8.

Customs 15. Ledgers of imports and exports, Ireland, vols. 71-78.

Customs 16. Customhouse reports: imports, exports, shipping, America. Ports from Quebec to Bermuda, 1768-73, one volume.

Customs 17. State of Navigation, Great Britain, vols. 1-13.

Customs 21. Miscellaneous papers. Volume 16 has retained copies of "out letters" from the Commissioners of Customs, Boston. Volumes 70-78 have the register of seizures in Great Britain, 1767-75.

Treasury 1. Bundles of "in letters" to the Treasury Board in Great Britain. Has extensive reports from the American Board of Customs Commissioners. Very valuable. Bundles 429-516.

Treasury 11. Customs officers in America, instructions, etc., vol. 28.

Treasury 28. Treasury Board in England. Entry book of "out letters" to Customs officers in America including the West Indies, vol. 1.

Treasury 38. Customs accounts of receipts and expenditures, vols. 269, 357, 363, 374.

Treasury 64. Miscellaneous reports of conditions of trade, opinions of the Attorney-General on customs problems in America, vols. 252, 273-76, 283.

British and American Magazines

The magazines of the period are important sources of political and governmental information. They give relatively little space to purely literary material. The following were used: *The American Gazette, A Collection of all of the Authentic Addresses, Memorials, Letters, etc., Which Relate to the Present Disputes Between Great Britain and Her Colonies, etc.* (London, 1774); *Annual Register* (London, 1763-76); *The General Magazine, or Complete Repository of Arts, Sciences, Politics and Literature, Comprehending a Great Variety of Valuable Original Writings in Prose and Verse, and a Faithful Compendium of all Such Occurances as May be Deemed Worthy the Attention of the Public* (London, 1776); *The Gentleman's Magazine and Historical Chronicle* (London, 1765-70); *The London Gazette, Published by Authority* (London, 1765-75); *The Oxford Magazine or University Museum Calculated for General Instruction and Amusement on a Plan Entirely New, etc.* (London, 1768-70); *The Pennsylvania Magazine or American Monthly Museum* (Philadelphia, 1775); *The Royal American Magazine* (Boston, 1774).

Newspapers

These have been examined on an imperial basis. It was found that a single file was not important except for the information it gave of local shipping, prices, and goods offered for sale. Important news items were copied from one newspaper to another. By examining a series of files it became apparent that the Empire in 1760-73 was essentially a unity. The commonly held economic and political ideals come to light in this mass of material as nowhere else. The files examined are listed below.

Some files were not complete.

England

> *London Daily Advertiser*, 1766-74.
> *London Chronicle*, 1765-75.

Nova Scotia

> *The Halifax Gazette*, 1765-66

Massachusetts

> *Boston Chronicle* (The first New England newspaper published twice a week. Strongly Tory), 1767-69.
> *Boston Evening Post*, 1765-75
> *Boston Gazette or Country Journal*, 1765-75.
> *Boston Post Boy and Advertiser*, 1765-75. (Carries the name *Massachusetts Gazette and Boston Post Boy*, 1769-75.)
> *Essex Gazette, Salem*, 1768-73.
> *Massachusetts Spy*, Boston, 1770-75.

Connecticut

> *Connecticut Courant*, Hartford, 1769-75.
> *Connecticut Gazette*, New Haven, 1766-67.
> *Connecticut Journal* and *New Haven Post Boy*, New Haven, 1767-75.
> *New London Gazette*, New London, 1766-67.

Rhode Island

> *Providence Gazette and Country Journal*, 1765-75.

New York

> *New York Gazette or Weekly Post Boy*, 1765-67.
> *New York Journal or General Advertiser*, 1766-75.
> *New York Mercury*, 1765-68.
> *Rivington's New York Gazetteer, or the Connecticut, New Jersey, Hudson's River and Quebec Weekly Advertiser* (strongly Tory), 1773-75.

Pennsylvania (All published at Philadelphia)

> *Pennsylvania Chronicle and Universal Advertiser*, 1768-75.
> *Pennsylvania Gazette*, 1765-75.
> *Pennsylvania Journal and Weekly Advertiser*, 1765-75.
> *Pennsylvania Packet and General Advertiser*, 1771-73.

Maryland

> *Maryland Gazette*, Annapolis, 1765-75.
> *Maryland Journal and the Baltimore Advertiser*, 1773-75.

Virginia

> *Virginia Gazette*, Williamsburg, Purdie, 1766-75.
> *Rind's Virginia Gazette*, Williamsburg, 1766-75.

North Carolina

> *North Carolina Gazetteer and Weekly Post Boy*, Wilmington, 1765-75.
> *Cape Fear Mercury*, Wilmington, 1773-75.

South Carolina (All printed at Charleston)
    South Carolina Gazette, 1765-75.
    South Carolina Gazette and Country Journal, 1765-75.
    South Carolina and American General Gazette, 1765-74.
Georgia
    Georgia Gazette, Savannah, 1765-75.

CONTEMPORARY HISTORIES OF THE REVOLUTION

The generation that participated in the Revolution left considerable historical literature. The basic material drawn upon by most of them was that compiled by Edmund Burke for the *Annual Register*, supplemented by personal information secured in various ways. The personal contribution frequently is important. Not a single writer ascribed the Revolution to the Navigation Acts.

Almon, John
    The Remembrancer or Impartial Repository of Public Events. 17 vols., London, 1775-84.
Boucher, Jonathan
    A View of the Causes and Consequences of the American Revolution in Thirteen Discourses. Dedicated to Washington. London, 1797.
Chalmers, George
    An Introduction to the History of the Revolt of the American Colonies; Being a Comprehensive View of Its Origin; Derived from the State Papers Contained in the Public Offices in Great Britain. London, 1782.
——. *Opinions on Interesting Subjects of Public Law and Commercial Policy Arising from American Independence.* London, 1785.
Drayton, Henry
    Memoirs of the American Revolution From its Commencement to the Year 1786, Inclusive; as Relating to the State of South Carolina, and Occasionally Relating to the States of North Carolina and Georgia. 2 vols., Charleston, 1821.
Galloway, Joseph
    Historical and Political Reflections on the Rise and Progress of the American Rebellion; in Which the Causes of that Rebellion are Pointed Out, and the Policy and Necessity of Offering to the Americans a System of Government Founded on the Principles of the British Constitution, are Clearly Demonstrated. London, 1780.
Gordon, William
    History of the Rise, Progress, and Establishment of the Independence, of the United States of America; Including an Account of the Late War, and of the Thirteen Colonies from their Origin to that Period. 4 vols., London, 1787.
——. *History of the Origin, Rise and Progress of the War in America Between Great Britain and Her Colonies, From its Commencement in 1764.* London, 1780.
Holroyd, John Baker (Lord Sheffield)
    Observations on the Commerce of the American States, With an Appendix. 2d ed., London, 1783.

Hubley, Bernard
> *The History of the American Revolution; Including the Most Important Events, and Resolutions of the Honorable Continental Congress During That Period; and Also the Most Interesting Letters and Orders of His Excellency General George Washington, Commander in Chief of the American Forces.* Northumberland, Pa., 1805, Vol. 1.

Hutchinson, Thomas
> *The History of the Province of Massachusetts Bay; From the First Settlement Thereof in 1628 to 1774.* 3 vols., Boston and London, 1764-1828.

——. *Impartial History of the War in America Between Great Britain and Her Colonies; From Its Commencement to the End of 1779.* Appendix with authentic papers. London, 1780.

Macpherson, David
> *Annals of Commerce, Manufactures, Fisheries, and Navigation, etc.* 4 vols., London, 1805.

Murray, Rev. James, of Newcastle
> *An Impartial History of the Present War in America, Containing an Account of Its Rise and Progress, the Political Springs Thereof, with Various Successes and Disappointments on Both Sides.* Newcastle upon Tyne, 1778-80.

Pitkin, Timothy
> *A Statistical View of the Commerce of the United States of America.* Hartford, 1816.

Ramsay, David
> *A History of the American Revolution.* 2 vols., Philadelphia, 1789.

——. *The History of the Revolution in South Carolina from a British Province to an Independent State.* 2 vols., Charleston, 1784.

Reynal, Abbé Guillaume Thomas François
> *The Revolution in America.* Edinburgh, 1783.

Stedman, Charles
> *The History of the Origin, Progress, and Termination of the American War.* 2 vols., London, 1794.

Warren, Mrs. Mercy (sister of James Otis and wife of Gen. James Warren)
> *History of the Rise, Progress and Termination of the American Revolution, Enterspersed with Biographical, Political and Moral Observations.* 3 vols., Boston, 1805.

Williamson, Hugh
> *The History of North Carolina.* 2 vols., Philadelphia, 1812.

Winterbotham, W.
> *An Historical, Geographical, Commercial and Philosophical View of the United States of America, and of the European Settlements in America and the West Indies.* 4 vols., London, 1795; New York, 1796.

CONTEMPORARY CONTROVERSIAL BOOKS AND PAMPHLETS

The best sources of information for public opinion on issues as they arose is the ephemeral pamphlet literature of the period. This needs to be examined on an empire-wide basis, because many of the English pamphlets were reprinted in the colonies and the colonial pamphlets were very generally re-printed in England as well as in other colonies. Any important pamphlet soon acquired wide circulation. No effort has been made to trace republication. The arrangement in the following list is by years, as that gives the best idea of the importance of an issue and the extent of public participation in its discussion. Long descriptive titles have been abridged.

PUBLISHED PRIOR TO 1764

Decker, Sir Matthew
> *An Essay on the Causes of the Decline of the Foreign Trade, Conse-quently of the Value of the Lands of Britain and of the Means to Restore Both.* London, 1750.

Anonymous
> *A Short View of the Smuggling Trade Carried on by the British Northern Colonies in Violation of the Acts of Navigation and Several Other Acts of Parliament.* London, 1751.

——. *Scheme for the Settlement of a New Colony to the Westward of Penn-sylvania.* Philadelphia, 1755.

——. *A Letter to a Member of Parliament on the Importance of the American Colonies and the Best Means of Making Them Most Useful to the Mother Country.* London, 1757.

Burke, William
> *Remarks on a Letter Adressed to Two Great Men. In a Letter to the Author of That Piece.* London, 1760.

Franklin, Benjamin
> *The Interest of Great Britain Considered with Regard to Her Colonies.* London, 1760.

Pulteney, William and Douglas, James
> *A Letter Addressed to Two Great Men (Duke of Newcastle and William Pitt).* London, 1760.

Rutherford, John
> *Importance of the Colonies to Great Britain.* London, 1761.

Anonymous
> *The Comparative Importance of Our Acquisitions from France in America, With Remarks on a Pamphlet [by Edmund Burke] Entitled, An Examination of the Commercial Principles of the Late Negotiations in 1761.* London, 1762.

Bollan, William
> *Coloniae Angliae Illustrae, or the Acquest of Dominion, and Plantations of the Colonies, Made by the English in America: With the Rights of the Colonies Examined, Stated and Illustrated.* London, 1762, Part I.

Anonymous
> *Some Hints to People in Power on the Present Melancholy Situation of our Colonies in North America.* London, 1763.

Dalrymple, John
> *An Appeal to Facts; In a Letter to the Right Honorable Earl Temple.* London, 1763.

1764

Anonymous
> *An Essay on Trade of the Northern Colonies of Great Britain in North America.* London, 1764.

——. *Reasons Against the Renewal of the Sugar Act, As it Will be Prejudicial to the Trade Not Only of the Northern Colonies But to That of Great Britain Also.* Boston, 1764.

An American
> *An Essay in Vindication of the Continental Colonies of America From a Censure of Mr. Adam Smith in His Theory of Moral Sentiments, With Some Reflections on Slavery in General.* London, 1764.

Fitch, Thomas
> *Reasons Why the Colonies in America Should Not be Charged With Internal Taxes, by Authority of Parliament, Humbly Offered for Consideration, In Behalf of the Colony of Connecticut.* New Haven, 1764.

Huske, John
> *Copy of a Letter to a Committee of Merchants in Boston.* Westminster, 1764.

Otis, James
> *The Rights of the British Colonies Asserted and Proved.* Boston, 1764.

Pownall, Thomas
> *Administration of the Colonies.* London, 1764.

Smith, William
> *An Answer to Mr. Franklin's Remarks on a Late Protest.* Philadelphia, 1764.

Thatcher, Oxenbridge
> *The Sentiments of a British American.* Boston, 1764.

1765

Anonymous
> *A Letter to the Author of the Halifax Letter; Occasioned by His Book, Entitled, A Defence of That Letter.* Has no place of publication, 1765.

——. *A Letter to the Earl of Bute Relative to the Late Changes That Have Happened to the Administration.* London, 1765.

——. *A Letter to a Member of Parliament Wherein the Power of the British Legislature and the Case of the Colonists are Briefly and Impartially Considered.* London, 1765.

——. *Oppression—A Poem, By an American, With Notes by a North Briton.* London, 1765.

——. *A New Collection of Verses Applied to the First of November, A. D., 1765, &c. Including a Prediction That the S—p A—t Shall not Take Place in North America. Together With a Poetical Dream, Concerning Stamped Papers.* New Haven, 1765.

——. *The Rights of the British Colonies Considered, the Administration and Regulation of the Colonies Exploded, and the Best Means Recommended to Make the Colonies Most Useful to the Mother Country.* London, 1765.

——. *The State of the Nation, With a Preliminary Defense of the Budget.* London, 1765.

Church, Benjamin
Liberty and Property Vindicated and the St—pm—n Burnt. Hartford, 1765.

Cooper, Sir Grey
The Merits of the New Administration Truly Stated in Answer to Several Pamphlets and Papers Published Against Them. London, 1765.

Dickinson, John
The Late Regulations Respecting the British Colonies on the Continent of America Considered. In a Letter From a Gentleman in Philadelphia to His Friend in London. Philadelphia, 1765.

——. *A Reply to a Piece Called the Speech of Joseph Galloway, Esq.* London, 1765.

Dulany, Daniel
Consideration on the Propriety of Imposing Taxes on the British Colonies for the Purpose of Raising a Revenue by Act of Parliament. Annapolis, 1765.

Dummer, Jeremiah
A Defence of the New England Charters. London, 1765.

Elliott, Andrew
A Sermon Preached Before His Excellency, Francis Bernard, Esq., Governor, the Honorable His Majesty's Council, and the Honorable House of Representatives of the Province of the Massachusetts Bay in New England, May 29, 1765. Boston, 1765.

Fothergill, John
Considerations Relative to the North American Colonies. London, 1765.

Galloway, Joseph
The Speech in Answer to the Speech of John Dickinson, Esq., Delivered in the House of Assembly of the Province of Pennsylvania, May 24, 1764. London, 1765.

Grenville, George
The Regulations Lately Made Concerning the Colonies, and the Taxes Imposed Upon Them Considered. London, 1765.

Hopkins, Stephen
Brief Remarks on the Halifax Libel on the British-American Colonies. Boston, 1765.

——. *Rights of Colonies Examined.* Providence, 1765.

Howard, Martin, Jr.
A Defense of the Letter from a Gentleman of Halifax, To His Friend in Rhode Island. Newport, 1765.

Jenyns, Soame
The Objections to the Taxation of Our American Colonies by the Legislature of Great Britain, Briefly Considered. London, 1765.

Knox, William (Agent for Georgia and later secretary to Hillsborough and Germain)
The Claim of the Colonies to Exemption From Internal Taxes Imposed

by Authority of Parliament Examined; From a Gentleman in London to His Friend in America. London, 1765.

Lloyd, Charles

An Honest Man's Reasons for Declining to Take Any Part in the New Administration, In a Letter to the Marquis of . . . London, 1765.

——. *A Critical Review of the New Administration.* London, 1765.

Massachusetts

A Brief State of the Services and Expenses of the Province of the Massachusetts Bay in the Common Cause. London, 1765.

Mauduit, Israel

Some Thoughts on the Method of Improving and Securing the Advantages Which Accrue to Great Britain from the Northern Colonies. London, 1765.

Otis, James

Brief Remarks on the Defense (by Martin Howard, Jr.) *of the Halifax Libel on the British American Colonies.* Boston, 1765.

——. *Considerations on Behalf of the Colonists. In a Letter to a Noble Lord.* London, 1765.

Palmer, John

An Essay on the Constitution of England. London, 1765.

Rogers, Major Robert

Concise Account of North America, Particularly of the Interior Country, Never Before so Accurately and Minutely Described by any Author. London, 1765-66.

Stamp Act

Copies and Extracts of Newspapers Printed in New England in the Months of September, October, and November, 1765, and Referred to in the Letters Transmitted from Francis Bernard, Governor of the Massachusetts Bay, to the Lords Commissioner for Trade and Plantations. London, 1765.

Whately, Thomas

Remarks on the Budget, or a Candid Examination of the Facts and Arguments Offered to the Public in That Pamphlet. London, 1765.

——. *The Regulations Concerning Colonies and the Taxes Imposed Upon Them Considered.* London, 1765.

1766

Almon, John

A Collection of the Most Interesting Tracts, Lately Published in England and America, on the Subject of Taxing the American Colonies and Regulating Their Trade. London, 1766.

Anonymous

The Answer at Large to Mr. Pitt's Speech. London, 1766.

——. *An Application of Some General Political Rules to the Present State of Great Britain, Ireland and America. In a Letter to the Right Honorable Earl Temple.* London, 1766.

——. *Authentic Account of the Proceedings Held at New York, etc.* Place of imprint not given, 1766.

——. *The British Antidote to Caledonian Poison*
and
The Scots Scourge; Being a Compleat Supplement to the British Antidote to Caledonia Poison. 6th ed., London, 1766.

——. *The Charters of the Following Provinces of North America; viz: Virginia, Maryland, Connecticut, Rhode Island, Pennsylvania, Massachusetts Bay, and Georgia. To Which is Prefixed a Faithful Narration of the Proceedings of the North American Colonies, in Consequence of the Late Stamp Act.* London, 1766.

——. *Considerations on the American Stamp Act and On the Conduct of the Minister Who Planned It.* London, 1766.

——. *Considerations Upon the Rights of the Colonies to the Privileges of British Subjects. Introduced by a Brief Review of the Rise and Progress of English Liberty and Concluded With Some Remarks Upon the Present Alarming Situation.* New York, 1766.

——. *Correct Copies of the Two Protests Against the Bill to Repeal the American Stamp Act With Lists of the Speakers and Voters.* Paris, 1766.

——. *The Crisis. Or a Full Defence of the Colonies.* London, 1766.

——. *An Essay on the Constitution of England.* London, 1766.

——. *An Examination of the Rights of the Colonies Upon the Principles of Law. By a Gentleman of the Bar.* London, 1766.

——. *Free and Candid Remarks on a Late Celebrated Oration, With Some Few Occasional Thoughts on the Late Commotion in America. In a Letter To* [evidently Pitt]. London, 1766.

——. *The General Opposition of the Colonies to the Payment of the Stamp Duty and the Consequence of Enforcing Obedience by Military Measures, etc. In a Letter to a Member of Parliament.* London, 1766.

——. *Justice and Necessity of Taxing the American Colonies Demonstrated Together With a Vindication of the Authority of Parliament.* London, 1766.

——. *The Late Occurrences in North America and Policy of Great Britain Considered.* London, 1766.

——. *A Letter From a Gentleman in London to His Friend in the Country Relating to the American Stamp Act With Mr. P--t's and Other Speeches on the Occasion.* London, 1766.

——. *A Letter to the North American, on Occasion of His Address to the Committee of Correspondence in Barbados. By a Native of the Island.* Barbados, 1766.

——. *The Necessity of Repealing the American Stamp Act Demonstrated, or a Proof that Great Britain Must be Injured by That Act. In a Letter to a Member of the House of Commons.* London, 1766.

——. *A Plain and Seasonable Address to the Free Holders of Great Britain on the Present Posture of Affairs in America.* London, 1766.

——. *The Proceedings of the North American Colonies in Consequence of the Stamp Act.* London, 1766.

——. *Reflections on Representation in Parliament, Being an Attempt to Show the Equity and Practicability of Establishing a More Equal Representa-*

tion Throughout Great Britain, But Also of Admitting the Americans to a Share in the Legislature, etc. London, 1766.

——. *The Rights of Parliament Vindicated on Occasion of the Late Stamp Act in Which is Exposed the Conduct of the American Colonists; Addressed to All the People of Great Britain.* London, 1766.

——. *A Short and Friendly Caution to the Good People of England.* London, 1766.

——. *A Short View of the Political Life and Transactions of a Late Right Honourable Commoner, To Which is Added a Full Refutation Under the Sanction of a Very Popular Nobleman, Entitled an Enquiry Into the Conduct of a Late Right Honourable Commoner.* London, 1766.

——. *Some Important Observations Occasioned by and Adapted to the Publick Fast Ordered by Authority, Dec. 18, A.D., 1765.* Newport, 1766.

——. *Some Strictures on the Late Occurrences in North America.* London, 1766.

——. *The True Interest of Great Britain With Respect to Her American Colonies, Stated and Impartially Considered, By A Merchant of London.* London, 1766.

——. *What Should Be Done: or Remarks on the Political State of Things. Addressed to the Present Administration, the Members of the House of Commons, and the Good People of England. Inscribed to Sir Joseph Mawbey, Bart. Member in Parliament for the Borough of Southwark.* London, 1766.

A. B.
A Letter From a Merchant in London to His Nephew in North America, Relative to the Present Posture of Affairs in the Colonies. London, 1766.

Appleton, Nathaniel.
Repeal of the Stamp Act. Sermon Preached in Cambridge May 20, 1766. Boston, 1766.

Barbadian
An Essay Towards the Vindication of the Committee of Correspondence in Barbados; In a Letter to a Friend. By a Barbadian. Barbados, 1766.

Bland, Richard
An Inquiry Into the Rights of the British Colonies. Williamsburg, 1766.

Bollan, William
A Succinct View of the Origin of Our Colonies With Their Civil State— With Observations on the Commercial, Beneficial and Perpetual Union of the Colonies With This Kingdom. (Extracts from an essay lately published entitled *The Freedom of Speech and Writing, etc.*) London, 1766.

Chauncy, Charles, D.D.
A Discourse on "The Good News From a Far Country." Boston, 1766.

Cooper, Samuel
The Crisis, or A Full Defence of the Colonies in Which it is Incontestibly Proved that the British Constitution Has Been Flagrantly Violated in the Late Stamp Act and Rendered Indisputably Evident that the Mother Country Cannot Lay any Arbitrary Tax Upon the Americans Without Destroying the Essence of Her Own Liberties. London, 1766.

Country Gentleman

A Parallel Drawn Between the Administration in the Four Last Years of Queen Anne and the Four First of George The Third. London, 1766.

Dickinson, John

An Address to the Committee of Correspondence in Barbados Occasioned by a Late Letter From Them to Their Agent in London. Philadelphia, 1766.

Devotion, Ebenezer

The Examiner Examined. A Letter From a Gentleman in Connecticut to His Friend in London, etc. New London, 1766.

Emerson, Joseph

A Thanksgiving Sermon Preached at Pepperrell, July 24th, 1766, A Day Set Apart by Public Authority as a Day of Thanksgiving on the Account of the Repeal of the Stamp Act. Boston, 1766.

Fitch, Thomas (Governor of Connecticut)

Some Reasons That Influenced the Governor to Take and the Councillors to Administer the Oath Required by the Act of Parliament, Commonly Called the Stamp Act. Hartford, 1766.

Franklin, Benjamin

Examination of Dr. Franklin Before an August Assembly Relating to the Repeal of the Stamp Act. Philadelphia, 1766.

Grenville, Richard

An Application of Some Political Rules to the Present State of Great Britain, Ireland and America. In a Letter to the Right Honourable Earl Temple. London, 1766.

Gentleman at the Bar

An Examination of the Rights of the Colonies, Upon Principles of Law. London, 1766.

Hopkinson, Francis

Dissertation on the Reciprocal Advantages of Perpetual Union Between Great Britain and Her American Colonies. Philadelphia, 1766.

Hopkins, Stephen

The Grievances of the American Colonies Candidly Examined. London, 1766.

Ingersoll, Jared

Mr. Ingersoll's Letters Relating to the Stamp Act. New Haven, 1766.

Lloyd, Charles

A True History of a Late Administration. London, 1766.

——. *A Short History of the Conduct of the Present Ministry With Regard to the American Stamp Act.* London, 1766.

Massachusetts

A Bill Entitled An Act For Granting Compensation to the Sufferers in the Late Times, and Extracts of a Letter from Henry L. Conway and Two Letters from Denys De Berdt. Boston, 1766.

Mauduit, Jasper

The Legislative Authority of the British Parliament With Respect to North America, and the Privileges of the Assemblies There, Briefly Considered by J. M. of the Inner Temple. London, 1766.

Mayhew, Jonathan, D.D.
The Snare Broken, A Thanksgiving Discourse Preached at The Desire of the West Church in Boston, N.E., Friday, May 23, 1766, Occasioned by the Repeal of the Stamp Act. Boston, 1766.

Morgan, John and others
Four Dissertations on the Reciprocal Advantages of a Perpetual Union Between Great Britain and Her American Colonies: Written for Mr. Sargents' Prize Medal, etc. Boston, 1766.

Patten, William
A Discourse Delivered at Halifax, July 24, 1766, On the Day of Thanksgiving to Almighty God, Throughout the Province of Massachusetts Bay in New England for the Repeal of the Stamp Act. Boston, 1766.

Ray, Nicholas
The Importance of the Colonies of North America and the Interest of Great Britain With Regard to Them Considered Together With Remarks on the Stamp Duty. London, 1766.

Scott, Rev. James (Anti-Sejanus)
A Short History of the Conduct of the Present Ministry With Regard to the Stamp Act. London, 1766.

Stamp Act.
The Speech by Mr. P——t— and Several Others, etc. London, 1766.

Pitt, William
The Celebrated Speech of a Celebrated Commoner. London, 1766.

——. *The Speech of Mr. Pitt, and Several Others, in a Certain August Assembly on a Late Important Debate: With an Introduction of the Matters Preceding It.* Philadelphia, 1766.

——. *An Appendix to the Speech of Mr. Pitt, Now Earl of Chatham, Upon the Stamp Act, etc.* Dublin, 1766.

Stamp Act Congress (New York, 1765)
Proceedings of The Congress at New York (October 7-25, 1765). Annapolis, 1766.

Stillman, Samuel
Good News From a Far Country. A Sermon Preached at Boston, May 17, 1766, Upon the Arrival of the Important News of the Repeal of the Stamp Act. Boston, 1766.

Throop, Benjamin
A Thanksgiving Sermon, Upon the Occasion of the Glorious News of the Repeal of the Stamp Act; Preached in New Concord, in Norwich, June 26, 1766. New London, 1766.

Steele, Joshua
An Account of a Late Conference on the Occurrences in America in a Letter to a Friend. London, 1766.

Todd, Nicholas
Good Humour, Or A Way With the Colonies, Wherein is Occasionally Enquired Into Mr. Pitt's Claim of Popularity and the Principles of Virtuous Liberty as Taught in the School of Mr. Wilkes and Other Peripateters. London, 1766.

Tucker Josiah

A Letter From a Merchant in London to His Nephew in North America, Relative to the Present Posture of Affairs in the Colonies. London, 1766.

Watts, Stephen

An Essay on the Reciprocal Advantages of a Perpetual Union Between Great Britain and Her American Colonies. Philadelphia, 1766.

Zubly, J. J.

The Stamp Act Repealed. A Sermon Preached in the Meeting at Savannah in Georgia, June 25, 1766. Savannah, 1766.

1767

Anonymous

An Address to the People of England; Shewing the Advantages Arising From the Frequent Changes of Ministers; With an Address to the Next Administration. London, 1767.

——. *The Commercial Conduct of the Province of New York Considered And the True Interest of That Colony Attempted to be Shown in a Letter to the Society of Arts, Agriculture and Economy.* New York, 1767.

——. *A Free Appeal to the People of Great Britain on the Conduct of the Present Administration Since the Thirteenth of July, 1766.* London, 1767.

——. *An Authentic Account of the Proceedings of the Congress Held at New York in 1765 on the Subject of the American Stamp Act.* London, 1767.

——. *A Letter to G. G.* London, 1767.

——. *The Present State of Great Britain and North America With Regard to Agriculture, Population, Trade and Manufactures.* London, 1767.

——. *Two Papers on the Subject of Taxing the British Colonies in America.* London, 1767.

——. *A New and Important Collection of Interesting Letters From the Public Papers, Many of Them Written by Persons of Eminence.* London, 1767.

——. *A View of the Several Changes Made in the Administration of Government Since the Accession of His Present Majesty.* London, 1767.

Blyth, Owen

The Charters of the Following Provinces of North America: Virginia, Maryland, Connecticut, Rhode Island, Pennsylvania, Massachusetts, Georgia; to Which Are Prefixed a Faithful Narrative of the Proceedings of the North American Colonies in Consequence of the Late Stamp Act. London, 1767.

Lloyd, Charles

The Conduct of the Late Administration Examined, etc. With an Appendix Containing Original and Authentic Documents. London, 1767.

Keith, Sir William

Two Papers on the Subject of Taxing the British Colonies in America. London, 1767.

Mitchell, John

The Present State of Great Britain and North America. London, 1767.

Postlethwayt, Malachy

Britain's Commercial Interest Explained and Improved, In a Series of

Dissertations on Several Important Branches of Her Trade and Policy.
2 vols., London, 1767.

Shute, Daniel
   Pastor of the Third Church at Hingham. A Sermon Preached to the Ancient and Honorable Artillery Company in Boston, New England, June 1, 1767, etc. Boston, 1767.

1768

Anonymous
   A Collection of Tracts From the Late Newspapers, etc., Containing Particularly the American Whig. A Whip for the American Whig, With Some Other Pieces on the Residence of Protestant Bishops in the American Colonies and in Answer to the Writers Who Opposed It, etc. Vol. 1. New York, 1768.
——. *The Constitutional Right of the Legislature of Great Britain to Tax the British Colonies in America Impartially Stated.* London, 1768.
——. *The First Measures Necessary to be Taken in the American Department.* London, 1768.
——. *The Following Address Was Read at a Meeting of Merchants at the Lodge in Philadelphia, on the 25th of April, 1768.* Folio Broadside. Philadelphia, 1768.
——. *The Power and Grandeur of Great Britain Founded on the Liberty of the Colonies and the Mischiefs Attending the Taxing Them by Act of Parliament.* New York, 1768.

Bollan, William
   Continued Corruption, Standing Armies, and Popular Discontents Considered; and the Establishment of the English Colonies in America With Various Subsequent Proceedings, etc. London, 1768.
——. *An Epistle From Timoleon to All the Honest Freeholders and Other Electors of Members of Parliament.* London, 1768.

Canning, George
   A Letter to the Right Honorable Wills, Earl of Hillsborough, on the Connection Between Great Britain and her American Colonies. London, 1768.

Dickinson, John
   Letters of a Farmer in Pennsylvania to the Inhabitants of the British Colonies. Boston, 1768.

Downer, Silas
   A Discourse Delivered in Providence, R. I., July, 1768, at the Dedication of the Tree of Liberty. Providence, 1768.

Fleming, Caleb
   The Friendship and Virtue of Jonathan and David, A Political Sermon, Which Never Was, Nor Ever Will be Preached. London, 1768.

Grenville, George (Also ascribed to Knox, William)
   The Present State of the Nation, Particularly With Respect to Its Trade, Finances, etc. Addressed to the King and Both Houses of Parliament. London, 1768.

Laurens, Henry

> *Extracts From the Proceedings of the High Court of Vice-Admiralty in Charleston, South Carolina, Upon Six Several Informations Adjudged by the Honourable Egerton Leigh, Esq., Sole Judge of That Court and His Majesty's Attorney-General in the Said Province, in the Years 1767-1768.* Charleston, 1768.

Livingston, William

> *A Letter to the Right Reverend Father in God, John, Lord Bishop of Landoff Occasioned by Some Passages in His Lordships Sermon on the 20th of February, 1767, In Which the American Colonies are Loaded With Great and Undeserved Reproach,* Boston, 1768.

Loyal Patriot

> *Some Observations of Consequence in Three Parts, Occasioned by the Stamp Tax, Lately Imposed on the British Colonies.* Place of imprint not given, 1768.

Massachusetts

> *True Sentiments of America Contained in a Collection of Letters Sent From the House of Representatives of the Province of Massachusetts Bay to Several Persons of High Rank in This Kingdom.* London, 1768.

Pacificus (John Dickinson?)

> *To the Public.* Philadelphia, July 16, 1768.

P-wn-ll, Th-m-s

> *The Speech of Th-m-s P-wn-ll, Esq., Late G-v-rn-r of This Province in the House of Commons in Favor of America.* Boston, 1768.

1769

Anonymous

> *Boston, 25 January, 1768, A Dialogue Between Sir George Cornwall, a Gentleman, Lately Arrived From England With Design to Travel Incognito Through the Continent of America and Mr. Flint.* London, 1769.

——. *Britannia's Intersession for the Deliverance of John Wilkes, Esq., From Persecution and Banishment to Which is Added a Political and Constitutional Sermon and a Dedication to Lxxx Bxxx (Lord Bute),* London, 1769.

——. *A Collection of the Letters of Atticus, Lucius, Junius and Others With Observations and Notes.* London, 1769.

——. *Considerations on the Dependencies of Great Britain With Observations on a Pamphlet, Entitled, The Present State of the Nation.* London, 1769.

——. *Copies of Proceedings in the Several Assemblies [of the British Colonies of North America] in Consequence of the Resolutions of Parliament in the Last Session.* Boston, 1769.

——. *An Inquiry Into the Nature and Causes of the Present Disputes Between the British Colonies in America and Their Mother Country.* London, 1769.

——. *A Letter to the Right Honorable the Earl of Hillsborough on the Present Situation of Affairs in America.* London, 1769.

——. *Observations on Several Acts of Parliament Passed in the 4th, 6th and 7th Years of His Present Majesty's Reign.* Boston, 1769.

——. *Observations on the Review of the Controversy Between Great Britain and Her Colonies.* London, 1769.

——. *The Present State of Liberty in Great Britain and Her Colonies, By An Englishman.* London, 1769.

——. *Private Letters From an American in England to His Friends in America* (pictures America as rich, prosperous, has all the good people, England deserted, overrun by Scots, trouble all comes from repeal of Stamp Act). London, 1769.

——. *Remarks on the Appendix to the Present State of the Nation.* London, 1769.

——. *The Repository: or Half-Yearly Register Containing Whatever is Remarkable in the History, Politics, Literature and Amusement of the Year 1768.* London, 1769.

——. *The Rights of the Colonies and the Extent of the Legislative Authority of Great Britain Briefly Stated and Considered.* London, 1769.

——. *The True Constitutional Means for Putting an End to the Disputes Between Great Britain and the American Colonies.* London, 1769.

Adams, Amos, A.M. (Pastor of First Church of Roxbury)
A Concise, Historical View of the Difficulties, and Hardships and Perils Which Attended the Planting and Progressive Improvements of New England: With A Particular Account of Its Long and Destructive Wars, Expensive Expeditions, &c. Boston, 1769.

Adams, Samuel
An Appeal to the World: Or A Vindication of the Town of Boston, etc. Boston, 1769.

Bancroft, Edward
Remarks on the Review of the Controversy Between Great Britain and Her Colonies; In Which the Errors of its Author Are Exposed and the Claims of the Colonies Vindicated Upon the Evidence of Historical Facts and Authentic Records. To Which is Subjoined a Proposal for Terminating the Present Unhappy Disputes With the Colonies. London, 1769.

Bernard, Francis
Letters to the Ministry: From Governor Bernard, General Gage, and Admiral Hood, and Also Memorials to the Lords of the Treasury From Commissioners of the Customs, With Sundry Letters and Papers Annexed to the Memorials. Boston, 1769.

Burke, Edmund
Observations on a Late State of the Nation. London, 1769.

Butler, George B.
The Case of Great Britain and America; Addressed to the King and Both Houses of Parliament. London, 1769.

Canning, George
A Letter to the Right Honorable the Earl of Hillsborough on the Present Situation of Affairs in America. London, 1769.

Church, Benjamin
An Address to a Provincial Bashaw. O Shame Where is Thy Blush, By a Son of Liberty (Poem, 27 stanzas). Printed in (the Tyrannis Administration of St. Francisco) Boston, 1769.

Cluny, Alexander
   The American Traveler: Or Observations on the Present State, Culture, and Commerce of the British Colonies in America. By an Old and Experienced Traveler. London, 1769.

Erskine, John
   Shall I Go to War With My American Brethern? A Discourse From Judges XX and 28th; Addressed to all Concerned in Determining that Important Question. London, 1769.

Hollis, Thomas
   The True Sentiments of America: Contained in a Collection of Letters Sent from the House of Representatives of the Province of Massachusetts Bay to Several Persons of High Rank in this Kingdom; Together With Certain Papers Relating to a Supposed Libel on the Governor of that Province, and a Dissertation on the Canon and Feudal Laws. Dublin, 1769.

Hoven, Jason
   Election Sermon, May 31st, 1769. Boston, 1769.

Knox, William
   Controversy Between Great Britain and Her Colonies Reviewed. The Several Pleas of the Colonies, in Support of Their Right to all the Liberties and Privileges of British Subjects, and to Exemption from the Legislative Authority of Parliament, Stated and Considered, &c. London, 1769.

Langrishi, Sir Hercules
   Considerations on the Dependencies of Great Britain; With Observations on a Pamphlet Entitled "The Present State of the Nation." London, 1769.

Laurens, Henry
   Appendix to the Extracts, etc. Charleston, S. C., 1769.

Leigh, Sir Egerton
   The Man Unmasked: Or the World Undeceived, in the Author of a Late Pamphlet, Intitled "Extracts From the Proceedings of the High Court of Vice-Admiralty in Charleston, South Carolina, &c." With Suitable Remarks on that Masterly Performance. Charleston, 1769.

Mauduit, Israel
   A Short View of the History of the Colony of Massachusetts Bay; With Respect to Their Charter and Constitution. London, 1769.

Murray, James
   Sermons to Asses. Philadelphia, 1769.

Phelps, Richard
   The Rights of the Colonies and the Extent of the Legislative Authority of Great Britain Briefly Stated and Considered. London, 1769.

Ramsay, Allan
   Thoughts on the Origin and Nature of Government, Occasioned by the Late Disputes Between Great Britain and Her American Colonies. London, 1769.

Whateley, Thomas
   Considerations on the Trade and Finances of this Kingdom and On the

Measures of Administration; With Respect to Those Great National Objects Since the Conclusion of the Peace. London, 1769.

Zubly, John Joachim

An Humble Inquiry Into the Nature of the Dependency of the American Colonies; and the Right of Parliament to Lay Taxes on the Said Colonies. By a Freeman of South Carolina. A House Divided Against Itself Cannot Stand. Charleston, 1769.

1770

Anonymous

A First Letter to the Duke of Grafton. London, 1770.

——. *The Importance of the British Dominion in India Compared With That in America.* London, 1770.

——. *Letter From a Merchant in Philadelphia to His Friend in London, Dated November 26, 1769.* London, 1770.

——. *A Letter to the King.* London, 1770.

——. *The New Present State of Great Britain: To Which is Added Lists of All the Civil and Ecclesiastical and Military Offices in Great Britain.* London, 1770.

——. *A Short Description of the Province of South Carolina, With an Account of the Air, Weather, and Diseases in Charleston, Written in 1763.* London, 1770.

Baldwin, Samuel (of the Custom-House, London)

A Survey of the British Customs, Containing the Rates of Merchandize as Established by 12 Char. II, c. 4, and Other Statutes, etc. London, 1770.

Boston Merchants

Observations on Several Acts of Parliament Passed in the Fourth, Sixth, and Seventh Years of His Present Majesty's Reign. Boston, 1770.

Boston

An Account of the Late Unhappy Disturbance at Boston in New England Extracted from Depositions that Have Been Made Concerning it by Persons of All Parties; With an Appendix Containing Some Affidavits and Other Evidence Relating to This Affair Not Mentioned in the Narration of it That Has Been Published at Boston. London, 1770.

——. *Additional Observations to a Short Narrative on the Horrid Massacre in Boston, Perpetrated in the Evening of the 5th of March, 1770. Appendix With Depositions.* Boston, 1770.

——. *A Letter From the Town of Boston to C. Lucas, Esq., One of the Representatives of the City of Dublin in Parliament; Enclosing a Short Narrative, etc.* Dublin, 1770.

Boston Massacre

A Fair Account of the Late Unhappy Disturbance at Boston in New England, etc. London, 1770.

——. *The Trial of William Weems, James Hartigan, Wm. McCauley, Hugh White, Matthew Killroy, William Warren, John Carrol, and Hugh Montgomery, Soldiers in His Majesty's 29th Regiment of Foot, For the Murder of Crispus Attucks, Samuel Maverick, James Caldwell, and Patrick Carr, etc.* (Shorthand Report). Boston, 1770.

Bowdoin, James and others
> A Short Narrative of the Horrid Massacre in Boston, Perpetrated in the Evening of the Fifth of March, 1770. London, 1770.

Burke, Edmund
> Thoughts on the Cause of the Present Discontents. London, 1770.

Cunningham, J.
> An Essay on Trade and Commerce Containing Observations on Taxes, etc. London, 1770.

Edes and Gill
> North-American Almanac and Massachusetts Register (has much political material). Boston, 1770.

Goddard, William
> The Partnership: Or the History of the Rise and Progress of the Pennsylvania Chronicle &c. Wherein the Conduct of Joseph Galloway, Esq., Speaker of the Honourable House of Representatives—Mr. Thomas Wharton, Sen. and Their Man, Benjamin Towne, my Late Partners, With My Own, is Properly Delineated and Their Columnies Against Me Fully Refuted. Philadelphia, 1770.

Knox, William
> The Controversy Reviewed. London, 1770.

Lathrop, John (Pastor 2nd Church, Boston)
> Innocent Blood Crying to God From the Streets of Boston. A Sermon Occasioned by the Murder of Mssrs. Gray, Maverick, Caldwell, Attucks, with Carr Since Dead and Monk Judged Unrecoverable, and Several Others Badly Wounded by a Party of Troops Under Captain Preston, on the Fifth of March, 1770. London, 1770.

Lee, Arthur
> The Political Detection: Or the Treachery and Tyranny of Administration, Both at Home and Abroad: Displayed in a Series of Letters, Signed Junius Americanus. London, 1770.

Maryland
> The Proceedings of the Committee Appointed to Examine Into the Importation of Goods by the Brigantine Good Intent, Capt. Errington, from London, In February, 1770. Annapolis, 1770.

Maseres, Francis
> Considerations on the Expediency of Admitting Representatives From the American Colonies Into the British House of Commons. London, 1770.

Massachusetts
> A Continuation of the Proceedings of the House of Representatives of the Province of the Massachusetts Bay Relative to the Convening, Holding and Keeping the General Assembly at Harvard College in Cambridge. Boston, 1770.

——. Extract of a Letter From the House of Representatives of the Massachusetts Bay to Their Agent, Dennys De Berdt, Esq., With Some Remarks. London, 1770.

——. The Proceedings of the Council and the House of Representatives of the Province of the Massachusetts Bay, etc. Boston, 1770.

Morris, Robert (Lincoln's Inn)
    A Letter to Sir Richard Aston, Kn't; One of the Judges of His Majesty's Court of King's Bench and Late Chief Justice of the Common Pleas in Ireland, Containing a Reply to His Scandalous Abuse, and Some Thoughts on the Moderate Doctrine of Liberals. London, 1770.

Wheelock, Matthew
    Reflections Moral and Political on Great Britain and Her Colonies. London, 1770.

                                    1771

Anonymous
    Considerations on the Policy, Commerce and Circumstances of the Kingdom. London, 1771.
——. *Heads of a Proposed Bill or Magna Charta of England, Mentioned in a Letter Addressed to the People of Great Britain Lately Published and as Laid before L. N—— (North) and L. H.—— (Holland).* London, 1771.
——. *A Letter to the People of Great Britain on the Present Alarming Crisis, Pointing Out the Most Elligible Means for Limiting the Number of Place-men and Pensioners, in Parliament and Putting an End to Bribery and Corruption, to Obviate the Dangers Which Now Threaten This Kingdom.* London, 1771.

Hawles, Sir John, Knight (Solicitor General to the Late King William)
    The Englishman's Right: A Discourse Between a Barrister At Law and a Juryman, etc. London, 1771.

Husbands, Herman
    A Fan for Fanning and a Touch Stone to Tryon; Containing an Impartial Account of the Rise and Progress of the So Much Talked of Regulation in North Carolina. Boston, 1771.

Lovell, James
    An Oration Delivered April 2, 1771, at the Request of the Inhabitants of the Town of Boston to Commemorate the Bloody Tragedy of the Fifth of March, 1770. Boston, 1771.

                                    1772

The Censor. November 23, 1771–February 22, 1772.
    This is a reprint of articles published in the newspapers at the time. Boston, 1772.

Dalrymple, Alex
    Measures to Be Pursued. London, 1772.

Hargrove
    An Argument in the Case of James Somersett, a Negro, Lately Determined by the Court of King's Bench: Wherein it is Attempted to Demonstrate the Present Unlawfulness of Domestic Slavery in England, to Which is Prefixed a State of the Case. London, 1772.

Jenyns, Soame
    Scheme for Coalition. London, 1772.

1773

Anonymous

The Advantages of a Settlement Upon the Ohio in North America. London, 1773.

Almon, John

A Collection of Tracts on the Subjects of Taxing the British Colonies in America and Regulating Their Trade. 4 vols., London, 1773.

Amor Patriae (Thomas Crawley).

A Second Appeal to the Justice and Interests of the People on the Measures Respecting America. By the Author of the First. London, 1773.

Allen, John

An Oration Upon the Beauties of Liberty or the Essential Rights of the Americans: Delivered at the Second Baptist Church in Boston Upon the Last Annual Thanksgiving, Dec. 3, 1772. Humbly Dedicated to the Right Honourable the Earl of Dartmouth. Boston, 1773.

Belknap, Jeremy

Sermon on Military Duty Preached at Andover, Nov. 10, 1772, Before His Excellency, John Wentworth, Esq: L.L.D. Governor of His Majesty's Province of New Hampshire, at a Review of the Second Regiment of Foot of Said Province. Salem, 1773.

Boston

News of the Meeting at Faneuil Hall—5000 Present, December 2, 1772. News Handbill, Boston, 1773.

Church

An Oration Delivered March 5, 1773. Boston, 1773.

Massachusetts

Committee Report on Hutchinson Letters, June 15, 1773. Boston, 1773.
——. *Representations of Governor Hutchinson and Others Contained in Certain Letters Transmitted to England and Afterwards Retrieved From Thence and Laid Before the General Assembly of the Massachusetts Bay. Together With Resolves of the Two Houses Thereon.* Boston, 1773.

Mather, Samuel

An Attempt to Show that America Must be Known to the Ancients; Made at the Request and to Gratify the Curiosity of an Inquisitive Gentleman: To Which is Added an Appendix Concerning the American Colonies and Some Modern Management Against Them. By an American Englishman. Boston, 1773.

Rush, Benjamin

An Address to the Inhabitants of the British Settlements in America Upon Slave Keeping, By a Pennsylvanian. Philadelphia, 1773.
——. *A Vindication of the Address to the Inhabitants of the British Settlements, on the Slavery of the Negroes in America: In Answer to a Pamphlet Entitled, "Slavery Not Forbidden by Scripture; Or a Defence of the West-India Planters From the Aspersions Thrown Out Against Them by the Author of the Address."* Philadelphia, 1773.

Skillman, Isaac

The American Alarm, or the Bostonian Plea for the Rights and Liberties of the People, Humbly Addressed to the King and Council, and to the Constitutional Sons of Liberty in America: By the British Bostonian. Boston, 1773.

——. *An Oration On the Beauties of Liberty, etc.* Boston, 1773.

Somers, John
  The Security of Englishmen's Lives; Or the Trust Power and Duty of Grand Juries of England. London, 1773.

Watson, Samuel
  The Gentlemans and Citizens Almanack, For the Year of Our Lord, 1773. Dublin, 1773.

1774

Anonymous
  Abstracts of the Principal Regulations Contained in the Acts of Parliament Relative to the Trade of the British Plantations. Charleston, S. C., 1774.

——. *A Collection of Letters and Essays in Favour of Public Liberty. First published in the Newspapers in the years 1764-65, 66, 67, 68, 69, and 1770. By an amicable band of wellwishers to the Religious and Civil Rights of Mankind, in three volumes.* London, 1774.

——. *A Free and Calm Consideration of the Unhappy Misunderstandings and Debates; Which Have of Late Years Arisen and Yet Subsist, Between the Parliament of Great Britain, and These American Colonies, etc.* Salem, 1774.

——. *Americanus Examined and His Principles Compared With Those of the Approved Advocates For America, By a Pennsylvanian.* Philadelphia, 1774.

——. *An Argument in Defence of the Exclusive Rights Claimed by the Colonies to Tax Themselves; With a Review of the Laws of England Relative to Representation and Taxation, etc.* London, 1774.

——. *Answer to Considerations on Certain Political Transactions of the Province of South Carolina.* London, 1774.

——. *The Interest of the Merchants and Manufacturers of Great Britain, in the Present Contest With the Colonies Stated and Considered.* London, 1774.

——. *The Right of the British Legislature to Tax the American Colonies Vindicated and the Means of Asserting that Right Proposed.* London, 1774.

——. *The Rights of the English Colonies Established in America Stated and Defended, etc.* London, 1774.

——. *A True State of the Proceedings in the Parliament of Great Britain and in the Province of Massachusetts Bay, Relative to the Giving and Granting the Money of the People of That Province and of all North America, in the House of Commons; in Which They Are Not Represented* (Seems to have been prepared by Massachusetts). London, 1774.

Adams, John
  History of the Dispute With America From Its Origin in 1764 (written in the year 1774). London, 1784.

Bernard, Francis
  The Causes of the Present Distractions in America Explained in Two Letters to a Merchant in London. London, 1774.
——. *Principles of Law and Polity Applied to the Government of the British Colonies in America: Written in the Year 1764.* London, 1774.
——. *Select Letters on the Trade and Government of America, and the Principles of Law and polity Applied to the American Colonies.* London, 1774.

Boucher, Jonathan
  A Letter From a Virginian to the Members of the Congress to be Held at Philadelphia, on the First of September, 1774. Boston, 1774.

Cartwright, John
  American Independence the Interest and Glory of Great Britain—etc., etc. London, 1774.

Continental Congress
  Extracts From the Votes and Proceedings of the American Continental Congress, Held at Philadelphia on the 5th of September, 1774. Williamsburg, 1774.

Cooper, Myles
  The American Querist: or Some Questions Proposed Relative to the Present Disputes. By a North American. Boston, 1774.
——. *A Friendly Address to All Reasonable Americans on Consequences of Opposing the King's Troops and of a General Non-importation in America.* New York, 1774.

T. Crowley
  Dissertations On the Grand Dispute Between Great Britain and America. London, 1774.

Dickinson, John
  A New Essay (by the Pennsylvania Farmer) On the Constitutional Power of Great Britain Over the Colonies in America With Resolves of Committees For the Province of Pennsylvania and Their Instructions to Their Representatives in Assembly. Philadelphia, 1774.

Draper, William
  Thoughts of a Traveller Upon Our American Disputes. London, 1774.

Drayton, William Henry
  Letter From Freeman of South Carolina To the Deputies of North America, Assembled in the High Court of Congress at Philadelphia. Charleston, S. C., 1774.

Drinker, John
  Observations On the Late Popular Measures; Offered to the Serious Considerations of the Sober Inhabitants of Pennsylvania. Philadelphia, 1774.

Duché, Jacob
  Observations On a Variety of Subjects: Literary, Moral, and Religious: In a Series of Original Letters, Written by a Gentleman of Foreign Extraction Who Resided Some Time in Philadelphia. Philadelphia, 1774.

Hamilton, Alexander
  A Full Vindication of the Measures of the Congress From the Columnies of Their Enemies in Answer to a Letter Under Signature of A. W.

Farmer; Whereby His Sophistry is Exposed, His Cavils Confuted, His Artifices Detected, and His Wit Ridiculed: In a General Address to the Inhabitants of America and a Particular Address to the Farmers of N. Y. New York, 1774.

Hancock, John
March 5, Oration, 1774. Newport, R. I., 1774.

Hopkins, Francis
A Pretty Story Written in the Year of Our Lord, 2774, by Peter Grievous, Esq. Williamsburg, 1774.

Hutchinson, Governor, and Oliver, Lieutenant Governor
Letters, Assembly Address, Proceedings of the Lord's Committee of Council, the Substance of Mr. Wedderburn's Speech Relating to the Letters. London, 1774.

Jefferson, Thomas
A Summary View of the Rights of British America; Set Forth in Some Resolutions Intended For the Inspection of the Present Delegates of the People of Virginia Now in Convention. Williamsburg, 1774.

Johnson, Samuel
The Right of the British Legislature to Tax the American Colonies Vindicated; and the Means of Asserting That Right Proposed. London, 1774.

Lee, Arthur
An Appeal To The Justice And Interests of the People of Great Britain in the Present Disputes With America. By an Old Member of Parliament. London, 1774.
——. *A True Story of the Proceedings in the Parliament of Great Britain and in the Province of Massachusetts Bay Relative to Giving and Granting Money of the People of That Province, and of All America in the House of Commons, in Which They Are Not Represented.* London, 1774.

Lee, General Charles
Strictures On a Pamphlet Entitled a "Friendly Address To All Reasonable Americans on the Subject of Our Political Confusions." Addressed to the American People. Philadelphia, 1774.

Leigh, Sir Egerton
Considerations on Certain Political Transactions of the Province of South Carolina; Containing a View of the Colonies Legislatures. London, 1774.

Livingston, Philip
The Other Side of the Question: Or a Defense of the Liberties of North America; In Answer to a Late Friendly Address to All Reasonable Americans on the Subject of Our Political Confusions. By a Citizen. New York, 1774.

Massachusetts
Letter From Boston Town Meeting To Other Towns. News Handbill. Boston, July 26, 1774.
——. *Notice to Towns in Regard to the Observance of the Solemn League and Covenant.* News Handbill, Boston, June 10, 1774.
——. *Solemn League and Covenant.* News Handbill, Boston, 1774.

Nichols, Robert Carter (Treas. of Va.)

Considerations on the Present State of Virginia Examined. Williamsburg, 1774.

Prescott, Benjamin

A Free and Calm Consideration of the Unhappy Misunderstandings and Debates Which Have of Late Years Arisen and Yet Subsist Between the Parliament of Great Britain and the American Colonies: Contained in Eight Letters, Six Whereof are Directed to a Gentleman of Distinction in England, Formerly Printed in the Essex Gazette; The Other Two, Directed to a Friend. Salem, 1774.

Quincy, Josiah, Jr.

Observations on the Act of Parliament Commonly Called the Boston Port Bill; With Thoughts on Civil Society and Standing Armies. Boston, 1774.

Report of the Lords Committees Appointed by the House of Lords: To Inquire Into the Several Proceedings in the Colony of Massachusetts Bay, in Opposition to the Sovereignty of His Majesty in His Parliament of Great Britain, Over That Province; And Also What Hath Passed in This House Relative Thereto From the First Day of January 1764. London, 1774.

Robinson, Matthew-Morris

Considerations On the Measures Carrying On With Respect to the British Colonies in North America. London, 1774.

Seabury, Samuel

A View of The Controversy Between Great Britain and Her Colonies Including a Mode of Determining Their Present Disputes, Finally and Effectually and of Preventing All Future Contentions in a Letter to the Author of a Full Vindication of the Measures of the Congress From the Columnies of Their Enemies. New York, 1774.

——. *Free Thoughts on the Proceedings of The Continental Congress, etc.* Signed A. W. Farmer. New York, 1774.

Sewall, Jonathan

A Brief Review of the Rise and Progress, Services and Sufferings of New England, Especially the Province of Massachusetts Bay; Humbly Submitted to the Consideration of Both Houses of Parliament. London, 1774.

Sharp, Granville

A Declaration of the People's Natural Right to a Share in the Legislature; Which is the Fundamental Principle of the British Constitution. London, 1774.

Sherwood, Samuel

A Sermon: Containing Scriptural Instructions to Civil Rulers and All Free-born Subjects: Also an Appendix Stating the Grievances the Colonies Labour Under, by the Rev. Ebenezer Baldwin of Danbury. New Haven, 1774.

Shipley, Jonathan (Bishop of St. Asaph)

A Speech Intended to Have Been Spoken on the Bill for Altering the Charters of the Colony of Massachusetts Bay. London, 1774.

Tennent, William
  An Address Occasioned By the Late Invasion of the Liberties of the American Colonies By the British Parliament. Philadelphia, 1774.
Tucker, Josiah
  Four Tracts With Two Sermons on Political and Commercial Subjects. Glocester, 1774.
Virginia
  Instructions to Their Delegates to The Continental Congress. News Handbill. Williamsburg, 1774.
Wilkins, Isaac
  Short Advice to the Counties of New York. New York, 1774.

1775

Anonymous
  An Answer to a Pamphlet Entitled Taxation No Tyranny; Addressed to the Author and to Persons in Power. London, 1775.
——. *Authentic Papers From America Submitted to the Dispassionate Consideration of the Public.* London, 1775.
——. *A Defence of the Resolutions and Address of the American Congress in Reply to Taxation No Tyranny.* London, 1775.
——. *Constitutional Considerations on the Power of Parliament to Levy Taxes on the North American Colonies.* London, 1775.
——. *The First Book of the American Chronicles of the Times.* Boston, 1775.
——. *A Full and Circumstantial Account of the Dispute Between Great Britain and America. Containing: I. A View of the Several Acts of Parliament Which the Americans Object To; II. The Lengths They have Gone in Rebellion.* Glasgow, 1775.
——. *A Letter to the People of Great Britain in Answer to That Published by the American Congress.* London, 1775.
——. *A Letter to the Right Hon. Lord Camden, On the Bill Restraining the Trade and Fisheries of the Four Provinces of New England.* London, 1775.
——. *A Letter to the Right Honourable Lord M—— on the Affairs of America; From a Member of Parliament.* London, 1775.
——. *The Pamphlet Entitled "Taxation No Tyranny" Candidly Considered and Its Arguments and Pernicious Doctrines Exposed and Refuted.* London, 1775.
——. *A Plain State of the Argument Between Great Britain and Her Colonies.* London, 1775.
——. *A Plan for Conciliating the Jarring Political Interests of Great Britain and Her North American Colonies and for Promoting a General Reunion Throughout the Empire.* London, 1775.
——. *A Proposal for the Present Peace and Future Government of the British Colonies in North America.* London, 1775.
——. *The Reply of a Gentleman in a Select Society, Upon the Important Contest Between Great Britain and America.* London, 1775.
——. *Resistance No Rebellion: In Answer to Dr. Johnson's Taxation No Tyranny.* London, 1775.

——. *A Short View of the Lord High Admiral's Jurisdiction And of the Several Acts for Regulating and Restraining the Trade of the British Plantations, and of the Commissions of Vice-Admiralty Courts There; Together With the Heads of a Bill for the Better Regulating the Same.* London, 1775.

——. *Some Candid Suggestions Towards Accommodation of Differences With America.* London, 1775.

——. *Some Reasons for Approving of the Dean of Gloucester's Plan of Separating from the Colonies: With a Proposal For a Further Improvement.* London, 1775.

——. *The Speeches in the Last Session of the Present Parliament Delivered by Several Advocates in the House of Commons in Favour of the Rights of America.* New York, 1775.

——. *Taxation Tyranny.* London, 1775.

——. *Three Letters to a Member of Parliament, on the Subject of the Present Dispute With Our American Colonies.* London, 1775.

——. *The Supremacy of the British Legislature Over the Colonies Candidly Discussed.* London, 1775.

——. *To the People of North America, By "A Native of the British West Indies."* (Asks not to be boycotted. They cannot do what continental colonies are doing. May starve if cut off from trade.) News Handbill, place of imprint not given, 1775.

——. *Thoughts Upon the Present Contest Between Administration and the British Colonies in America, Addressed to the Merchants of the City of London and All the Sea-port, Trading, and Manufacturing Towns in Great Britain and Ireland.* London, 1775.

——. *The Triumph of the Whigs or T'Other Congress Convened.* New York, 1775.

——. *Tyranny Unmasked. An Answer to a Late Pamphlet Entitled Taxation No Tyranny.* London, 1775.

Barry, Henry
    The Advantages Which America Derives From Her Commerce, Connection and Dependence on Britain. London, 1775.

——. *The Strictures (by Charles Lee) to a Friendly Address (by Myles Cooper) Examined.* Place of imprint not given, 1775.

Burke, Edmund
    Speech on Concilliation With the Colonies, March 22, 1775. New York, 1775.

Campbell, John (Agent for Georgia, 1765-75)
    Political Essays on the Present State of the British Empire. London, 1775.

Cartwright, John
    American Independence; The Interest and Glory of Great Britain. New edition, Appendix. London, 1775.

——. *Letter to Edmund Burke, Esq: Controverting the Principles of American Government, Laid Down in His Lately Published Speech on American Taxation Delivered in the House of Commons on the 19th of April, 1774.* London, 1775.

Chandler, Thomas Bradley
    What Think Ye of Congress Now? Or an Enquiry How Far the Americans are Bound to Abide by and Execute the Decisions of the Late Congress. New York, 1775.
First Continental Congress
    Journal of the Proceedings of the Congress Held at Philadelphia, September 5, 1774. Containing the Bill of Rights; A List of Grievances; Occasional Resolves; the Association; A Memorial to the Inhabitants of the British American Colonies and an Address to the Inhabitants of the Province of Quebec. London, 1775.
Dalrymple, Sir John
    The Address of the People of Great Britain to the Inhabitants of America. London, 1775.
Duché, Jacob
    The Duty of Standing Fast in Our Spiritual and Temporal Liberties: A Sermon, Preached in Christ Church, July 7, 1775, Before the First Battalion of the City and Liberties of Philadelphia and Published at Their Request, Dedicated to George Washington. Philadelphia, 1775.
Galloway, Joseph
    A Candid Examination of the Mutual Claims of Great Britain and the Colonies; With a Plan of Accommodation on Constitutional Principles. New York, 1775.
——. *A Plan of a Proposed Union Between Great Britain and the Colonies.* Philadelphia, 1775.
Glover, Richard
    The Substance of the Evidence on the Petition Presented by the West India Planters and Merchants to the Honorable House of Commons, 16th March, 1775. London, 1775.
Gordon, William (Pastor 3rd Church in Roxbury)
    A Discourse, Preached December 15, 1774, Being the Day Recommended by the Provincial Congress, and Afterwards at the Boston Lecture. Boston, 1775.
——. *Remarks Upon a Discourse, etc.* Boston, 1775.
Hamilton, Alexander
    The Farmer Refuted, or a More Impartial and Comprehensive View of the Dispute Between Great Britain and the Colonies; Intended as an Answer to a Letter from A. W. Farmer, Entitled A View of the Controversy, etc. New York, 1775.
Hewes, Joseph
    A Collection of Occurences and Facts. Known by Living Evidences and Also Recorded in a Public Manner in Printed and Written Papers, Now in Being and Indisputably True; With Reflections Thereon. Providence, R. I., 1775.
Hunt, Isaac
    The Political Family: Or a Discourse Pointing Out the Reciprocal Advantages Which Flow From an Uninterrupted Union Between Great Britain and Her American Colonies. 2 Pitchers Afloat—"If we strike we break." Philadelphia, 1775.

Honaway, Jonas (Heartman)
> *Common Sense in Nine Conferences Between a British Merchant and a Candid Merchant of America.* London, 1775.

Johnson, Samuel
> *Taxation No Tyranny. An Answer to the Resolutions and Address of the American Congress.* 4th ed., London, 1775.

Lee, Arthur (an old member of Parliament)
> *An Appeal to the Justice and Interest of the People of Great Britain in the Present Disputes with America.* London, 1775.

——. *A Second Appeal to the Justice and Interests of the People on the Measures Respecting America; By the Author of the First.* London, 1775.

Lee, Charles
> *Strictures on a Pamphlet Entitled "A Friendly Address to All Reasonable Americans, etc."* Philadelphia, 1775.

Leonard, Daniel
> *The Origin of the American Contest With Great Britain; Or the Present Political State of the Massachusetts Bay in General and the Town of Boston in Particular, etc.* New York, 1775.

Lind, John
> *An Englishman's Answer to the Address From the Delegates to the People of Great Britain; In a Letter to the Several Colonies Which Were Represented in the Late Continental Congress.* New York, 1775.

London
> *The Address, Petition and Remonstrances of the City of London, to the King, in Favor of the Americans and Their Resolves, July 5, 1775.* London, 1775.

——. *To the Honorable the Commons of Great Britain; The Petition of the Merchants and Traders of the City of London, Interested in the American Commerce.* London, 1775.

Macaulay, Catherine
> *An Address to the People of England, Scotland, and Ireland on the Present Important Crisis in Affairs.* London, 1775.

Mein, John
> *Saggittarius' Letters and Political Speculations Extracted From the Public Ledger, Printed by Order of Selectmen and Sold at Donation Hall For the Benefit of Distressed Patriots.* Boston, 1775.

Pulteney, Wm.
> *Thoughts on the Present State of Affairs With America.* London, 1775.

Reynal, Guillaume Thomas François
> *The Sentiments of a Foreigner on the Disputes of Great Britain With America. Translated From the French.* Philadelphia, 1775.

Robinson, Matthew-Morris
> *A Further Examination of Our Present American Measures and of the Reasons and the Principles on Which They Are Founded.* Bath, England, 1775.

Shebbeare, John
> *An Answer to the Printed Speech of Edmund Burke, Esq. Spoken in the House of Commons, April 19, 1774: In Which His Knowledge in Polity,*

Legislature, Humankind, History, Commerce, and Finance, Is Candidly Examined, &c.: And His Arguments are Fairly Refuted; Addressed to the People. London, 1775.

Thomas, Isaiah
New England Almanac (Has copy of Association). Boston, 1775.

Toplady, A. M.
An Old Fox Tarred and Feathered: Occasioned by What is Called Mr. John Wesley's Calm Address to Our American Colonys. By an Hanoverian. London, 1775.

Tucker, Josiah, Dean of Gloucester
An Humble Address and Earnest Appeal to Those Respectable Personages in Great Britain and Ireland Who by Their Great and Permanent Interest in Landed Property, Their Liberal Education, Elevated Rank and Enlarged Views are the Ablest to Judge and the Fittest to Decide Whether a Connection With or a Separation From the Continental Colonies of America be Most for the National Advantage and the Lasting Benefit of Mankind. Gloucester, 1775.

——. *"A Letter to Edmund Burke, Esq., In Answer to His Printed Speech,"* . . . *in the House of Commons, March 22, 1775.* Gloucester, 1775.

Wesley, John
A Calm Address to Our American Colonies. London, 1775.

West, Benjamin
The New England Almanac (has an account of the rise of the controversy with England). Providence, R. I., 1775.

Wilkins, Isaac
An Alarm to the Legislature of the Province of New York; Occasioned by the Present Political Disturbances in North America: Addressed to the Honourable Representatives in General Assembly Convened. New York, 1775.

Zubly, John Joachim
Great Britain's Right to Tax Her Colonies Placed in the Clearest Light. By a Swiss. Philadelphia, 1775.

1776

Anonymous
The Plain Question Upon the Present Dispute With Our American Colonies. London, 1776.

——. *Remarks on the Different Opinions Relative to the American Colonies: Addressed to Lord North.* London, 1776.

——. *Reflections on the American Contest in Which the Consequences of a Forced Submission and the Means of a Lasting Reconciliation are Pointed Out; Communicated by a Letter to a Member of Parliament Some Time Since and Now Addressed to Edmund Burke by A. M.* (probably Samuel Seabury). London, 1776.

Champion, Joseph
Reflections on the State of Parties, on the National Debt and the Necessity and Expediency of the Present War With America. London, 1776.

Germain, Lord George

    The Rights of Great Britain Asserted Against the Claims of America; Being an Answer to the Declaration of the General Congress, Eighth Edition, To Which is Now Added a Refutation of Dr. Prices' State of the National Debt. London, 1776.

Lind, John

    An Answer to the Declaration of the American Congress. London, 1776.

McPherson, James

    The Rights of Great Britain Asserted Against the Claims of America: Being an Answer to the Declaration of the General Congress. London, 1776.

Paine, Thomas

    Common Sense: Addressed to the Inhabitants of America on the Following Interesting Subjects. Philadelphia, 1776.

Poplicola, Historicus

    America Poised in the Balance of Justice. In This Research the Present Dissention Between the Mother Country and Her Colonies is Considered in a New Light, and Supported by Arguments Quite Different From Those Held Forth by the Parliamentary Speakers, and Polemical Writers on Either Side of the Question. London, 1776.

Tucker, Josiah, Dean of Gloucester

    A Series of Answers to Certain Popular Objections Against Separating From the Rebellious Colonies, and Discarding Them Entirely; Being the Concluding Tract on the Subject of American Affairs. Gloucester, 1776.

AFTER 1776

Almon, John

    Prior Documents. A Collection of Interesting Authentic Papers Relative to the Dispute Between Great Britain and America, Shewing the Causes and Progress of that Misunderstanding, 1764-1775. London, 1777.

Anonymous

    Essays, Commercial and Political, on the Real and Relative Interests of Imperial and Dependent States, Particularly Those of Great Britain and Her Dependencies. Newcastle on Tyne, 1777.

——. *The Case Stated, on Philosophical Grounds, Between Great Britain and Her Colonies.* London, 1777.

Galloway, Joseph

    Examination Before the House of Commons in a Committee on the American Papers: With Explanatory Notes. London, 1779.

Hartley, David, M.P.

    Letters On the American War: Addressed to the Mayor and Corporation (etc.) of Kingston Upon Hull. London, 1779.

Anonymous

    An Essay on the Interests of Britain in Regards to America: Or an Outline of the Terms on Which Peace May be Restored to the Two Countries. London, 1780.

——. *Authentic Rebel Papers Seized at St. Eustatius, 1781.* London, 1781.

REFERENCES FOR BIBLIOGRAPHY

1. Most of Bancroft's discussion of the Navigation Acts is in his *History of the United States* (1st ed., Boston, 1834-74), II, 43-47, 122, 157-58, 198-99; V, 159; VI, 72, 290.

2. One of the widely used reading books on the Revolution was published by Samuel Williams in 1824 (Walpole, N. H.). It contains no reference to the Navigation Acts. The evolution of the Navigation Acts as a cause of the Revolution can best be traced in the widely used Peter Parley-Goodrich school histories of the United States.

3. Justin Winsor, *Narrative and Critical History of America* (Boston, 1886-89), VI, Chap. 1, "The Revolution Impending."

4. *Ibid.*, pp. 9-10.

5. *Ibid.*, pp. 63-64.